The Book of *est*

ALSO BY LUKE RHINEHART

The Dice Man

The Book of
est

Luke Rhinehart

Holt, Rinehart and Winston

NEW YORK

An Owl Book

Published by Holt, Rinehart and Winston,
383 Madison Avenue, New York, New York 10017.

Published simultaneously in Canada by Holt, Rinehart and
Winston of Canada, Limited.

Library of Congress Cataloging in Publication Data

Rhinehart, Luke.
     The book of *est*.

     Includes bibliographical references.
     1.   Erhard seminars training.   I.   Title.
RC489.E7R48   158   76–4728
ISBN Paperback 0–03–018326–X

Printed in the United States of America
10   9   8   7   6   5   4   3

Portions of chapters one through four of this book contain
material based in part on unpublished lectures created and
copyrighted by Werner Erhard and used by the author
with his permission. No material created and copyrighted
by Werner Erhard may be used or disseminated in any
medium or language without his prior written authorization. No portion of this book which is based on the afore-
said material may be used in motion picture, television or
stage versions, or in any other non-print media, without
the prior written authorization of the author and of
Werner Erhard.

ISBN 0-03-018326-X

ACKNOWLEDGMENTS

I'd like to thank Morty Lefkoe and Ted Long for assisting me in making this book as accurate as possible. Their patient and often extensive discussions with me regarding the *est* data and processes used in this book with *est*'s permission have helped me greatly in my effort to capture the spirit of an *est* training. I was especially impressed that not once did they suggest any changes because of something that might make *est* look bad; their major concern, rather was that *The Book of est* be accurate. I'd also like to thank my wife, Ann, whose writing and critical talent contributed considerably to the quality of the book.

CONTENTS

FOREWORD

Luke Rhinehart has written an engaging, dramatic reenactment of the *est* training—a fictionalized re-creation of what takes place during the four days. He presents his experience of the training from his own point of view, while taking care to keep the facts basically accurate.

As Archibald MacLeish said some time ago in "The Poet and the Press," merely reporting facts does not always convey the truth. Instead of reporting literally on what takes place, Luke chose a novelist's approach and used it brilliantly to communicate clearly to the reader both a sense of being in the training room and the spirit of what takes place there.

What Luke has written reminds me of a porthole looking onto a busy pool. It is one specific point of view through which you can see what is happening. After a while the porthole fades from your awareness, and while you are still viewing from a particular porthole, you have some sense of being in the pool.

Luke not only shares his own experience of the training, he also presents the experience of other people whom he has re-created as composite characters in his dramatization.

I enjoyed reading Luke's book. It allowed me to get a sense of what someone taking the *est* training might experience. I support Luke Rhinehart totally.

WERNER ERHARD
Founder, Erhard Seminars Training

INTRODUCTION

est, the Erhard Seminars Training, is currently the fastest-growing and most important, original, and controversial "enlightenment" program in the United States. The *est* Standard Training consists of two long weekend sessions lasting over sixty hours, during which 250 people are shouted at, ordered around, insulted, lectured, and introduced to various "processes" (exercises in observation during altered states of consciousness). As a result they come to share intimate experiences, discover hidden aspects of themselves, and are eventually led, miraculously enough, to the experience of "getting it": seeing at last what life really is and being able to let it work.

Since its creation in 1971, *est* has expanded with explosive force, almost doubling its number of graduates each year. By the fall of 1976 demand for the training has so outstripped *est's* ability to supply it that thousands of people who have signed up for the training are sometimes having to wait months to receive it. Already over 100,000 people have graduated from the two-week training. These include hundreds of psychologists and psychotherapists and numerous "name" personalities—John Denver, Peter Max, Valerie Harper, Cloris Leachman, Yoko Ono, Roy Scheider, Jerry Rubin—many of whom have become enthusiastic supporters of the program.

est makes use of the best techniques of many different traditional religious and psychotherapeutic disciplines. Its purpose is to bring people over two weekends to a unique experience that transforms their lives. Many graduates find that their "problems" tend to evaporate as they begin to take total responsibility for all they experience; their goals in life are clarified, their concentration is sharpened, and for the first time, it often seems, their lives begin to work.

After taking the *est* training myself for the first time, I realized that it is indeed an extraordinary training, one which, in a short time, has remarkably powerful effects on people's lives. It clearly deserved a book, but certainly not the normal expository work such a subject usually receives. Although I have done graduate work in psychology, worked for several years in mental hospitals, read widely in Western psychologies and Eastern religions for over a decade, and have a PhD from Columbia University, I felt that a scholarly or academic book about *est*, while interesting, would be counterproductive. "Understanding" and "beliefs," I had effectively learned from both Zen and *est*, are barriers to liberation. "Knowledge" about *est* would in many cases prove to be a barrier to people's choosing to *experience* the *est* training.

For *est* to work, the training must be experienced. One can, of course, come to believe one understands *est*, or to see *est*'s relation to gestalt therapy or scientology. One can learn facts about *est*: number of graduates, methods used, programs offered. This book will offer some such facts. But understanding and information have nothing to do with the essence of *est*. One can read *about* the training, just as one can read about LSD, but one shouldn't then expect to have a dramatic awakening.

The problem is that *est* is not a religion, not a therapy, not an academic course, and not a belief system. It might best be described, if it can be described at all, as theater—as living theater, participatory theater, encounter theater. Once we begin to see *est* in these terms, much that fails to fit the scheme of therapy or religion or science begins to make sense.

Certainly the unemotional behavior of the *est* assistants,

the dramatic entrance of the trainer, the loud stage voice that he and his staff assistants inevitably use, the raised platform, and the comic and dramatic monologue developed for the trainer by Werner are all quite theatrical. The analogy might seem to break down in that the members of the audience are the principal performers in the many dramatic encounters between trainer and trainees. But experiencing our "acts" and experiencing ourselves as *actors* is one of the results of the *est* training: our minds "play" us the way a puppeteer strings his puppets or a master director manipulates his actors. And of course participatory theater has long integrated the audience into the play.

Seeing the trainer as a master actor playing an assigned role along with the bit-player assistants permits us to evaluate his acts and words much more intelligently than if we misinterpret him as being a scholar or scientist giving a lecture. The trainer contradicts himself a dozen times during the training and is quite effective while doing so; a scientist who contradicts himself has failed. The trainer emphasizes that his audience should not *believe* what the trainer says and then argues with trainees who take exception to his authoritarian pronouncements— inexplicable behavior for a "reasonable" man. The trainer badgers and insults the beliefs of the trainees—action permissible in an actor but not normally tolerated in a fellow human being (and since the trainees don't experience the trainer as an actor, they often don't tolerate his insults).

If the training can best be described as participatory theater, it can also best be presented to a reading audience as drama. A book that summarizes the *est* training by describing its "philosophy" and analyzing what some people call its "therapy" may perpetuate precisely the way of life that *est* itself attempts to explode: namely, the adherence to the mind's belief systems. "In life, understanding is the booby prize" is a frequently heard *est* aphorism. Experiencing the training itself is the *only* way to get what the training offers, but the closest approximation to the training is a dramatization.

The majority of this book, then, consists of a re-creation of the highlights of the four days of the *est* training, presented, as nearly as possible, as a trainee would experience them. The training normally lasts fifteen to twenty hours a day, and as a result every trainee suffers from periods of "unconsciousness"— times when he is so bored, angry, involved in his own fantasies, or simply exhausted that he is unable to *experience* or recall what is happening in the training itself. Moreover, the training itself involves a considerable amount of repetition: of the notions of *est*, of the various meditative-like processes, and of the kinds of sharing of the trainees. Such repetition is essential for the success of the training but would be ineffective and ultimately alienating in the medium of a book. Hence, I have omitted some material to avoid a repetitiveness that here in print would not work, and have indicated lapses of time and consciousness by using ellipses and space breaks.

The reader should be quite clear that although this book dramatizes the highlights of the training and attempts to give you the vicarious experience of being at a training, this is a book, and the *est* experience cannot result from reading any book.

None of the trainees, or their names, words, or experiences re-created here are intended to represent any actual trainee. All are the product of a novelist's irrepressibly fantasizing mind. The names of the two trainers are also fictional, but their words convey notions of *est* reiterated in all trainings and their interchanges with the trainees are created to capture the spirit of the training.

Graduates of *est* who have read my re-creation of the training report, "Yes, you've really captured the way it was." Then each one inevitably adds, "and why didn't you put in more of . . . ," and each suggests something else. I have taken the training two full times, in three different cities, with five different trainers. *My* experience varied from day to day, and the training appeared to vary somewhat from trainer to trainer and from audience to audience. Interviews with scores of graduates seem to uncover scores of other trainings.

Introduction

No matter how objectively I have tried to present my fictional dramatic reenactment of the *est* Standard Training, I am only presenting the training as *I* experienced it, evaluated it, and then chose to re-create it. Moreover, for the sake of capturing the essential spirit of the training and for the purposes of dramatic effect, I have taken a few minor liberties with the exact sequence of events of the training. Another writer, equally sincere and objective, if asked to present the training in 200-odd pages, might re-create a very different training. And if you somehow managed to read three such books, and then you yourself *took* the training, lo and behold, a fourth training would appear—yours alone.

Part 1

THE TRAINING

"What is est?" asked the stranger.

"It's gestalt encounter therapy with the touchy-feely left out," said a guest who hadn't taken est.

"It's scientology without the hocus-pocus," said a second such guest.

"It's packaged Zen," said a third.

"It's Werner's way of earning a living," suggested a fourth.

"It's a scientific kick in the balls," said a recent est graduate.

"It's two weekends of madness to create saner weekdays," said a second est graduate.

"It's a car," said the third graduate.

"A car?" asked the stranger, now totally bewildered.

"Just a car," the graduate went on. "You can use it to get where you're going faster or use it to explore new places."

"I see," said the stranger, frowning.

"Or," said a fourth graduate, "you can just lie down in front of it and let it run over you and then blame the car."

1

DAY ONE

The Great Ripoff, or "I Paid $250 for This?"

"Knock, knock!" suddenly came from within the soul.

"Who's there?" asked the Seeker, surprised and frightened.

"It's God," came the Voice from within.

"Prove it!" said the Seeker.

And the silence returned.

One day the sun, after proceeding in its usual methodical way up the sky, at about 11:17 A.M. Eastern Standard Time, stopped. It was three days before anyone in Manhattan noticed.

We mingle nervously in the corridor outside the large hotel ballroom early on Saturday morning. We don't know much about what's going to happen in the training about to begin. Most attended something called a "guest seminar" or "special guest event" and learned some of the impressive things that seem to happen to people who take the *est* training. All but a few of us attended a three-hour "pre-training" the previous Monday in which the ground rules or "agreements" governing the training were discussed. We've been told we won't be able

3

to pee, eat, or smoke for a long time and that knowledge keeps many of us occupied.

Mingling with the early arrivals, we notice that underneath the occasional yawn a pleasant excitement of anticipation runs side by side with a nervousness in some people bordering on dread. Several people are afraid the training won't work for them. Actually the cause of fear in most is probably the opposite—*what if est works?* What if we were to take the training and were to *change*, become different, lose interest in our present games, our familiar problems, our act, our enduring personal relationships, and . . . and . . . A terrifying thought.

Being sophisticated and intelligent people, many of us engage in sophisticated and intelligent conversation—guaranteed to communicate nothing of our emotions and little of our intellect, but with *style*.

"How'd you get into this?" Jack asks Jennifer.

"My daughter took the training and began keeping her room neat and clean. I couldn't believe it."

"Yeah. A friend of mine says he's increased his sales thirty percent. But what really impressed me was the guy seems to know what he's doing now. He's suddenly sure of himself. He tried to explain it to me but it all comes out *est* gobbledygook."

"I know what you mean. My daughter has been so busy talking about 'creating spaces' for me and her sisters and everybody else you'd think she was renting apartments."

The doors of the training room open and a stony-faced young man with an *est* name tag pinned to his chest announces in clear, even tones: "You may enter the training room now. There will be no talking in the training room. There will be no smoking in the training room. Go to the main table on the right and pick up your name tag. Name tags are arranged alphabetically by last names. On the left is a table where you are to check all timepieces. Then you may enter the training room. There will be no talking in the training room. There will be no smoking in the training room. Go to the main table . . ."

We trainees bunch together at the entrance of the room like

sheep at a barn door and then file through past several other *est* assistants, all of whom seem fiercely robotlike, but who in fact reveal quite neutral, expressions, fierce only compared to the social smile expected. The name tags arranged alphabetically are picked up one by one by the trainees—each proclaims in large letters the existence of CHUCK, MARCIA, TINA, JIM, and so on. In smaller letters, barely legible, are last names. Most people check their watches at the other table and then wander nervously through a second set of doors into a large meeting room in which 254 chairs are arranged in eight rows in a gentle arc facing a raised platform.

The hotel room is extravagantly decorated in Versailles modern: garish red curtains compete with a garish purple rug. Chandeliers hang brightly from a plain white ceiling. On the platform—roughly thirty feet wide, twelve feet deep, and one foot higher than the floor—are two upholstered high stools, a small lectern, a larger lectern with a pitcher and metal insulated jug, and two blackboards, one on each side of the platform, each angled slightly toward the center of the room with legs taped to the carpet of the platform. The lecturer's paraphernalia seem distinctly out of place among the chandeliers and shimmering curtains.

est assistants keep informing those entering to take seats at the front and toward the center, toward the front and toward the center, and people file forward and begin filling the seats.

"I don't really think I need this," a woman labeled Tina whispers after a while to Jean sitting beside her. "I mean I'm perfectly happy. But *est* did wonders for my ex-husband, and who knows, maybe it'll do something for me."

"My psychiatrist says he investigated *est*," Jean replies quietly, "and couldn't find anything wrong with it. Coming from him that rates as high praise."

"Why are *you* taking the training?" Tina asks her neighbor to her right, a middle-aged man labeled Stan.

"Oh, I guess because my life's all fucked up," Stan replies mildly. "My wife and I split up a year ago and I've sort of lost a sense of direction. Whatever *est* does it seems to make people feel they know what's going on and what they want."

"That's true," comments Tina. "My husband's going on a safari in Africa this summer, something he talked about for fifteen years, and now suddenly he's actually doing it. When I—"

"MY NAME IS RICHARD MORRISON AND I AM HERE TO ASSIST YOUR TRAINER," suddenly booms out a voice over the room. A tall, slender man dressed in neat clothes with light blue shirt and unbuttoned collar is standing on the platform looking out at the audience. A hush falls over the room. The 254 trainees are now arranged neatly in the eight rows, each row with two middle sections of eleven seats each and two side sections of five or six seats each, the sections separated by three aisles each five feet wide. The trainees look up intently at Richard. Behind the trainees' chairs stand seven or eight assistants, three of whom have microphones in their hands. In back of them are two more assistants seated at two tables. At the back of the room are tables with pitchers of water and paper cups.

"IT IS NOW 8:36," announces Richard in a loud voice. "YOUR TRAINING HAS BEGUN. Werner has developed certain ground rules for the training which you have agreed to follow. These ground rules exist for one reason: because they work. Following them will permit you to get the most results from the training. We want you to *choose* to follow these ground rules. In fact, you have already made agreements with *est*. You have agreed not to bring timepieces into the room. If you have a watch or timepiece in your possession at this time stand up now and go to the back of the room. An assistant there will take your watch and give you a ticket. Is there anyone in the room still possessing a watch?"

Two people raise their hands. One of them, a slim, attractive woman in her twenties, says to Richard in a soft voice:

"I've got a watch in my handbag, but I promise during the training not to look at it."

"YOU HAVE AGREED NOT TO BRING WATCHES INTO THE ROOM. GO TO THE REAR AND HAND IN YOUR WATCH."

"It's in my handbag," says Linda, "that's not the same as wearing it."

"THE HANDBAG IS IN THE ROOM. THE WATCH IS IN THE HANDBAG. YOUR AGREEMENT IS NOT TO HAVE A WATCH IN THE ROOM. TAKE YOUR WATCH TO THE BACK OF THE ROOM."

Flushed, the woman abruptly turns away from Richard, picks up her handbag, and marches quickly to the back of the room.

"LOOK AT THE PERSONS SITTING ON EACH SIDE OF YOU. IF YOU KNEW EITHER ONE BEFORE THIS MORNING, RAISE YOUR HAND. . . . GOOD. WOULD THE PERSON SITTING ON THIS SIDE OF THE OTHER [Richard points to his left.] STAND UP AND GO TO THE BACK OF THE ROOM."

"I've only known this person a few days," announces a woman named Anna. "Just since the pre-training meeting. Does that count?"

"IF YOU ARE SEATED NEXT TO ANYONE YOU KNEW BEFORE THIS MORNING RAISE YOUR HAND. THE PERSON SITTING ON THIS SIDE OF THE OTHER IS TO GO TO THE BACK OF THE ROOM."

Three or four individuals, after a brief period of confusion, go to the back of the room, where they are directed to new seats.

"You have all agreed to remain in this room as long as the trainer requires. THERE WILL BE NO BATHROOM BREAKS FOR ANYONE until the trainer says so, except for those with medical reasons, which we'll go into soon. There will be no smoking. There will be no reading in the room. There will be no note-taking or tape-recording devices in the room. No chewing of gum. There will be no talking. If you wish to communicate with the trainer or share something with the other trainees, raise your hand. If the trainer acknowledges you, you will stand up and wait until a microphone is brought to you by an assistant. You will take the microphone, hold it three inches from your mouth, and then communicate what you wish to communicate. Except when you have been acknowledged and are standing with a microphone, you will not talk. Is that understood? Yes, David. Stand up. Take the mike."

"Ah ... yeah," says David, a tall, distinguished-looking man in his thirties. "Look, we went over all these agreements during the pre-training meeting and frankly I haven't paid two hundred and fifty bucks to be reminded for half an hour that I can't smoke. Could we please begin the training?"

"THE TRAINING HAS ALREADY BEGUN. I AM HERE TO ASSIST THE TRAINER AND TO REMIND YOU OF ALL OF THE AGREEMENTS YOU HAVE MADE. IT WILL TAKE LONGER THAN HALF AN HOUR."

"It seems pretty stupid to me."

"Being reminded of agreements always seems stupid to people who don't keep agreements. I get that you think it's stupid. Do you get that my talking now is part of the training?"

"Someone said it's possible to get your money back some time. Is that true?"

"That is true. The trainer will eventually communicate to you about leaving and getting your money back."

"Good."

"Thank you," says Richard. "You will remain in your chairs at all times except when instructed to move from the chair by me or the trainer or except when called upon to communicate. At the end of each break you will take a different seat. If you feel you have to vomit raise your hand and an assistant will bring you a bag. If you need a tissue raise your hand and an assistant will bring you a tissue. If you have to vomit, hold the bag close to your face and vomit. When you have finished vomiting an assistant will take your bag and give you a fresh one. You will not be excused to go to the bathroom except during the specific breaks announced by the trainer. You may not smoke in this room. During the course of this training, the next ten days, you will not drink alcohol, or use any drug, hallucinogen, or other artificial stimulant or depressant unless you have a medical prescription and the drug is absolutely necessary for your health. We recommend you not practice any meditation during this period. Yes, Hank."

"It's part of my business to have a friendly glass of beer or wine or Scotch with clients. Can I be excused from that particular part of the agreement?"

"YOUR CLIENTS WILL SURVIVE IF YOU DO NOT HAVE A BEER. KEEP THE AGREEMENT. Thank you.

"Some of you, because of medical disabilities, are on what we call the special-permissions list. Would anyone who . . ."

Assistant Richard spends fifteen minutes getting those who are on the special-permissions list (a physician indicates they have to go to the bathroom regularly, for example, or take certain medication on a regular basis) to move to the back row center and those who were sitting there to rearrange themselves elsewhere in the newly vacated seats. There are several more questions on subjects like smoking, alcohol, vomit bags, knitting, being able to remove one's suit jacket, chewing gum, closing one's eyes, timing of the breaks, length of this day's session, arranging for rides home, the definition of meditation, and a reminder by Richard of two or three other minor agreements made by the trainees.

Then, as suddenly as he had appeared, Richard marches off the platform down the center aisle to the back of the room. The platform is now vacant. The trainees remain respectfully if not fearfully silent.

Nothing happens. The stage remains empty. A few stir restlessly, but most, subdued by the long and repetitious reminder of the agreements and the frequent and often trivial questions about them, sit quietly. As four, five, then six minutes pass, a nervous tension mounts. The silence deepens. An occasional car horn from outside the hotel is all that can be heard.

And then, at last, a second man comes briskly up the same

center aisle, mounts the platform, goes to the small lectern, and opens up a large notebook he has brought with him. He is young, in his early thirties, neatly dressed, dark, and handsome. The name tag on his chest announces Don.

He looks out over the audience briefly, his look neither friendly nor hostile, then looks down at his notebook and begins leafing through the pages. His pants are pressed so well the crease looks as if it could cut through paper; his shoes gleam. His shirt is open at the collar. He doesn't look like Werner Erhard.

He studies his notebook at least a full minute, the silence deepening yet more. Then, a second time, he looks out over the trainees. He looks to his right for a moment, then straight ahead at the center sections, and then to his left. At last he speaks, his voice, like that of the assistant Richard, unnaturally loud, firm, and dramatic.

"MY NAME IS DON MALLORY. I AM YOUR TRAINER."

He pauses, and something about his total confidence and ease, the inordinate loudness of his voice, and the word *trainer* seems to send a small shiver through several of the trainees. The trainer's face shows no expression whatever, neither of warmth nor of coldness. Amazingly, through the next several hours, it will never show *any* emotion. His voice, however, unlike those of the assistants, will vary: he will shout sometimes; he will be normally loud most of the time; he will lower his voice dramatically at others. He will mimic voices and play parts, but always his *face* will remain stoically indifferent to everyone.

"I AM YOUR TRAINER," he continues in his intense, penetrating voice, "AND YOU ARE THE TRAINEES. I AM HERE BECAUSE MY LIFE WORKS AND YOU ARE HERE BECAUSE YOUR LIVES DON'T WORK."

He pauses and takes a single relaxed step to the right of his small lectern on which rests the notebook; he is looking slowly from right to left at the attentive trainees.

"Your lives don't work," he goes on firmly. "You have great

theories about life, impressive ideas, intelligent belief systems. You are all—every one of you—very *reasonable* in the way you handle life, and your lives don't work. You're assholes. No more, no less. And a world of assholes doesn't work. The world doesn't work. Just remember the madhouse of a city you've just come through to get here this morning and you *know* the world doesn't work. Just look at your own fucking lives and you know they don't work. You've paid two hundred and fifty dollars to take this training so your lives *will* work, and you'll spend most of the next ten days doing everything you can to make the training *not* work, so your lives can go on peacefully not working. You've just paid two hundred and fifty dollars to be here and you'll get *nothing* from this training."

The trainer again pauses and paces back now in front of the lectern, his dark eyes moving attentively over the trainees.

"Richard has just reminded you of the agreements you've made to participate in the training, and I can tell you from experience that we know that you all, ALL, are going to break some of them. Most of you already have. We asked you not to talk in this ballroom after entering and what happened? [A ripple of nervous, self-conscious laughter flows through the trainees.]

"It's quite simple. You all break agreements. That's one reason your lives don't work. You all live your lives under the theory that you're somebody special, a privileged character, and are thus free to cheat—on income taxes, stop signs, wives, husbands, expense accounts, and certainly on little trivial agreements with *est*. 'Sure,' you'll say to yourself sometime next week, 'What's the big hassle about a little glass of wine?' Or 'Why should I bother to do without a friendly joint?' *'est* is square and uptight, I don't have to play their game.' It's not reasonable to keep an agreement when it won't seem to hurt anyone when you break it, and since you're all reasonable people you'll break agreements.

"You'll all break them. You can't keep agreements, and your lives are so messed up you don't even *know* that you can't keep agreements. You lie to yourself. And the definition of a friend is somebody who agrees to go along with your lies if you'll go along with his. It's beautiful. And nobody's life works."

The trainer's voice is penetratingly intense, cold, and he moves his eyes over the trainees as if he were capable of looking through each one.

"I'm going to tell you what to expect in this training," he goes on. "There are two parts: I talk and you talk. Right now it's I talk; I talk and you listen. But let me make one thing clear: I don't want any of you assholes to *believe* a word I'm saying. Get that. Don't believe me. Just listen.

"What you're going to experience during the next ten days of this training is everything that you normally try hard *not* to experience. You're going to experience anger. Fear. Nausea. Vomiting. Crying. Submerged feelings that you lost touch with decades ago are going to come up. They're going to come up. Of course, you'll try hard to avoid them. Oh, how you assholes will try to avoid your real feelings. You'll go through boredom, unconsciousness, sleep. You'll experience incredible resentment, rage even, at me, at the other trainees, at the agreements. You're going to fall asleep. You're going to feel you have to piss in your pants. You're going to feel that if you don't get a cigarette or eat that piece of candy you snuck into the training, you're going to scream. You're going to feel that this training is the biggest ripoff since you last bought the Brooklyn Bridge. You're going to want to leave. Oh, how you're going to want to leave. Anything, anything, anything, to avoid having to BE HERE NOW with your actual experience. *Anything* to avoid having to give up your racket, give up your acts, your theories, give up the beautiful structured reasonable unworking mess you've made of your lives. You're going to experience the whole gamut of negative emotions until you begin to get that you'll do anything to keep from ending your acts and experiencing what's happening right here and now.

"You're also going to tell me all the rational reasons that what I say to you is stupid and I'm going to stand here and continue to call you an asshole and you are going to continue to be an asshole."

The trainer pauses yet a third time and moves back behind the lectern with his notebook. Although he uses his arms to emphasize certain points during portions of his rap, they hang now loosely at his sides. When he gestures, he gestures; when he doesn't, his arms and hands seem totally at peace. The trainer seems utterly nerveless, without mannerisms or habits.

"If you don't think you can take all this, then I want you to GET OUT. Go to the back of the room, turn in your name tag, and get out. We'll refund your money in full.

"But if you choose to stay, then you're choosing to keep the agreements and to experience the anger and nausea and boredom I've just described to you. And if you choose to stay and keep your sole in the room [He gestures toward his feet.] and follow instructions and take what you get, then I'll guarantee that on next Sunday you'll get it. You may sleep half the time and be angry the other half, but if you just keep your sole here in the room and follow instructions you'll get it. It will blow your minds . . .

"Not that you'll get better. You'll leave here exactly the same as when you began. Only you will be turned around one hundred and eighty degrees. You see, one of your problems— you'll admit it may cause a certain amount of difficulty—is that you're driving the car of your life using the rearview mirror to steer by. You're zooming through life with both your hot little hands and your hot little eyes glued firmly to the rearview mirror. A few accidents and wrong turns can be expected. And some of you ten days from now will begin to talk about how *est* performs miracles, when all we do in some cases is introduce people to the possible usefulness of the steering wheel. . . . Yes, Kirsten? Stand up. Take the mike."

Kirsten, a slender brunette with a slight Scandinavian accent, stands up and, bright-eyed, speaks rapidly into the microphone.

"I'm an actress when I can get work, in TV commercials,

and I'd like to share—isn't that the word?—that I'm both excited and nervous about being here. A girl friend of mine took *est* and it changed her life, it really has, but what I want to say is that I'm afraid I won't get it."

"Kirsten," the trainer responds as he moves over to the side of the room from which she is speaking, "all you have to do to get it is keep your sole in the room and stay with your experience."

"But I'm afraid my resistances are really tremendous. I mean I'll try to do what—"

"DON'T *TRY* TO DO ANYTHING," the trainer interrupts loudly. "You won't get it because you've *tried* to get it, you won't get it because you're intelligent and bright and reasonable, you won't get it because you're a *good* person. You'll get it for one simple reason: Werner has created the training so that you'll get it."

"Thank you," Kirsten says and sits.

"By the way," the trainer says, moving back to the center of the platform. "Kirsten has shown you what to do when you wish to say something. Now I will tell you what to do after someone has finished communicating. You do this. [He claps his hands together several times.] It is called applauding. You will acknowledge each trainee who has finished speaking by applauding. Do you understand? Good.

"I'm telling you all that you'll get it," the trainer resumes. "But don't think it will be easy. You assholes have been messing up your lives for from fifteen to seventy years and we can be quite confident you'll do your best to mess up this training the way you mess up everything else.

"The first way you'll try to mess it up is to pretend you're here because your husband wants you to be here, or your wife, or your Uncle Henry is paying for it, or the boss told you to take it, or a magazine article said it would be good for your asthma. That's asshole thinking. If you stay in this training I want you to get that *you're here because you choose to be here*. Right here, right now, I want you to *choose* either to be here in the training or to get out. If you choose to stay you're going to feel yourself insulted and harassed, you're going to get upset, you're going to want to leave, but you'll get it. But don't stay here because somebody told you to or because a magazine article or psychiatrist recommended it. Stay here only because *you* choose to stay. Otherwise, get out. Do you get that? I want you all to . . . All right, yes—Jack, go ahead. Take the mike."

Jack, a burly man with bushy hair and a colorful suit, stands up and speaks into the mike, his voice almost as loud as that of the trainer.

"I'm here because several people I respect, one of whom is a psychotherapist, recommended *est*, and their recommendation is good enough for me. What's wrong with that?"

"There's nothing wrong with that," says the trainer. "Do you choose now on your own to stay in the training?"

"Well, frankly, from what I've heard so far, *I*, well, might not, but no matter how stupid it seems up to now, since *they* recommended it . . ."

"YOU'RE AN ASSHOLE, JACK. That kind of thinking leaves the responsibility squarely in the lap of your friends. We want YOU to take charge of your life."

"I am in charge."

"THEN QUIT LETTING YOUR FRIENDS RUN IT. Do you choose, here and now, to stay in this room and take the training?"

"Sure, I just said . . . ," begins Jack.

"And you choose to stay because YOU . . . CHOOSE . . . TO STAY. Do you get that? Not because Tom, Dick, and Harry recommended that you stay, but because YOU CHOOSE to stay. Do you get that?"

Jack is briefly silent and then replies:

"Yeah. Well, yeah, I guess I understand. Yeah, okay . . . I'm staying because I've decided to stay."

"Good. Thank you. [Weak, scattered applause as Jack sits and the assistant with the microphone scurries down the aisle to his station at the back of the room]

"All right, assholes, less than half of you acknowledged Jack.

I want to see EVERY ONE of you acknowledge him. You can either applaud or throw money toward the stage. Either one. Got it? Let's hear it. [Loud applause, no money]

"Good. You're learning. Jack has chosen to stay. Big deal. I don't give a shit whether he stays or leaves. I don't give a shit whether any of you leave or not. There are twelve thousand people waiting to take the training. It's *your* lives, *your* aliveness that's at stake, not mine. My life works whether you take the training or go to a porno movie.

"It's up to you. It's up to you to choose to stay, to choose to transform your life. I'm not going to do it for you. Only you can do that. All I can do is play the trainer in the training. As a matter of fact you're perfect just the way you are, but you can't get that yet. But in any case we know you can't change your life trying the way you've been trying because that's why your lives don't work. All you can do is choose to take the training, keep your sole in the room, follow instructions, and take what you get. Or you can get out. Now. Full money back. It's your life, your choice, not mine . . ."

The trainer pauses and looks slowly over the room. Two hands are raised.

"Tom," the trainer, calling on one of them. "Stand up. Take the mike."

Tom, a young man, bearded, with glasses and prayer beads, has trouble holding the mike, then speaks:

"I was told this training was a Zenlike enlightenment program," he says in a gravelly voice, "and instead all I've heard for an hour is a very uncentered person—namely you—making a lot of stupid generalizations that may apply to some people but certainly not to all. I don't understand what's going on."

"That's great, Tom. You've already made more progress than most of the people in the room. If you assholes think you understand what's going on, you're living your assholeness to its fullest. And you, Tom, have come into this training with a beautiful theory about what *est* is—namely, a Zenlike enlightenment program—and you've decided not to pay attention to anything that doesn't fit your beautiful theory. Guess how much you're going to get out of it, going through life that way?"

"Maybe I'm mistaken about what *est* is supposed to be," says Tom, frowning. "But you're all wrong when you talk about nobody's life working. I know a false generalization when I hear one and I don't like it."

"Fine! I get that. I'm going to modify my false generalization. All the trainees except *you* are assholes because they live in belief systems that prevent them from experiencing aliveness and having their lives work. You're the exception. You've got a *beautiful* belief system and so we'll agree to call you a beautiful asshole."

Tom is stunned, and for a second, silent.

"You can call me all the names you want," he says after a moment. "The fact that you have to insult me is simply a symptom of your not being a centered person."

"I get that, Tom," the trainer says, walking to the edge of the platform and staring down at Tom, who is standing in the third row. "You believe I'm not a centered person because I call people who are assholes assholes, right? Tom, that's just another theory of yours. Another part of your belief system. Your mind tells you, 'Centered people do not call other people assholes.' That's your belief. Great! I get that. Now you can sit down knowing that I know you believe that I'm uncentered. And I can continue to stand up and be the trainer who reminds you people that you're here because your lives don't work. Okay?"

Tom, scowling, but his gravelly voice quite steady, replies:

"What good does it do to keep harping on the fact that our lives don't work? I thought *est* was supposed to create safe spaces so people could talk about themselves and you put down everybody who opens his mouth."

"The space in here *is* safe," the trainer says, stepping down off the platform and standing in front of the first row opposite Tom. "There's nothing wrong with being an asshole. Some of my best friends are assholes. [Nervous laughter] In fact, all of my best friends are assholes. And I don't put people down. I just make statements. If some of these statements make you feel down that's your contribution, not mine."

"It just seems to me that a Zen master wouldn't spend the first hour of *darshan* calling his disciples assholes."

"I wouldn't count on that, Tom. I've heard of some pretty tough Zen masters. A lot of them I know when they're not batting their monks over the head certainly do a lot of yelling. But look, if you want a Zen master, find a Zen master. If you want *est*, take *est*. The reason I keep telling you assholes that your lives don't work is simple: YOUR LIVES DON'T WORK! If they did, you wouldn't be here. I harp on it because you're all carrying around a whole lot of beliefs that try to convince you that your lives *do* work, that you're right, that you're right on. Unless a tiny glimmer of your stuckness, of the unworkingness of your lives, gets through to you, you'll continue to hide in the lies you live by, the lies which prevent your lives from working."

"But you can't change people by lecturing at them."

"Right! I get that. That's why I tell you not to believe a word I'm saying."

"Then why are you saying them?" Tom asks.

"I'm saying them because Werner has found that the trainer's saying them works."

This answer silences Tom for a moment, but then he resumes: "So we just sit here and take it?"

"Or stand up and take it. Either way. It works either sitting or standing. It probably works a bit better for people who stand: erect assholeness is always easier to see than seated assholeness."

"Jesus! You are one arrogant bastard."

"Great! Anything else, Tom?"

Tom stands slightly slumped with his head lowered for a few moments.

"No," he finally says. "I guess arrogant bastard sums it up."

"Thank you, Tom," says the trainer and Tom sits. The applause that follows is rather light.

"Okay, you assholes, you're not applauding. Either coins or clapping, I want you *all* to acknowledge Tom. Let's hear it. [Loud applause]

"Jean. Stand up."

Jean, an attractive, matronly woman in her late thirties, conservatively dressed, takes the microphone and speaks:

"I don't understand why there's all this fuss about applauding everyone who speaks. Couldn't we do without it?"

"No, we can't do without it."

"But why do we have to do it?"

"You have to do it because it's one of the ground rules. Look, I want everyone in here to know that he or she can stand up and say whatever he wants and no matter what he says, when he's finished we're going to acknowledge him with applause. We're not applauding someone because you agree with him— shit, that would just be assholes applauding assholeness—but rather to acknowledge his sharing with us his experience or his point of view—whether you like it or not. That's all."

"It seems silly to applaud someone who simply asks if he can take his suit jacket off, like that man did earlier."

"That's okay, Jean. Learn to live with silliness, that's what *est* is all about. Thank you. HEY! WHERE DO YOU THINK YOU'RE GOING?!"

A young woman has arisen from the front row and walked hastily across the front of the audience toward an exit in the rear. Looking pale and holding her hands to her mouth, she is led back to her seat in the front where she stands unsteadily.

"I'm going to vomit! I'm going to vomit!" she says.

"Take the mike, Marie."

"I want to go to the bathroom! I'm going to vomit!"

"The assistant just gave you a bag. If you have to vomit, vomit in the bag. Hold the mike for her, Richard."

"I don't know how to use it," says Marie, fumbling with the bag.

"You take the bag in your hands," says the trainer, seating himself for the first time in one of the two upholstered stools on the platform, "and you hold it up near your face. You can't miss. Go ahead, do that."

"I can't!"

"DO IT!"

(Silence)

"I can't breathe," announces Marie in a muffled voice with the bag over her mouth.

"Hold the fucking bag a few inches away from your face."

"I won't be able to hit it!"

"I don't care how good a fucking shot you are, put the bag closer to your face."

"I won't be able to breathe!"

"Look," says the trainer, leaning back in his chair. "If you want to breathe, breathe. If you want to vomit, hold the bag close to your face and vomit."

"Please, let me go to the bathroom."

"Sit down. Play yo-yo with your vomit bag, and don't try and see how good a shot you are. Thank you."

As Marie sits there is nervous applause.

"That girl's sick!" a voice shouts from the back of the room.

"SHUTTUP!" the trainer shouts back, and he stands up and moves to the front of the platform. "If you want to speak in this room you raise your hand and you don't speak until I call on you and the assistant has brought you a mike. You may then stand and speak anything you want. Get that, assholes?"

The question is answered with a complete silence. Then a hand is raised in the back of the room.

"All right," said the trainer. "John. Stand up. Take the mike."

The man who stands is the same one who shouted out earlier. He is an older man with thinning gray hair, glasses, and a slightly stooped posture.

"I'm upset," he says in an emotional voice. "I see no reason whatever for you to be so rude to people. You could have told that girl how to use that bag without insulting her and making fun of her every step of the way."

"Got it, John," says the trainer, ambling back to his chair

and sitting down again. "But let's see what happened. Marie wants to vomit. We give her a bag. We throw in free instructions on how to use it. You feel like standing up and defending outraged womanhood; Marie feels like feeling she has to vomit. We'll treat you both the same. You get a mike. She gets a paper bag."

"I'm not sick," says John.

"Great! No vomit bag for John."

"You could be polite. You could have helped her."

"Sure. That's just the game Marie's probably used to having people play when she creates a sickness: 'Poor Marie! Has to puke. Poor baby!' In *est* if somebody wants to puke we say 'Fine! Here's a bag. Have fun.' Amazing how few people end up actually choosing to use it."

John stands uncertainly for a moment and then sits.

"Thank you for sharing, John. [Applause] I think we failed to acknowledge Jean who was talking before Marie tried to leave the room. Would you acknowledge Jean? [Applause]

"All right then. Let me remind you before I go on that I don't want you to believe a word I say over this weekend, just listen. Because the reason your lives don't work is that you're all living mechanically in your belief systems instead of freshly in the world of actual experience." The trainer stands up again and moves toward the right-hand side of the platform. "You don't look at reality and then construct conclusions, no. No, you did that decades ago. You assholes are roboting through life with your conclusions, and with your conclusions developed decades ago you're constructing reality! No wonder you've lost all aliveness. No wonder your lives don't work.

"Look. If we put a rat in a maze with four tunnels and always put cheese in the fourth tunnel, after a while that rat will learn always to go to the fourth tunnel to get cheese. A human will learn to do that too. You want cheese? Zip zip zip down the fourth tunnel, there's the cheese. Next day you want cheese? Zip zip zip down the fourth tunnel and there's the cheese.

"Now after a while the Great God in the white suit moves the cheese to *another* tunnel. Zip zip zip goes the rat to the fourth tunnel. No cheese in the fourth tunnel. The rat comes out. Goes down the fourth tunnel again. No cheese. Rat comes out. Goes down the fourth tunnel again. No cheese. Comes out. Down the fourth tunnel again. No cheese. Comes out. Eventually the rat will stop going down the fourth tunnel and look elsewhere.

"Now the difference between rats and human beings is simple: THE HUMAN BEINGS WILL GO DOWN THAT FOURTH TUNNEL FOREVER! FOREVER! HUMAN BEINGS COME TO *BELIEVE* IN THE FOURTH TUNNEL. Rats don't believe in anything; they're interested in cheese. But the human being develops a BELIEF in the fourth tunnel and he comes to MAKE IT RIGHT TO GO DOWN THE FOURTH TUNNEL WHETHER THERE'S CHEESE IN IT OR NOT. The human being would rather be *right* than get his cheese.

"And you people are, unfortunately, human beings, and not rats, and thus all of you are RIGHT. That's why for a long time now you haven't been getting any cheese and your lives aren't working. You've got too many beliefs in too many fourth tunnels.

"Well, that's fine. That's why you're here. To blow up all your life-denying, cheese-denying beliefs so that you can begin locating what you really want. We're going to help you throw away whole belief systems, totally tear you down so you can put yourself back together in a way that lets life work.

"But don't think it's going to be easy. You've been dedicated assholes for decades, and you know you're RIGHT; your whole life is based on the principle that you're right. And the fact you're miserable, that your life doesn't work, that you haven't gotten much cheese since you were in the fourth grade—that makes no difference. You're RIGHT. Your fuckin' belief systems are the best that money can buy or minds can create; they're the *right* belief systems and the fact that your life is all messed up is just an unfortunate and unrelated accident.

"BULLSHIT! Your correct, intelligent, reasonable belief systems are *directly* related to your not getting any cheese. You'd rather be right than be happy and you've been marching down fourth tunnels for years to prove it.

"You *know* you've been spending your time in empty tunnels because every now and then—accidents *will* happen—you experience some cheese: a freedom, a joyfulness, an aliveness so different from your usual flow that you wonder whether someone slipped some acid in your morning orange juice. And 'Wow!' you say to yourself, 'This is great, I'm gonna hold onto this,' and you reach out to get a good grip on it and POP! it disappears. The harder you try to get it back again the worse you feel.

"YOU ASSHOLES, you'll NEVER get it by trying to get it where it just was. The Great God of Life in the white suit is *always* moving the cheese. You'll never be happy by trying to be happy, because your trying is totally channeled by your beliefs about the right place for cheese to be. As soon as you have an idea about what you want and exactly where it is, you've ruined your chance of being happy and alive, because an idea or belief *destroys* experience and you ain't *never* gonna be alive unless you live in the realm of experience . . .

"Yes, you there, Betty. Stand up."

Betty, an attractive young woman with red hair and bright orange slacks, stands up and in a definite Bronx accent speaks into the mike:

"I don't get why an idea about what I want should make it so tough for me to get it."

"Oh, you'll get it all right. You got an idea about what you want?"

"For sure."

"What is it?"

"I'd like to have my own house in the country for myself and my children."

"Fine."

"But you say that the *idea* will stop me from getting it."

"The idea will stop you from *experiencing* it. You may get a house in the country all right, but as long as you hold onto the idea of the kind of house that will be *right* for you and the types of experience the house will give you, you'll never experience the actual house you're in, and because you don't experience it, you'll never be happy with it. You'll spend your time trying to live in the house you have a belief in and never get to enjoy the real mud on the real rug in the real house."

"But I don't see what my wanting a house has to do with looking for cheese in a fourth tunnel."

"Well, Betty," says the trainer, striding across the platform to stand nearer to her, "that's not an easy thing to see because you yourself got stuck in your particular fourth tunnel a long time ago. Exactly why you think all the cheese is located in a house in the country is not something we can trace right now. There are a lot of people living now in the country who think that if they lived in the city, life would be better. Later, when we do what we call the 'truth process,' you may want to take as your item the tenseness or dissatisfaction you feel living where you do now and maybe you'll be able to reexperience what's so with you about houses."

"Why can't I believe that living in the country would be better for me and my children than living in the goddamn Bronx?"

"You may someday *experience* that country living is better, but until you've learned to make it in the Bronx, you'll never make it in the country. Every belief you have about something kills it. Have a belief about the kind of house you want, BANG! No house. Have a belief about God, Bang! No God.

"EXPERIENCE, you assholes!" the trainer shouts out at the trainees as he moves away from Betty. "You live so much in your fucking minds you've probably never lived in a *house* in your whole life. Thank you, Betty. [Applause]

"All right, you there. Jerry. Stand up."

Jerry is a big man with a brush cut. He must weigh close to

240 pounds and he looks like a truck driver except that his voice, when he now speaks, is quite fluent and precise.

"That is the most ridiculous piece of nonsense you've spoken so far," he says intensely.

"Which is that?" the trainer asks amiably.

"That having a belief in God kills God."

"Gets Him every time."

"One must have a belief in God in order eventually to experience Him."

"One must NOT have a belief in God in order *ever* to experience Him."

"But that's utter nonsense," Jerry says passionately, holding the mike too far from his mouth but being heard anyway because of the loudness of his voice. "All of the most religious figures in history have had great belief in God."

"BULLSHIT, Jerry. They had *experience* of God," the trainer shouts and moves to the edge of the stage nearer Jerry. "Do you have a belief in the existence of human beings?"

"That's a silly question."

"YOU'RE GODDAMN RIGHT IT'S A SILLY QUESTION! You've experienced human beings directly; you *know* them; beliefs are totally unnecessary."

"But I can have a belief in God and experience Him too!" exclaims Jerry.

"If you experience God, really experience God, you'll probably find that you can't come up with a single worthwhile belief about what you've experienced."

"Saint Thomas Aquinas wrote seventy-three volumes about God!"

"Well, we can be damned sure he didn't have much time to experience Him then. Look, Jerry, don't give me your goddamn belief systems. They don't work. If you want to share with me your actual experience of God, that I would be interested in, but ideas about God are deadly. They're so deep in the scale of nonexperience they're less substantial than ghosts."

"I believe God exists," Jerry says loudly. "That belief does not cause God to cease to exist."

"For you, as long as you live in your belief, it *does*, Jerry, it does. Look," says Don, coming down the aisle to stand right beside Jerry. "Let me tell you a little story. A friend of mine was studying and meditating with a Hindu yogi that's a very high being, and one day, after he'd been fasting for about twelve hours and meditating about six hours, he suddenly experienced a rush of the most dazzling and all-pervasive light he'd ever even vaguely heard about. He was overwhelmed. I mean this guy had tripped on every drug known to God and Timothy Leary and never experienced *anything* like the long overwhelming flood of light and joy he got that afternoon.

"So," says the trainer, walking back toward the platform and now addressing the whole audience again, "this guy naturally tells his best friend about his experience, his yogi being at that time in Europe.

"'You saw *God!*' the friend tells him enthusiastically. 'And if you fast some more and meditate more, you'll see Him again.'

"Well, my friend, who may have had a genuine experience of something we might want to call God, now develops a few definite *ideas* about God: He's bright, He's glowing, He's overwhelming, He comes after meditation and fasting. So he puts these beliefs into practice and guess what?"

The trainer pauses, looking slowly over the trainees and then stopping with his eyes back on Jerry.

"Guess what, Jerry. God ceased to exist. My friend has been meditating and fasting now off and on for two years since that experience, and he's gotten no further experiences of God. Of course he's got *ideas* about God, beliefs about God, but ask him if he'd trade them all in for *one single minute* of the experience he once had and you're damned right he would."

Jerry is silent now for almost a half minute.

"What did the yogi say to your friend about this matter?" he finally asks.

"The yogi just said, 'Good, you saw God. Don't try looking

for Him there again.' Remember, Jerry, God gets around. If we try to pin Him to light or mountaintops or guys nailed to crosses or skinny brown guys in loincloths sitting in the lotus position, we're just being assholes. Later today I'll make it very clear that those things we're *really* certain about, the things we really *know*, are way beyond belief systems. The only things people believe in are things they don't know. Ghosts, flying saucers, reincarnation, a perfect society, a faithful husband . . ."

"But we have to have beliefs," Jack is saying a half hour later.

"Who says so?" replies the trainer.

"I do, for one."

"Well, that's one of your beliefs, Jack, and that's one of the reasons you're all fucked up."

"But *you* have a belief that all beliefs are bad."

"Who says so?"

"I do."

"Well, that's just *another* of your beliefs, Jack, and just another reason that your life—"

"But don't you believe that all beliefs are bad?"

"NO, asshole."

"Do you believe that most beliefs are bad?"

"Nope."

"What do you believe?"

"NOTHING! That's what I've been saying for the last hour."

"But you either believe something is true or you believe that it's false."

"*You* may believe, not me."

"You've *got* to believe."

"I don't believe a thing I'm saying and I don't want you to either."

"Oh, well, then you're just playing with words."

"That's right, Jack. I'm playing with words and my life works, and you *believe* in words and that's why *they* play with *you* and run your life."

"I still don't get it."

"That's fine, Jack. Don't worry about it. If you got it *now*, think how bored you'd be for the next three days . . ."

"But you're telling me I've got to destroy my belief system and my whole life is based on my intellectual and moral beliefs and on my feeling that I should achieve the most intelligent beliefs. You'll never get me to give them up. If that's what the training is all about, I'll never get it."

"Oh, you'll get it all right, Jack," says the trainer, and his face reveals almost the hint of a smile. "Don't worry about that. Just keep your sole in the room, follow the instructions, and take what you get. Thank you, Jack. [Applause]

"Look, people," the trainer says, standing once more behind the small lectern on the center of the stage. "You'll all get it because I'm taking responsibility for communicating it to you. Right now you're all messed up about what communication is all about. You think you do your best to tell someone something and if they don't get it, tough shit. Or that you listen hard and if you don't get it, it's the other guy's fault.

"In here, communication means taking responsibility when you're communicating to see that the other person *gets* your communication. If he doesn't, it's *your* responsibility. And when you listen you *get* what the other person gives and then observe what you yourself may add to it.

"For example, Tom over here just called me an arrogant bastard. I got that. Let's say for the sake of discussion that when he called me that I observed I experienced a tiny rush of anger. If I felt that anger then, that was something *I* added. I would have to take total responsibility for the anger.

"I've been calling all of you assholes. Fine! Get it and note what you add to it: resentment, anger, bewilderment, depression, amusement, hatred, shame—whatever it is you add to being called an asshole. Whatever you add: that's part of your assholeness. Your mechanicalness. Just look at it. You resent my calling you an asshole? Great! You resent me. No big deal. Happens in the best of families. Just observe it and note it's yours; not mine. I give you the words, 'You're an asshole.' The rest is all your creation ..."

Time passes during the training, and no single trainee remains conscious through every moment. One of the impressive characteristics of the trainer is that he, no matter how boring or silly someone's objections may be, always seems to pay perfect attention. He seems able not only to listen to the words, but also to understand the emotional and attitudinal content latent within the words. Notions are hammered in over and over, objections voiced over and over, and we trainees drift into unconsciousness and then out again. Some trainees doze, many become annoyed over what seems endless repetition of trivial argument or ego-centered sharing.

"REASONABLENESS! Yes, REASONABLENESS!" The trainer is shouting in response to a trainee. He strides now to a blackboard and draws a horizontal line across the middle of the board. At the bottom he writes in big capital letters the word REASONABLENESS.

"That's one of the lowest forms of nonexperience," he says and writes the word NONEXPERIENCE just under the horizontal line and at the far right of the board. "And you people have been living most of your lives being reasonable and thus you've been living in the realm of nonexperience."

"So what do we try to do about it?" asks the trainee Lester, a tall man in his early twenties, with long brownish hair, who has been involved in an exchange with the trainer.

"You don't *try* to do anything," the trainer replies. "*Doing nothing* will eventually work but you can't get that yet. In fact, in your misguided efforts to achieve real experience, you do in fact occasionally rise to slightly higher levels of nonexperience: deciding ... hoping ... helping," and he writes these three words on the board above REASONABLENESS but below the horizontal line.

"But what's *above* the line?" asks Lester.

"Above the line is an *experienced* experience, and the first step above that line, the first real form of experience, involves simply accepting. If you want to get out of the realm of non-experienced experience, you've got to stop being reasonable, stop making decisions, stop hoping, and just *accept what is*. No more, no less. Accept what is. When you do that, the light bulb of experience is turned on. Until you do, it's turned off."

"It seems to me," says Lester, "that all experience is experience. How can there be anything called a nonexperienced experience?"

"Since all you've been doing for the last decade, Lester, is nonexperiencing experience, it's tough to recall the distinction. I get that. But look, at the simplest level, let's pretend you're making love to a woman."

"Okay by me."

"You're on top of her banging away, okay?"

"Got it!"

(Nervous laughter)

"And you're being reasonable."

"Oh, Jesus."

(Easier laughter)

"You're wondering whether the woman thinks the fact that you're balling her represents a commitment on your part to her. While you reasonably consider this, are you *experiencing* your experience?"

(Nervous laughter)

"Not what I'd rather be experiencing," Lester replies.

"And then you move to the next level," the trainer goes on. "You *decide* to make love with ostensible physical ardor but without verbal communication. You decide to bang her good but mum's the word. While you're deciding, *are you experiencing?*"

"No."

"You hope she's going to have an orgasm. While you're hoping, *are you experiencing?*"

"No."

"No. And we can also bet that every second you're wasting on hoping decreases the likelihood that she will have an orgasm. Finally, you decide to use your great lovemaking techniques, freshly developed from pages fifty-eight through one-forty-nine of *The Joy of Sex,* and *help* your girl friend have an orgasm. While you're busy trying to help her, *are you experiencing?*"

"Not when I'm *thinking* about helping her," Lester replies. "But when I'm actually helping her it seems it might be pretty groovy."

"It might be, Lester," says the trainer. "And if it is, it's because you've gone beyond hope—you've stopped hoping—and are now just *being there* with the woman, accepting what's happening, and not believing, deciding, hoping, or helping a damn thing. Do you get that?"

Lester stands there jiggling the mike back and forth for a moment and with his other hand brushes his hair away from his face.

"Yeah, okay, I get that," he replies. "But if just being there with a woman is in the realm of experience then I want to lay claim to having lived a few times in the realm of experience."

"That could be, Lester. Certainly one reason men and women are attracted to sex is that it's one of those experiences —almost getting killed is another one—that can shock people into aliveness.

"But don't count on it," the trainer goes on. "Most people don't even experience fucking. A lot of you assholes haven't fucked since you were sixteen. I don't care how many times you've jumped from one bed to another; you've been fucking in your minds. In fact, one reason that assholes go from one sex experience to another is that you're incapable of having a genuine *experience* with *one* person, so you think maybe sixteen might do it.

"The problem is that some time or another you had a really fine experience—a marvelous, *shared* love experience—and you know what you've done? You've used it to murder every potentially similar experience since. You've taken that marvelous shared lovemaking and put it in a little silver box, and every time your life brings you something similar your asshole mind says, 'Wow! This may be almost as good as the one in the silver box, let's look and see.' And you pry open the silver box while you're making love and take a peek. You spend so much time *comparing* that you never experience what's happening here and now."

"I get what you're driving at," Lester says, smiling. "But isn't most of life a *blend* of experience and nonexperience?"

"NO! No, goddamn it!" Don barks back at Lester. "Experience is either on or off. There ain't no such thing as 'slightly experiencing' something. Who the hell ever heard of someone slightly experiencing a pain in the back? You're either feeling it or you're not.

"Look. Let me finish this chart on the board by listing the other modes of experience beyond accepting. Next is witnessing or observing," and Don writes these words just above ACCEPTING, "and then participation or sharing, and finally up to something we call 'sourcing.' Don't worry about all of these now. They're all in the realm of fully experienced experience. That's all you have to know now.

"Now, if we make a scale of one to a hundred we might say that reasonableness is at the level of minus eighty on the scale of nonexperience. Deciding might be minus twenty. Hoping might be minus ten and helping minus five. On the other side of the line—that of experience—the scale will all be plus, from let's say plus five for accepting to plus one hundred for sourcing. Got it?" Don asks, looking up from his chalk work and striding forward to the edge of the platform.

"Okay," he goes on, moving quickly back to the blackboard. "How do we go from minus five over to the plus side?"

"You go through zero," Lester answers promptly.

"Right! You go through zero. You have to go through *nothing*." Don writes a zero and the word NOTHING next to the horizontal line. "You have to go through nothing," he repeats. "I want you to *get this*: something is either experience or nonexperience; it's either plus or it's minus. The light bulb is on or it's off. And to get from nonexperience to experience you have to go through *nothing*."

A trainee named Sandy raises his hand and is acknowledged by the trainer.

"So," he says, frowning, "you're arguing that if we learn from this training to stop trying to change, then we'll change."

"That's not it, Sandy," the trainer replies, taking a long sip from his thermos and then holding the thermos in front of him in both hands. "I've already told you, you'll get nothing from this training; nothing will be changed. As it says in our pamphlets, 'The purpose of the *est* training is to transform your ability to experience living, so that the situations you have been trying to change or have been putting up with clear up just in the process of life itself.' And I warned you that the word 'transform' doesn't mean 'change,' it means for us in this context something like 'transubstantiate' or 'alter the substance of' your ability to experience living. Change implies only modification of form. We're talking about something as radical as the difference between plus one and minus one. Going from minus five to minus one—we can call that change. But going from minus one to plus one—that represents a one-hundred-and-eighty-degree turnabout. That represents a transformation of your ability to experience living. And to get from minus one to plus one you've got to go through nothing."

"Well, I think your semantic distinction is not that basic. The important thing is we can hope to change."

"No! I don't want you to hope to change. Hope is fully in the realm of nonexperience. And I don't want you to change. You're perfect the way you are. Just stay in the room and take what you get ... then later you can tell me whether what you get constitutes change or not ..."

Our buttocks ache at this point, our shoulders ache, our stomachs have been growling for an hour and a half, our bladders announce that their needs are being neglected, and we are beginning to feel that if we hear the word *experience* one more time we may have to raise our hands and share a scream. How can the goddamn trainer keep talking? And *he* already knows all this stuff. And why can't I have one little cigarette? What the hell time can it be getting to be? Did they design these hotel chairs for maximum discomfort? Why don't all of us assholes agree to agree with everything Don says so we can all go out and have supper?

"... Tell me something you *really* know how to do," the trainer is saying. "Andy, go ahead."

"I really know how to box," says Andy, a compact young man in his twenties.

"Fine. How do you box?"

"You gotta stay in a crouch, keep your gloves up, keep your attention on both the guy's hands and torso at once. Then you—"

"Fine. But how do you box?"

"You keep your left—if you're not a southpaw—in front of your face—like this—and your right hand a little lower—like this. Then ... you box."

"But that's what I want to know: how to box."

"I can give you lessons."

"But how do I box?"

"It takes too long to explain."

"How long?"

(Silence)

"A couple of years."

"But I thought boxing was something you knew *really* well? It takes you two years to let me know *how?*"

"Longer, if you're any good," Andy replies.

"Thank you, Andy. [Applause] I want you to tell me about something you *really* know. Tania?"

"I know how to sing," announces Tania.

"Fine. Tell me how to sing."

Tania stares at the trainer for a long moment.

"You ... you open your mouth—no, it's done like this—" and Tania breaks out into a lovely soprano rendition of the opening phrases of 'Ave Maria.' She stops after only ten seconds. "That's how you sing."

The trainees applaud loudly.

"Great," says the trainer. "But *how* do you sing?"

"I can't explain it in words."

"You mean, something you *really* know, you can't tell me how to do?"

"Not singing," replies Tania.

"Thank you. Jed?"

(Applause for Tania)

Jed, a plump middle-aged man in a wrinkled suit, takes the mike.

"I really know how to walk," he announces.

"Fine. Tell me how to walk."

"Like this," Jed answers and he walks back and forth four strides up and down the aisle next to which he has been sitting.

"I see you, but *how* do you walk?"

"You lift first one leg, then the other."

"Fine, but how do you *walk*?"

"You lift your left leg, you know, by bending your knee, so that the left foot rises about four inches off the floor. Then you sort of shift your weight forward and let the foot fall forward back to the floor and ... [Jed is studying his own walking very carefully.] as your left leg stiffens 'you begin to bend the right knee and lift your right foot off the ground ..."

"Okay, but *how* do you *walk*?"

Jed stares at the trainer.

"I just showed you."

"I *saw* you walking, but I want to know *how* to walk."

"I told you: you lift your left leg ..."

"But *how* do you lift your left leg?"

Again Jed stares.

"You . . . uh . . . lift your . . . uh . . . left leg."

"But *how?*"

"Oh, Jesus, I don't know how."

"I thought lifting your leg was something you really knew?"

"It is, damn it, but it's not something you can tell about."

"Thank you, Jed. [Applause] Someone else? Bill?"

Bill, a gangly man with a handlebar moustache and huge head of hair, has a smile on his face as he stands.

"What do you really know?" the trainer asks Bill.

"I *really* know how to be an asshole."

(Laughter)

"Fine," says the trainer. "Tell me how to be an asshole?"

"Get into a dialogue with an *est* trainer."

(Laughter)

"But can you tell me how to *be* an asshole?"

"No problem," Bill replies. "Just be yourself."

(Laughter)

Don is smiling too now when he says: "That's fine. But *how* can I be an asshole?"

"I said, 'Just be yourself.' "

"No, Bill, that won't work. It so happens that anyone who just *is* himself has *ceased* to be an asshole. But thank you for sharing. [Applause]

"Look, when you *really* know something, with complete certainty and reliability, then beliefs about it, or thinking about it, or feelings about it, are all irrelevant: you just *know*, so thoroughly, that beliefs and thoughts and feelings are not necessary and words are inadequate . . .

"In terms of certainty, we only cross the line into something really reliable when we get out of beliefs and feelings and simply observe. When you go beyond the level of observing, you get to the level of what we call realization—that's when you have an 'ah-ha!' experience. . . . All right—Rick, is it?—go ahead, stand up, take the mike."

Rick is a short, squat man with thick gray hair, and he wears boots and a striking purple shirt open at the collar. He is standing in the middle of one of the middle sections and speaks with obvious irritation.

"Ah've ... where do Ah hold this dumb thing? Here? Can you hear me? ... Ah've ... flown in from El Paso, Texas, to take this here training and Ah'm *damned* if Ah know if Ah know what's goin' on. You folks are talkin' the *craziest* nonsense Ah've *eveh* heard. What the *hell* do y'all mean by this talk of levels of experience and levels of certainty? And what the *hell* is this business of your not knowing how to *walk*? Far as Ah'm concerned everybody here who's talked makes just as much sense as you do. Though that surely ain't much. Far as Ah'm concerned, believin' somethin' and thinkin' about somethin', and doing somethin' are a lot better'n just sitting 'round *lookin'* and waitin' for some damned fool 'ah-ha!' experience to come along."

(Laughter and applause)

"I get that, Rick," says the trainer. "We're talking about certainty, right?"

"Damned if Ah know half the time *what* you're talkin about."

"What's your job?"

"Ah raise beef. Ah've got a thousand head of some of the best cattle in west Texas."

"Fine. Now let's say that *I* have a *belief* that raising cattle to slaughter them is morally wrong. I'm certain that what you're doing is evil."

"Well, Ah don't give a good goddamn what you think," says Rick.

"I said I *believe* it. My next level of certainty would be that I *think* raising beef is bad."

"Ah still don't give a shit."

"Right. What I'm going to *do* is write a letter to the governor of Texas denouncing your ranch."

"Lots of luck," Rick says with a big grin. "The governor of Texas butchers more cattle in a week than Ah do in a year."

(Laughter)

"I *feel* very strongly that slaughtering cattle is cruel."

"Feel any damn way you like."

"Now, Rick, what happens if I stop believing and thinking and doing and feeling about your business, and just *go* to your ranch and *observe?*"

"You'd be showin' a bit of sense."

"RIGHT! And you see the diagram on the blackboard showing the levels of certainty?"

Rick squints toward the left blackboard on which are printed levels of certainty—BELIEF ABOUT, THINK ABOUT, DO ABOUT, and FEEL ABOUT below a horizontal line and OBSERVATION, REALIZATION, CERTAINTY OF NOT KNOWING, and NATURAL KNOWING above it—the chart analogous to the one on the other board showing levels of experience.

"Yeah, Ah see it."

"That's all it's saying. That the higher up we go on that scale, the more certain and reliable is the knowledge we have. When we reach the highest level of certainty we're at something we call 'natural knowing'—something like the way Jed knows walking or Tania knows singing. And you can see now that the lowest form of certainty lies in the realm of belief."

"Depends on the belief, don't it?" Rick says.

"NO, you asshole! *All* belief is the least reliable form of knowing. Belief represents *un*certainty. People believe in God because they have no real certainty about Her. Where there is a natural knowing of God, there is no need for belief. The highest form of certainty is something you know so thoroughly and so naturally that it's impossible to put into words."

"Yeah, well, Ah get that," Rick says firmly. "That's why Ah find all the word business Ah been hearing in here a lot of manure."

"It *is* manure. Everything I say is manure. I've warned you about that several times, haven't I?"

"Y'have?"

"I've said don't believe a word I say."

"Then why do you say them?"

"Why do you pump dirty water from a pond and squirt it into a stable?"

"To clean out the shit."

"Well guess what? That's why I have to pour words at you assholes . . ."

"All right, now we're going to do a *process* and then we're going to take a break."

There is a great heave of groans and sighs and scattered applause.

"First, I'm going to tell you *how* you're going to do the process, and then you're going to do it. I want you to listen carefully now as I tell you what I'm going to say and what you're going to do in the process, but DON'T, ASSHOLES, BEGIN YET TO DO IT. Do you understand? Good.

"First, I will instruct you to remove your glasses and contact lenses, place any article on your lap onto the floor beneath your chair, and sit comfortably with your arms and legs uncrossed. I will ask you to place your hands on your thighs and to close your eyes. Then I will instruct you to 'enter your space,' which simply means to *be* quietly in your mind wherever you are in your mind. Next I will say 'locate a space in the toes of your left foot,' and after giving you sufficient time to locate a space in the toes of your left foot, I will acknowledge you by saying 'fine' or 'good' or 'thank you' and ask you next to 'locate a space in the bone of your left foot.' After five or six seconds I will say 'good, locate a space in the bone of your left ankle.' Such instructions and acknowledgments will continue until you have located spaces in parts of every area of your body, up both legs, through your torso to the top of your head, and up both arms to the shoulders. I will also ask you to observe any tension you may experience in the muscles in the forehead between the eyes, in the jaw, in your tongue . . ."

For perhaps fifteen more minutes the trainer describes in full detail the coming process and answers questions from the trainees about the process. As he goes over the instructions and begins to answer questions the tension in the room begins to drain. People are stretching and turning in their seats, yawning, exercising their eyes and fists. Several people begin whispering to each other.

"HEY!" shouts the trainer. "There's no talking in this room except when I say so. Get that. And shuttup!"

And he goes on.

At last he begins the process.

Eyes closed, we sit quietly.

"I want you to locate a space in the toe of your left foot ... good. ... Locate a space in the bone of your left foot ... fine. ... Locate a space in the bone of your left ankle ... fine. ... Now locate a space in the toe of your right foot ... good. ... Locate a space in the bone of your right foot ... fine. ... Now locate a space in your right ankle ... good. ... Locate a space in your left shinbone ... fine. ... Now locate a space in your left knee ... fine. ... Locate a space in your right lower leg ... good ... Locate a space in your right shinbone ... good. ... Now locate a space in your right knee ... fine. ... Locate a space in your left thigh bone ... fine ..."

The effect of the trainer's loud voice is not at first relaxing, but since most of the trainees have become fatigued by the energetic interchanges between themselves and Don, the repetitiousness of the process instructions and acknowledgments soon has a hypnotically unwinding effect. The effects of the gradual relaxing into a less conscious state vary considerably among trainees. Before ten minutes have passed and the trainer is still locating spaces only in the left thigh, we hear a woman softly crying. By the time he reaches the diaphragm and gives the instruction to follow the inhale and exhale of the breath, another louder sobbing is heard. Later, a man's rhythmic snoring. But the process goes on and on, and for twenty-five minutes the trainer's voice—still loud and intense —guides the trainees in locating spaces and relaxing muscles, in the forehead, jaw, and tongue. The women who were crying come to stop crying but another woman's sniffling can be heard, and the man's snoring continues with the soft regular systole and dystole of an ocean's surf.

When the entire body has been gone over and the muscles

of the face totally relaxed and the trainees have taken three deep breaths and R E L A A A A X E D on the exhale, the trainer begins to read a long set piece of prose poetry, a long declaration of self-affirmation, a saying yes to life and the expanding powers of the individual.

I am and have been okay. . . .
I can do and be whatever I want to do or be
Providing it does not bring harm to other human beings.
It is all right for me to be this way.
I love and have been loved and am loving.
I recognize this and accept this.
I can aspire to and have a higher state of awareness
  and consciousness. . . .
It is all right for me to do this . . .

The affirmation goes on and on for almost five minutes.

When the bodies of most of the trainees are completely relaxed and the process is over, the trainer asks the trainees to re-create the room around us in our mind's eye, and then slowly he brings us back into the garish reality of the hotel ballroom.

When our eyes are open, Richard is standing on the platform ready to assist in the logistics of the long-awaited first break. He mechanically describes the locations of three different sets of bathrooms in the hotel, though most of us undoubtedly feel we could probably locate a rest room even if there was only one in the whole universe and that one camouflaged. There is to be no eating during this break, and all trainees are expected to be back in our seats in precisely thirty minutes. To our amazement we learn that the time is now 4:05—except for a short bathroom break, we have been with the trainer for over eight consecutive hours. No wonder asses ache. And then we are released.

"Charlotte? Stand up," says the trainer after the break.

Charlotte stands and takes the mike. She is very young and blonde, wearing blue denim jeans and a blouse.

"Well, what happened to me during the process," she says animatedly, "is that ... well, I just relaxed ... I mean totally let go, and it felt *great*. And then when you brought us out of it, the room seemed so *beautiful*. I mean the rug, the colors of the rug were just terrific. It was like a grass high if you know what I mean. I really enjoyed it."

"Thank you, Charlotte. [Applause] Mike."

"This is the first time I've said anything," Mike says in a deep voice, "and it's simply that nothing happened with me in the process. It seemed a big waste of time."

"Thank you, Mike."

"Can I ask a question?"

"Save it till after the sharing, Mike."

"Okay."

"Thank you. [Applause] Tom?"

Tom, the young bushy-haired, beaded, gravelly voiced man who earlier called the trainer an arrogant bastard, stands and takes the microphone.

"It was interesting," he says. "I do a lot of meditating and I must admit that what you did with all those 'locate a spaces' is put me into the same blissed-out state I usually don't reach until after an hour of deep breath-counting. I was pretty surprised. It was okay."

"Thank you. [Applause] Jennifer? Take the mike."

Jennifer is a woman in her forties, plump and with a weary expression on her face.

"I'm afraid I'm one of those who cried. I don't know why. I was doing the process just like you said and then when you got to the abdomen, as soon as you said 'locate a space in your abdomen' I was suddenly crying. It was ridiculous. I don't have the slightest idea why I was crying ..."

"That's okay, Jennifer," Don says. "Just follow instructions and take what you get. Did you resist your crying?"

"No," Jennifer says. "It was strange. It was a very quiet crying. I felt like you had pushed some button in my abdomen and some gentle faucet had been turned on. It was strange."

"Thank you, Jennifer. [Applause] Tim. Take the mike."

Tim, a small, balding man wearing glasses, speaks in a tight voice that quavers.

"Uh . . . first I'd like to say that I'm . . . scared to be standing up talking. In fact," he clears his throat, "I'm scared shitless. [Scattered applause] But about the process . . . I found that as soon as you said 'go into your space'—even before you talked about locating a space in your left foot—I mean at the very *beginning* of the process—I felt panic. I was trembling during the whole thing. I don't think I located a single space. . . . I spent all the time trying to stop feeling so afraid. I wasn't scared before anytime during the whole day. This is off the wall! I can barely hold the mike."

"That's okay, Tim," Don says, moving from the center of the platform to the right front edge. "Later today and tomorrow we'll talk about handling things like that. You'll be able to look at your fear, and by being really with it, it'll disappear. But don't cling to that life raft I just threw you. Stay with your experience. I don't expect you to get what I just said right now. For the time being just be with your fear, observe it, don't fight it. Okay? Thank you for sharing. [Applause] Kathy?"

"Nothing special happened to me," says Kathy, a tall woman with short, curly hair. "But I'd like to share that someplace near the end of the process, I think I had an 'ah-ha' experience." She smiles and several people laugh. "It was during locating a space in my right buttock—which was aching like hell at the time. It was the most vivid thing that had happened to me all day. I felt in touch with my body and really in touch with life."

"Thank you, Kathy. [Applause] David? Take the mike, please."

"I'd like to know what the purpose of the process was," says

David, a distinguished-looking man with thick, curly black hair and wearing dark, horn-rimmed glasses.

"No purpose," Don replies mildly. He is sitting on the stool, feet resting on the lower rung and one arm relaxed across his chest. "It's just part of the training."

"I mean, were we supposed to experience light? Or break down crying? Or just get some rest?"

"You were supposed to follow the instructions and take what you get. What did you get, David?"

"I didn't get anything," David says, frowning and adjusting his glasses. "But of course I didn't follow the instructions either. I spent most of the time wondering what we were doing it for and the rest daydreaming about eating *coq au vin.*"

"That's what you got, David. I get that you got you didn't follow instructions, wondered why we were doing the process, and imagined eating. If you want to live the rest of your life in the mind, go ahead, but if you'd like to *experience* something I suggest you begin by following instructions. Thank you. [Applause] Sally ..."

And on goes the sharing. It is strange to experience the quiet sincerity with which people are sharing what happens to them: so different from the clashes with the trainer before the process and the break. Has *he* changed or have we?

"You are perfect," Don is saying, pacing from left to right across the platform perhaps an hour later, "but there are barriers preventing you from experiencing and expressing your perfection. We have called this the first notion of *est.*

"And the second has to do with one of those barriers blocking you from feeling and expressing your perfection. Stated simply it's this: resistance leads to persistence. If you try to resist something or change something, it will become more solid. The only way to get rid of something is just to let it be. This doesn't mean to ignore it. Ignoring is actually a form of rejection and resistance. To ignore anxiety or anger is one of the asshole ways to try to eliminate it. To let something be means to observe it, stay in touch with it, but make no effort to change it.

"The third related notion is one you'll never believe, but since we don't want you to *believe* it, we can go right ahead and say it: the re-creation of an experience makes the experience disappear. Reexperiencing something to completion disappears it. Jennifer? Stand up."

"You say that trying to change something makes it persist," says Jennifer, the plump woman who cried earlier. "But I thought people were taught to learn to control their emotions. Doesn't that mean trying to resist and change them?"

"YES! And you know damned well it doesn't work. The whole world has been trying to change things for centuries and they still persist. How many wars to end war have we fought?"

"But if trying to control things doesn't work," Jennifer says slowly, "then why do human beings keep trying to do it?"

"BECAUSE HUMAN BEINGS ARE ASSHOLES!" the trainer shouts almost into Jennifer's face. "Look, I know it's a paradox and not easy to get, but the effort to control or change something absolutely *ensures* its persistence. If you're angry and begin to get angry at your anger and try to change it, your anger will persist. If you're feeling tense and try to relax, you'll continue to be tense. If you have a headache and try to change it, your head will continue to ache as long as you're trying to get rid of it. . . . Thank you, Jennifer. All right, David?"

(Applause)

"I don't understand then," David says, standing tall and erect in the front of the room, "how change *ever* occurs."

"We're not talking about *change*," the trainer says sharply. "We're talking about whether something persists or not. If you try to change your tenseness you may change the form of the tenseness, but the tenseness will still persist. You won't be able to disappear it. The substance will remain the same."

"All right then," says David, "Then I don't understand your theory about how anything ceases to persist."

"IT'S NOT A THEORY, ASSHOLE!"

"Then what is it? Idea, notion—no matter what you call it, it's really a theory or belief."

"No! You may *make* it into a theory or belief, but that's not what I'm putting out. What I'm putting out is the words 'Trying to change something leads to its persisting,' and these—"

"That's a statement of belief," says David, his face flushed.

"It's a statement of my direct experience."

"How does that differ from a belief?"

"Like night and day, asshole. A belief is a statement that does NOT COME OUT OF EXPERIENCE. 'Christ died and on the third day rose from the dead.' That's a statement too, but it has nothing to do today with anyone's direct experience. It's a belief."

"Okay, then, you can call your statement a notion," David says. "I still don't see how, according to your notion, anything ceases to persist."

"It's simple: the re-creation of an experience makes the experience disappear."

"What does *that* mean?"

"To re-create an experience, you get totally in touch with it, you rebuild it element by element until it is entirely restructured and—paradox—it disappears."

"Now how in God's name can you rebuild something like tenseness?"

"Well, I'll tell you one thing, David," says the trainer, moving away from David back to the center of the platform. "You first have to get in touch with the elements of tenseness. You can't re-create a house unless you know about wood and brick and nails and shingles. So too you can't re-create tenseness or any other experience unless you know what it's made of."

"Tenseness isn't like a house, it's a . . . an abstraction."

"No. It's a word people use to try to describe certain kinds of experience. Because people don't know their experience, because they're living in the realm of nonexperience, they don't really know *any* of the elements of tenseness."

"Well, then," says David, "we're back where we started. You can't re-create tenseness without knowing the elements and no one knows the elements."

"No, you're still not getting it. Everyone has experienced tenseness at least once and what we want for them is to experience it again. If they'd stop resisting it, stop trying to change it, and just be with it, observe it, they would in fact re-create the experience of tenseness and it would disappear."

"Impossible!"

"Of course it's impossible. I never said it was anything else. In a couple of hours you'll see one person after another come up on this platform with me and each one will say that he's tense or tired or has a headache, and you know what? I'll ask him to observe and re-create his tension or tiredness or headache and it'll disappear. It'll disappear. Totally impossible. Total nonsense. Only it works."

"I'll believe it when I see it."

"DON'T BELIEVE IT NO MATTER HOW MANY TIMES YOU SEE IT!" the trainer shouts in David's face. "*Experience* it when you see it."

"Well, since I won't see it in any case, the semantical difference—"

"FUCK YOUR SEMANTICAL DIFFERENCES. I'M talking about REAL differences and it's only your asshole reasonableness that keeps you from experiencing them."

"I'm not going to argue with you," David says, and he hands the mike back to the assistant and sits down.

"You're getting smart," the trainer replies, striding across the platform. "You can't win in here. Nobody wins in here except me. Unless I decide to *let* you win. It ought to be perfectly clear to everyone now that you're all assholes and I'm God. Only an asshole would argue with God. I may let you be Gods too but that'll come later. Thank you, David. Yes, Marie?"

(Applause)

"Do you mean that this morning when I wanted to vomit, that I shouldn't have resisted but just vomited?" asks Marie, the slight, attractive girl who earlier tried to leave the room. "When you felt nauseous you probably panicked and tried to change it, right?"

"Yes."

"And what happened?"

"It got worse."

"IT GOT WORSE. IT PERSISTED, ASSHOLES.... What happened after I finished showing you how to use the bag?"

Marie stands quietly for a moment without answering. She is still in the front row although now off to the far left of the room.

"Well ... I ... uh ... gradually stopped feeling sick."

"Fine. What did you experience just after you sat down and I started talking to someone else?"

Again Marie stands in silence.

"I ... remember vividly seeing how clean the inside of the paper bag was. I also noticed that it was big enough to take ... whatever I might give it.... I also felt that I would have no trouble using it ..."

"Go on."

"And ... well ... I didn't have to vomit anymore."

(Silence)

The trainer strides away from Marie to the center of the platform.

"She didn't have to vomit anymore. You *know* why? Do *any* of you assholes know why? Chuck?"

"Because she was so emotionally upset with you, the anger dominated the nausea," answers Chuck.

"BULLSHIT!" roars the trainer. "Marie, were you angry and upset with me?"

"No," Marie replies promptly.

"No. Then *why* did Marie suddenly stop feeling sick? Angela?"

"Because ... I think I've got it," begins Angela uncertainly. "Because when she ... when she saw that the paper bag was big enough and felt she could use it, and maybe too that you didn't care whether she vomited or not—that seems to me important—then she was free to vomit. She didn't have to resist it. She didn't have to change it."

Marie and Angela are both standing, and the trainer lets Angela's answer hang there in the room for all of us to hear.

"Yes," he says with a strange mildness. "Exactly. She didn't have to resist it." And then he abruptly shouts. "SHE DIDN'T TRY TO CHANGE IT, ASSHOLES! She accepted it, got in touch with it, and it disappeared." He stands in the exact center of the front of the platform staring neutrally out over the audience for almost half a minute. Then he concludes: "Thank you, Angela. Thank you, Marie," and the trainees applaud loudly.

"Trying to change an experience makes it persist. Re-creating an experience—accepting it, being with it, observing it—makes it disappear. All bullshit. All nonsense. It works. Yes, Jerry."

Jerry, the big man with a brush cut who argued about his "belief" in God, stands up immense in the fourth row on the aisle and speaks.

"I've got a habit of getting angry with people who try to push other people around, especially who try to push *me*. The anger's justified a lot of the time, but I got this morning that I think I'd rather not bother to be right about it, I'd rather not be angry.

"And in fact I've learned to *control* it pretty well. For example, I've got a boss who's real pompous and when he orders me to do something I'd love to tell him he's being unfair. . . . Frankly I'd love to punch him in the mouth. But instead I say 'Yes, sir,' and go do what he wants, counting my breaths like crazy, and looking forward to a drink at lunchtime. The anger is kept under control. That is, when it arises, I successfully change it into something which will permit me to avoid doing something I might regret."

"So each time you've been trying to resist and change your anger?" the trainer asks Jerry.

"Of course," Jerry replies. "And I have."

"And is your anger persisting?"

(Silence)

"Yes . . . ," begins Jerry uncertainly, "but not the way . . ."

"YOU'RE GODDAMN RIGHT IT PERSISTS! AND IT'LL PERSIST THE REST OF YOUR FUCKING LIFE AND YOU *KNOW* IT."

"But I've *changed* it," insists Jerry, looking uncomfortable and shifting his big bulk uneasily.

"You've modified it. But it still persists. You haven't disappeared it."

"What am I supposed to do? Tear the boss to pieces?"

"Stop resisting your anger and start observing. Stop trying to eliminate your anger, just witness it, be with it, get in touch with exactly what anger is for you, your bodily sensations, feelings, your attitudes."

"What good will that do?"

"None whatsoever. Except that your anger will probably disappear."

"Huh."

"Look," the trainer goes on, looking over the audience. "You people all know you've been *trying* to *change* your lives for years and they DON'T CHANGE. The things you work on persist. It's not that you're weak or not trying hard enough. It's just that you're assholes, that's all. You're using the wrong method. If you don't like something about yourself or someone else, the thing to do is just observe it, experience it, get in touch with it. You say your boss is an irritable pompous bastard? FINE! Wonderful! See how many specific manifestations of his irritability, pomposity, and bastardry you can observe and experience. He makes you angry? Great! Exactly how? What is your anger? Weigh it, measure it. See what color it is. See what muscles it is affecting, what sensations it produces in what parts of your body. Really get in touch with your exact bodily sensations and feelings in relation to your boss. Presto! You know what will happen?"

"I'll get a headache," says Jerry.

(A few trainees laugh.)

"That's exactly what usually happens, right?" says the trainer.

"That's what always happens," comments Jerry.

"You know what your head is trying to tell you? It's trying to tell you to STOP RESISTING AND PAY ATTENTION. If you would groove to the boss you'd find it would be groovy."

"You mean the boss will cease to be a pompous jerk?"

"You will cease to experience him as a pompous jerk."

Jerry frowns.

"You just told us that we were getting fully in touch with his being that," he says.

"That's right."

"If we're in touch with it, how can we cease to experience it?"

"The *only* way to cease to experience something is to get in touch with it. It's a totally impossible paradox: if you *fully* experience something, then the experience will disappear and you'll have a new one."

"I just don't understand."

"That's because you're in your asshole mind. I don't want you to understand it. Understanding gets the booby prize. Just try it and experience it. You can even experience away your being an asshole . . ."

Jerry stiffens.

"Maybe it's you that's the asshole," he says.

"Great. Now just get in touch with your anger. See what you're experiencing *right now*."

"You're a stupid fascist."

"THAT'S NOT AN EXPERIENCE, ASSHOLE!" the trainer shouts at Jerry a few feet away. "THAT'S A BELIEF! LOOK! LOOK AT YOUR EXPERIENCE. I want you to observe and be in touch with what you're feeling right now."

"I'm mad."

"That's closer. Exactly what are you *feeling* right now?"

Jerry hesitates and then appears to examine himself.

"My muscles are tense and my stomach churning and you're a fascist."

"Good! Two experiences and a belief!" says the trainer, now standing right next to Jerry and seeming small in comparison. "Which muscles are tense?"

"My arm muscles and my jaw muscles. My stomach muscles. Abdomen."

"Great. Which jaw muscles?"

"The ones . . . well . . . the ones . . . through here," says Jerry, pointing up beside his ear.

"Good. Where is the tenseness in your belly?"

"Uh . . . here," Jerry replies, pointing to just above his belly button.

"How far in is this tenseness?"

"About two inches."

"Good. Is it a pain or pressure or what?"

"It's . . . uh . . . just sort of a sensation, a tenseness."

"Fine. Describe what's happening now with your arm muscles."

Jerry glances automatically at his left arm.

"They're still a little tense."

"You've got two fucking miles of arm muscles. Where?"

"Actually, it's in my fingers and up here around the shoulder."

"Great. Tell us exactly what sensations you have in your fingers."

Jerry wiggles his fingers.

"Actually they're . . . okay now."

"Fine. Now look at your abdomen again. Describe what you're experiencing there."

"A little heaviness above the navel."

"Well, how big is the heaviness?"

"About a golf ball now."

"How far in is it?"

". . . It's kind of fuzzy. . . . Maybe two inches."

"Great. What color is it?"

"Color?"

"What color is this heaviness?"

Jerry spends a long time with his head lowered, looking within.

"No ... I just can't say."

"Okay. Tell me what *size* the heaviness is now."

Jerry hesitates again.

"It's ... uh ... well ... actually there's nothing there now. There's no more heaviness."

"I see," says the trainer, still standing only two feet away from Jerry. "Are you still experiencing anger at me?"

Jerry smiles shyly.

"No," he says.

"Are you still experiencing me as a stupid fascist?"

Jerry smiles.

"Just as you asked me the question I felt a rush of resentment but I realize that ... basically ... no. A fascist maybe, but not stupid."

"You got in touch with your anger and it disappeared?"

For a moment Jerry stands uneasily in silence, shifting his considerable weight from foot to foot. Then he shakes his head and grins.

"It sure did disappear."

"What would have happened five minutes ago, if, when you were angry, I told you to try to control yourself, to change your anger into peacefulness, your resentment of me into love for me?"

"I would have told you to stick it up ... I would have remained angry."

"The anger would have persisted?"

"Yeah ..."

"Thank you ..."

For our second process, we assume comfortable positions with arms and legs uncrossed and follow the instructions of the trainer in locating spaces throughout our bodies. Before twenty minutes have passed the continual background chatter of most of our minds—"yamayama" in *est* terms—has quieted, and one or two people are crying and a few sleeping. We relax the muscles in our foreheads, jaws, and tongues. We breathe deeply. We listen to the long affirmation of life read to us by the trainer.

Finally we are asked to create for ourselves an idyllic beach on which we can play and feel completely relaxed. The trainer assists us in seeing and feeling the sand dunes, the reeds, the seashells, the hotness of the sand, the line of seaweed running parallel to the water line, the blue sky blotched with clouds, the pieces of bleached driftwood, the crushed empty beer can, the charcoal remains of a fire, the gulls circling above a decaying fish. He assists us in hearing the cries of the gulls, the hissing and crash of the surf, and in feeling the warm saltiness of the seawater washing about our feet. A tape recording begins to play the sounds of waves crashing rhythmically against our beach, and we are asked to play there ... however we feel like playing ...

And many many fantasy-filled minutes later we are at last given our long-promised ninety-minute break to eat dinner. Like schoolchildren held too long after class by a strict teacher, the trainees scatter out into the streets outside the hotel as if onto a playground.

Around the tables at the various restaurants scattered in the vicinity of the hotel, many of the trainees are somewhat subdued. Whether it is exhaustion from the long day, serenity produced by the second guided meditation on our "beaches," or a vague dread that most of our normal dinnertime talk with new acquaintances will be ego-inspired game-playing is not easy to determine ...

"Harold? Stand up. Take the mike," says the trainer after the dinner break.

"What happened to me at the beach was first enjoyable and then frightening. I was *there*, I could really hear the waves and feel the water, and then you said play at our beach and I figured I'd play with my two children. But when I tried to get them onto the beach with me they wouldn't come, they just wouldn't materialize. Next I tried to get a couple of my business buddies. Nothing. Nobody would materialize. It was weird. And I realized that I never really play with anyone. Ever. It isn't that they won't play with me. I never play with them . . ."

Barbara: ". . . I don't understand why I feel this nausea. . . . Both times, in both processes, as soon as you've finished with locating spaces in our legs I began to feel sick to my stomach. . . . There are no thoughts . . . no memories . . . just nausea. . . . Why?"

David: ". . . and when you asked us to play I was suddenly running along the beach, just jogging along at the edge of the surf. And you said 'play' and I thought this isn't playing, I've got to imagine myself playing, but I kept running, the running was so vivid, just running down the beach, not running away from anything, not running toward anything, just running along my beach, running . . . and not playing . . ."

Jennifer: "I didn't cry this time. I just sat in the sand and watched the waves come curling in and slide along the sand and it felt good. And when it was time to play I built a sandcastle, and I did something this time that I have never done in real life. I built the sand castle right close to the waves rather than way back. I knew when the tide came in it would destroy what I was building, but somehow it didn't matter . . . it made me happy. . . . When a wall got washed away it was as nice as building it . . ."

Robert: ". . . I mean how the fuck is anyone supposed to play at a beach when the lady next to me is throwing up all over the place? The whole process is ridiculous. The damn tape recorder sounded like the IRT subway train coming in and was about as relaxing as that. . . . I didn't get anything but irritability and wondering what the fuck I was doing lying on the floor playing silly mind games . . ."

Angela: "I've never smelled. Never in my life have I been able to distinguish odors. . . . And yet when you said 'decaying fish' . . . I *smelled*, for the first time in my life. [Angela is glowing with excitement and then she smiles self-consciously.] I smelled something. I know it will seem strange but . . . the smell of the decaying fish was beautiful . . . just beautiful."

Hank: "I just wanted to say that I didn't get anything out of the process. I thought it was a waste of time. Mainly I slept . . ."

Tom: ". . . So that was sure one groovy beach. The sky was as blue as it ever gets on grass and I could even feel the sun hot on my belly. But the funny thing was, when you asked us to play I began wading out into the ocean. And then swimming. I mean not piddling around in the surf like I usually do, but swimming straight out, straight out into the fuckin' ocean, straight out. . . . I mean, wow, that was really heavy. I'm glad you pulled us back into the room before it was too late . . ."

"You're all murdering life," the trainer is saying later on, after more sharing. "You're all trying to change yourselves, all trying to change what is, and thus you're never actually *living* what is. You're killing who you are every day of your lives by not being *who* you are . . . where you are . . .

"You're all liars," he goes on after taking a sip from the metal thermos that usually rests on the large lectern. "And lying about where you're at prevents you from getting to where you intend to go.

"Look, let's say I'm a good typical normal human being standing here in the exact center of this platform. Being a good normal human, I'm totally out of touch with where I really am. I lie. I have a belief that I'm a radical, a leftist. I lie that I'm actually on the left-hand side of the platform and far to the front . . . definitely far to the front—over there, that corner over there.

"Great! I'm in the center of the platform and I lie to myself that I'm on the left forward corner.

"Now look what happens. I want to get to the right front corner of the platform. I think I'm over there in the left front corner, so I think I have to walk due west thirty paces. Fine. I walk west thirty paces. . . . And look what happens . . .

"I FALL OFF THE PLATFORM FLAT ON MY FACE!" the trainer shouts as he mock-falls off the far edge of the platform. As he returns to the center of the stage he seems to be staring fiercely at the audience.

"You lie. You lie about where you *are* so that when you try to change where you are you just make a royal mess of things. You might just as well know that you can't possibly get from here to there unless you're actually *here* in the first place . . .

"You lie. You sense you're stuck and want to break out, but you can't possibly go where you want to go until you find out where the fuck you actually *are*. Trying to change a thing leads to the persistence of that thing. The only way you're ever going to eliminate anything is to *observe*, find out *what* it is and *where* it is. The complete experiencing of that thing, being totally with it, leads to its disappearing . . .

"Tonight we're going to do a few processes in which you will completely *experience* your tiredness or your headaches and they will disappear. No big deal. Tomorrow you'll get to experience some really big things in your lives and *they'll* disappear, at least for some of you. Observation and re-creation of things disappears them. Obviously impossible. Obviously nonsense. Who'd like to be first?"

A nervous laughter ripples across the room. Several hands are raised.

"David?" says Don, pointing to the tall, well-dressed man who has often argued with him.

"It's still not clear to me," says David, "why resistance is not the best strategy to invoke against obviously undesirable things."

"Well, David, since you seem to be a very rational and in-

tellectual man, with a reading acquaintance with a wide variety of belief systems, you might recall that the Chinese knew
all about this business five thousand years ago. They called it
yin-yang. If somebody pushes and you push back you'll very
likely have pushing forever. You can't have darkness without
light. Darkness only exists because of the 'resistance' of light.
Good can only exist with the resistance of 'bad'—and 'bad' can
exist *only* because of the resistance of 'good.' Up exists because
of the pull of down. Eliminate the resistance, eliminate the
polarity, eliminate the effort to change and presto! You've got
nothing. NOTHING. And when you've got nothing then you
really have something."

"You seem to be saying that a good person should stop trying to avoid the bad."

"That's right, David."

"That's bullshit."

"That's right, David, and your countertheory is Daveshit.
Good people have been trying to eliminate badness for a million years and it doesn't work. It doesn't work."

"It works better than not doing anything."

"Not so, David. I know the myth is that if we all believed in
doing good and avoiding evil that all would be well. But the
sad truth is that the man who kills his neighbor always believes
in good and evil—his own good and his neighbor's evil . . .

"It's doing *nothing* that works. You may not be able to get
that yet, but the Taoists knew it four thousand years ago . . ."

"But who's tired? Anyone in the room tired?"

A score of groans and a dozen hands go up.

"Fine. Who would be willing to come up here and have their
tiredness disappear? All right, Sam? Come on up."

Sam, a rumpled man with a lunging gait, comes from his
seat at the side of the room up onto the platform. Sam's eyes
seem red and he does look tired. He sits down in one of the

two high stools and automatically slumps forward. He glances briefly up to his right at the trainer and then down again at the feet of the people in the front row.

"Sam, are you willing for your tiredness to disappear?"

"Yes. I am."

"Fine. Close your eyes.... Go into your space.... Tell me, Sam, are you tired?"

"... Yes."

"Good. Where do you experience tiredness?"

"In my shoulders ..."

"Fine. Where else do you experience tiredness?"

"In my neck ... In my lower legs ..."

"Good. Where else do you experience tiredness?"

"In my shoulders ... my upper back ... my eyes ... my eyes are tired ..."

"Okay. What are you experiencing right now in your shoulders?"

"... Heaviness."

"Where?"

"In my ... across the back part ... upper part ..."

"Fine. Describe the heaviness."

Sam is sitting more erect now, obviously concentrating on his inner sensations.

"Well," he begins, "actually right now ... it's not there."

"Fine. Describe to us how your eyes feel."

"Little burning sensations in each eye."

"Okay. How strong a burning sensation?"

"Just little flashes like."

"How many flashes per second?"

"Mmmmm ... they've sort of stopped," Sam says softly, and he suddenly opens his eyes wide and stares out at the audience. "In fact, I feel great," he concludes.

"Are you tired?"

"No. It's all gone. I feel great."

"Fine. Thank you, Sam."

Sam steps down to light applause. Several trainees look skeptical, and a half-dozen hands are raised.

"When did you plant Sam?" someone shouts.

The trainer apparently doesn't hear. He calls on Jerry, the big man whose anger at the trainer was "disappeared" earlier.

"It seems to me," says Jerry, looming up immense in the middle of the fourth row, "that all that happened was that after Sam got up on the platform he found what he was doing interesting . . . and thus he wasn't bored and tired anymore."

"Fine, Jerry," the trainer replies, going to the lectern to get a drink from his thermos. "I get that. But remember, this process is intended to show you how little you assholes ever *observe*. Do you get that Sam, sitting down, was experiencing tiredness and was undoubtedly not liking it and that he got up here and *observed* it and he found he *wasn't* tired?"

"Maybe, but I'm not sure observation is what disappeared it."

"Great. It's ridiculous to think that his looking at and describing his tiredness would disappear it, isn't it?"

"Yes."

"Especially to disappear it so fast."

"Yes."

"And it may come back again for Sam in another ten or fifteen minutes . . ."

"Right."

"All that is sometimes our problem in the training. We get people up here who say they're exhausted, have been exhausted for four hours, and we ask them to describe their tiredness and thirty seconds later they say, 'Oh, it's all gone, I feel great.' Or a person has had a headache all day and we get them sitting up here and relaxed and we ask them how big their headache is and they say, 'What headache?' [Laughter]

"And sometimes, half an hour after they've sat down they manage to get their headache again. We bring them up here and presto! it disappears. Our problem is that the fuckin' process works so fast—the process of ceasing resistance ending persistence—that you assholes *know* it's all a fake . . ."

"All right, let's make a list of the causes of a headache. You mentioned, Beverly, that you were experiencing tension which was giving you a headache. Are there any other causes of a headache?" The trainer goes to the blackboard and quickly writes TENSION in the top left corner. "Anyone else? Yes, Marcia?"

"I often have sinus headaches, especially during flu season."

"Fine. Let's put SINUS under TENSION. Tim?"

"A hangover."

"Right! Hangover!" The trainer writes HANGOVER under SINUS. Many hands are popping up. He points to another.

"Eyestrain causes headaches."

"Good. Eyestrain." As he writes, he asks Marcia to come up and help him write on the board. A young woman goes up, smiling and looking a little awkward at first, but quickly getting into the serious business of writing down the myriad "causes" of headaches.

"John?" says the trainer, beginning to recognize hands more quickly.

"Anger."

"Right, anger. Got that, Marcia? Yes . . . Cliff?"

"Genuine disease," he says pointedly.

"That's too vague," says Don. "Give me a specific disease."

"Okay, polio," he says distinctly.

"Right, polio." Don points to another in the back. "Ann?"

"From worrying too much."

"Okay, worry."

The assistants are scurrying up and down the aisles with the mikes, sometimes not making it fast enough. But the trainees are entering into it and speaking up louder. They're on "safe ground."

"Yes, Mike."

"A stomachache will cause a headache."

Marcia writes STOMACHACHE.

"David?"

"Listening to the trainer."

"Right. Good: listening to the trainer. Get it down, Marcia. Bob?"

"A hit on the head," Bob says, smiling.

"Right. Hit on head."

"Carol?"

"Too much sun."

"Right. Andrea?"

"Overfatigue."

"Okay ... Jack, would you give Marcia a hand up here at the blackboard? Thank you." Jack goes up willingly. The pace quickens; the list grows. The apparent causes of a headache are endless: jealousy, noise, too cold outside, glare, feet hurt, anxiety, hatred, hypertension, fear, indigestion, poor posture, heat prostration, hunger, disorder, not enough sleep, depression, watching television too long, argument with spouse, too many children, riding the subway, faulty contact lens, excessive lovemaking, inflamed brain capillaries, lunch with the boss, tight hats, bad smells, guilty feelings ... The list spills over to fill the other blackboard.

"Okay. Good," finally concludes the trainer. "Let's take one of those headaches and do a process that will demonstrate that you people don't know how to *observe*. I don't mean one of your twenty-four-year headaches. I mean one that's been around for four or five hours, more or less. Is someone willing to come up here and sit in this chair [He has one hand on the arm of the high stool.] and be with their experience of a headache in front of the group?"

The hands that were so willing a few minutes ago to commit causes of headaches to the air disappear to about three.

"Fine, good. Joan. Will you come up here?" She rises and

passes to the platform. "How long have you had this head-ache?"

"About an hour."

"Are you willing to be with your experience of a headache in front of the group?"

"Yes," she says quietly. He directs her to the tall black plastic chair.

"Are you willing to experience out your headache now in front of everyone and if it disappears let it disappear, and if it remains let it remain?"

"Yes," she answers again.

"Okay, Joan. Relax, close your eyes, and go into your space." He gives her a minute. He is standing close to the chair, mike in hand, passing it from his mouth to hers as needed.

"Fine," he continues. "Are you ready?"

"Yes, I'm ready."

"Joan, describe your headache to us. Tell us what your experience of your headache is." He puts the mike near her mouth.

"Well, it's like a pressure in my head."

The trainer looks at the audience and back at Joan.

"Where in your head?" His hand with the mike moves to near her mouth.

"It's, uh, behind my eyes, behind my eyebrows."

"Fine. How big is it?" He is now concentrating neutrally on Joan. The audience is stirring less and less.

She thinks a moment. "It's the size of a brick, from temple to temple."

"What color is it?"

"Red."

"Fine. What shape is it?"

"Oblong with sharp edges."

"How far in behind your eyebrows is it?"

"About half an inch—and it goes in about two inches."

"Good. What size is your headache?"

She concentrates. "A brick," she answers.

"What color is it?"

(Pause)

"Sort of reddish orange."

"Good. What shape is it?"

"Rounded, smooth brick."

"How big is it?"

"Like a blackboard eraser."

"Great. What color is it?"

The audience is very quiet.

"It's orange with a little gray."

"What shape is it?"

Joan hesitates for some time. "It's fuzzy. Like a scoop of ice cream."

"Good. How big is it?"

"Maybe a golf ball."

"What color is it?"

She hesitates, seems to search. Finally, "Yellow, some gray."

"What shape is it?"

"Round."

"How big is it?"

She is quiet again for almost fifteen seconds. The audience is totally silent. "It's almost not there," she says, a little amused. "I guess the size of a pea."

"Fine. What color is it?"

"Umn . . . nothing, it's gone, it's not there."

She opens her eyes with a blank expression, closes them again, and then repeats: "It's gone . . ."

"Thank you, Joan," says the trainer; and the audience breaks out into long, loud applause.

2

DAY TWO
The Truth Shall Make You Free

"Well, Werner, yesterday I freed myself
from three more beliefs."
"That's very good," said Werner smiling.
"And today, so far as I know, you've only
added one new one."

"If all beliefs are illusions, Werner, your
statement that all fixed beliefs are illusions
is itself an illusion."
"Absolutely."
"Then what is one to believe?"
"Exactly."

"Who would be wrong if your life began
to work?"

—AN *est* KOAN

The next morning the hotel room is the same. The trainer is the same. The other trainees are the same. Even the assistants are the same. It's been less than eight hours since we were last in the room and everything is the same—and everything is different. The tension and fear that were present for so many during most of the first day are less palpable in the morning. People are smiling more and talking less. When the assistant Richard addresses the trainees in his robotlike way about our agreements, trainees tend to smile or giggle instead of tremble. The trainer comes to the platform quite informally this time and stands there looking over the trainees. He says simply:

"Hi."

The trainees respond with a few "Hi's" in return, and many relax with a yawn. The training had ended the first night at close to one A.M., after the disappearing of two more headaches and the sharing of many questions about the process. In the last hour or so the trainer had handled "rides"—permitted people to stand up, announce where they were going, and arrange to share cars or cabs. The handling of rides completed, Don had instructed each trainee to be thinking of some persistent, recurring barrier, some emotion or upset or compulsive action or physical pain or habit that he would like to experience out as other trainees had experienced out headaches and fatigue. He had also introduced three processes for us to do in bed before going to sleep: that of setting a mental alarm clock, which might permit awakening at a specific early hour without the aid of a physical alarm clock; that of preparing oneself to awaken alert, refreshed, and alive; and a third process designed to assist us to remember our dreams. He also suggested that anyone having trouble going to sleep simply begin locating spaces in the body as was done in the processes.

This morning the trainer glances only once at the notebook open on the small lectern and then announces that we will begin with some sharing about our experiences with the processes we might have tried overnight or sharing about anything.

And we share.

Three or four people who set a mental alarm clock report that they woke up within a few minutes of the time they had set their mental alarms for. Several trainees say that on just four or five hours' sleep they awakened more alive and energetic than they normally do on eight or nine hours' sleep.

Others report they slept right through their mental alarms—they woke up tired as usual . . .

Phil: ". . . I was worried about having to sleep without my usual Nytol or double Scotch. I've been something of an insomniac for years and if it takes me two hours to get to sleep with booze, TV, and Nytol, I figure without them I'll just be finally dozing off when the damn mental alarm clock I set will be waking me up. [Laughter] So I decided to try this process of yours. You know, locate a space in my left toe, and so on up the body. I figured at the least I'd get to locate a few hundred spaces I never knew existed. So, I located a space in my left big toe . . . and that's the last thing I remember before waking."

(Laughter and applause)

Marie: ". . . So I was really pleased that my mental alarm had woken me up on time and that I was feeling good and as I was sitting at the window looking out at the rain I suddenly felt pooped. I went back to bed and the next thing I knew the *real* alarm clock was waking me up."

The microphone is handed next to an older man seated in the back row wearing what looks like an expensive tweed jacket and a brown open-necked gabardine shirt. His white hair is full and wavy. He has a solid build and slight jowls in a square reddish face.

"I'm a writer," Stuart says in a tremulous voice. "I've had success with my work . . . but no matter how much success I may have had, still have, it hasn't been enough to erase the inner knowledge of my ultimate mortality. Over the last few years, I've had the realization, and it's overwhelming me, that I'm going to die. I'm sixty-three and no matter how much success I achieve I know I'm going to die. [He pauses and clears his throat.] I'm constantly causing my family and myself pain and unhappiness by pointing out this . . . impending reality. . . . I can't seem to live with it . . .

"I usually take a few drinks every evening to help me get to sleep. In the middle of the night, if I still haven't made it, I take a sleeping pill. I'm afraid to go to sleep, that's why I drink and take the pills. I'm frightened of going to sleep. I'm afraid if I go to sleep, I won't wake up! [Again he pauses.]

"Last night was one of the most horrible I've ever had. I couldn't sleep. I never slept. I kept my agreement until near dawn when I had two shots of Scotch . . ." His voice is trembling and he seems near tears. "I wish I knew what to do . . ." he goes on hesitantly and abruptly slumps back in his chair.

There is light, uncertain applause.

"Thank you, Stuart," says the trainer. "I want you to get one thing: don't fight your fear of death. Don't resist it. Don't fight death. When you die, you're dead; that much we know. More people have killed themselves resisting dying than any other known way. What's a stomach ulcer but resistance? What's a stroke but resistance? If you want to die as soon as possible I highly recommend you resist dying—all the time with all your might. The surgeon general ought to put out a notice: 'Resistance to dying is dangerous to your health.' Later today, Stuart, you'll see how you can handle your fear in the truth process. . . . Thank you."

(Applause)

Kirsten: ". . . So I thought I'd try to disappear some of the pain of my arthritis before I went to sleep. . . . But it didn't work. . . . I tried, but it didn't work."

Steven: "One reason I've never shared before is that I've always felt that I had to say something *significant.* [Some trainee laughter of recognition] You know, something that would impress everybody with how really bright or together I am. Or maybe with how *uniquely* messed up I am. . . . Well, I decided this morning I would get Don to call on me and then I'd share something that definitely would not get written down in the history books. [Laughter] What I'd like to share is that I enjoy being here and enjoy being with you people. . . . That's all."

"Under each chair you will find a pencil and a card to fill out," begins the trainer. "Don't reach under yet," he directs authoritatively, pausing to watch our attention shift back to him. "We're going to do a 'personality profile,' which most of you have seen demonstrated at the pre-training seminar."

For the next ten minutes he directs us in filling out the card and understanding what a "personality profile" is. Once we have reached under our chairs to get the cards and pencils, the first step is to choose a personality to do a profile on: a friend, spouse, lover, a boss, or whomever the trainee finds desirable as a subject. Listed are the name, hometown, age, height, build, complexion, and marital status of the acquaintance. Next the trainee is asked to choose three adjectives to describe the friend's personality—adjectives such as friendly, strongwilled, arrogant, shy, wishy-washy, competitive, aggressive, extroverted, stubborn, selfish, etc. Then the trainee is asked to list three things to which the friend has definite reactions. For example "food"—"he loves to eat"; "sports"—"thinks they're all a waste of time"; "women"—"he lusts after them"; "children"— "can't stand them"; etc. Last, the trainee lists three specific friends or relatives of the acquaintance, his relationship to them, and then his reactions to them. Thus: "Edgar—boss— respects and admires"; "Marcia—wife—alienated from, thinks he hates her but still connected"; "Josh—son—loves, loves to play with"; "Oscar—friend—likes to compete with." The trainees are assured that all of the cards will be destroyed at the end of the day's training.

When all of the cards have been filled out, they are handed in to the assistants and the trainer.

"Okay," begins the trainer in a loud but somewhat mild voice. "To assist us in this process we have an *est* graduate, Linda Martin, who will do the personality profile for us. Linda?"

An attractive young woman comes forward down the center aisle and takes one of the two stool-chairs. The audience applauds and she smiles. The trainer begins looking through the

250 profile cards the trainees have just filled out, smiling as he does so.

"If only your friends knew," he comments softly, and the trainees laugh.

"I didn't know we had so many doctors this time," he says after another thirty seconds. "I can tell by the handwriting."

"Okay," he suddenly announces. "This one should do. Would Jane MacDougal be willing to come up here and share with us about her friend and the personality profile?"

Jane is willing and is soon seated beside Linda in front of the trainees. She looks ill at ease.

"All right, Linda," directs the trainer. "Close your eyes, relax, and go into your space." He gives her a few minutes and goes on neutrally.

"I'm going to ask you about Carl Janson of Santa Barbara, California. Carl is thirty-two years old, five feet ten, one hundred seventy pounds, stocky build, dark complexion. He is married. Now, Linda, do you get anything at all about Carl?"

For many seconds, Linda, seated with eyes closed, says nothing. Then, abruptly, her face brightens.

"I got him!" she says.

Another brief silence.

"What do you get?" asks the trainer.

"I get him ... very intense, very energetic, he likes to *do* things. He really gets a kick out of doing things ..."

(Silence)

"Fine," says the trainer. "Jane, how does that fit your experience of Carl?"

Jane is silent a moment and then says, "Well, yes ... he certainly is intense. He doesn't always seem energetic but he does get a lot done ..."

"Anything more?"

"He also enjoys doing things."

"Good. All right, Linda, I'm going to read you two contrasting adjectives and I want you to see which one you get to be Carl. Okay?"

"Fine," says Linda.

"Do you get Carl as a strong character or a weak one?"

"He comes through very strong. I see him making his own decisions and being able to stick to them. He ... I ... he really is able to dominate his wife ..."

"Jane?"

Jane laughs loudly. "She's certainly right there," she says.

"Good. Linda, is he gregarious or is he quiet and shy?"

"He's very friendly. He likes to talk. He likes people. I see him enjoying parties. [She pauses.] I see him enjoying children.... I don't know if he has any children, but I see him enjoying children."

"Jane?" He holds the mike in front of her.

"Yes, he's really a talker!" She seems somewhat surprised. "And he has two children." She adds, "And he adores them." She is clearly impressed.

"Fine. Actually you've probably already answered this one: is he retiring or outgoing?"

"I would say he's outgoing, definitely. I see him glad-handing at parties, and at his business too."

"Jane?" He switches the mike.

"Yes, he is." Her hands are clasped in her lap tightly.

"Fine. Now we come to the second part, which is three things Carl has a definite reaction to. The first is food. Linda, do you get anything on food?"

Linda hesitates a moment. "He enjoys eating."

"Fine. Anything else?"

"He enjoys his food, he enjoys eating well. I see him rubbing his stomach after a good meal."

"Good. Jane?"

She nods yes, but does not seem absolutely certain. "Well, yes, I guess he likes food. Actually what I had in mind was he has an incredible sweet tooth. But I guess he likes all food."

"Fine. Okay, Linda. The next item is children. What do you get on children?"

"He likes them; he's a devoted father. [She pauses.] I see

him outdoors with . . . a boy . . . in the woods, with his son."

"Right, right," says Jane. "He's wonderful to his kids, and he often goes camping with his two boys."

"Good. Okay, Linda, what do you get about Carl's experience with cars?"

"I get that he . . . likes cars. . . . He has a real interest in them. I see him really enjoying showing off his new car."

"Jane?" The mike goes back to her.

"Well, I don't know," she says uncertainly. "I don't think he likes cars. His car has to be working perfectly or he's upset. He trades it in every few years. Of course, he certainly is proud of his new cars, that's true. He does show off the new one when he gets it."

"Fine. Okay Linda. The next item in the profile is Carl's reaction to three people. Are you ready?"

She nods yes.

"Okay. The first person on the list is his wife. What do you get?" He looks at us briefly, then neutrally concentrates on the mike and Linda.

"I definitely get that he is the boss, that he needs to be in control . . ."

"That's right," says Jane. "Absolutely."

"I see them doing things together . . . what *he* wants to do though."

Jane laughs. "Oh boy," she says.

"Fine," says the trainer. "What about his brother, Axel? What is Carl's experience of his brother?"

There is a long silence.

"I get warmth. A good warm feeling . . . I get that there is a good relationship between them. . . . I see them embracing, smiling and laughing together. . . . Carl is pounding his brother on the back."

"Jane?" He switches the mike.

"That's right. They get along really well." She is nodding her head slightly in agreement. "They're business partners and— amazing!—just last week they closed a big deal and Carl *was* pounding Axel on the back."

"Okay. Now Linda, what about John, his best friend? What's Carl's experience with John?"

She waits, then says, "I get feelings of ... competition. There is something there ..."

"Something more?"

She hesitates a moment. "I get negative, something between them ..." She trails off. "Some trouble ... it's strange."

"Anything else?" prompts the trainer.

A half minute goes by; finally she says, "No, that's it. That's all I get."

"Jane?"

"I'm amazed. Carl and John have been having a quarrel. They've been friends for years, but always seem to be at odds over something or other."

"Thank you, Linda."

There is applause.

"Jane," says the trainer, holding the mike to her, "is there anything you'd like to say about your experience of this personality profile?"

"Well, yes," Jane replies, smiling. "I thought Linda got Carl really well. She caught his enjoyment of things immediately and that thing about backslapping was really far out. I'd like to know how she does it."

"Linda?" asks the trainer, turning the mike to her.

"I don't know *how* I do it," Linda replies promptly. "I just try to get out of the way and take what comes. Sometimes it seems to hit the nail on the head, other times the other person thinks I'm off a bit."

"Do you actually *see* things?" Jane asks.

"Sometimes. The backslapping I saw. And Carl and a boy having fun camping in the woods. But with the brother at first all I got was warmth and with the friend all I ever got was bad vibrations."

"Fine," says the trainer, turning now to the audience. "Do any of you have any questions of either Linda, Jane, or me about the personality profile?"

About a half-dozen friendly questions are asked of Jane and

Linda, none challenging the process, and the seventh questioner says that he notices the questions this time are much less antagonistic than they had been after the personality profile the trainees had witnessed at the pre-training. After two further questions, Linda and Jane are permitted to return to their seats. Before the trainer can go on, David, the professorial young man who has frequently challenged the training, waves his hand so vigorously he is called upon. He stands up on the aisle of the fourth row in the center of the room and speaks with tense acidity:

"I can't let this nonsense pass without speaking up," he says. "I just can't."

"Go ahead, David. You've got the mike."

"I mean I hope everyone realizes that there are about two thousand ways this process could be rigged. You notice that the *trainer* chooses the personality card, the *trainer* reads off the adjectives, the trainer can encourage Linda or discourage her in her answers. The most amateurish magician could pull this sort of thing off without working up a sweat."

"Fine," says the trainer, leaning back in one of the chairs just vacated by the two women. "Anything else?"

"Yes," David goes on vigorously. "I was doing the process along with Linda and *I* got Carl almost as well as she did. When—"

"OH, YOU DID!?" shouts the trainer loudly and the audience laughs.

"But it doesn't *prove* anything," David almost shouts back.

"Have we said we were *proving* anything?" the trainer asks, still leaning back casually in his chair.

"Maybe not," David, quite flushed. "But the whole thing seems to be set up to imply we have mystical powers of perception which *est* will untap."

"There can't be anything mystical about them," says the trainer, "since *you* seem to have them too."

(Laughter)

"They're *not* mystical," David continues. "It's just a case of picking up the subliminal clues you and Jane are giving off. That is, if the whole thing isn't rigged. Besides she missed a few things. Has everybody forgotten that?"

"Do you have a question, David?"

"Well, what is it all supposed to prove?"

"Not a damn thing, David. Just keep your sole in the room and take what you get. If you get that we set Jane up with a bribe or something to pretend Linda had guessed her friend, fine! If you get it's all done with subliminal clues, great! No problem. We're not too bright, you see. We only do the personality profile because it works. Something is happening. *You* apparently saw it could be done. At graduation everyone in this room will get a chance to discover the same ability Linda has and then play the role of Linda, and, of course, that will obviously be a set-up. We'll simply bribe all the graduates."

"You mean at graduation we'll all try to guess someone's friend's personality?"

"You won't *guess*, David. You'll go into your space and someone will ask you the type of questions I asked Linda and you'll get what you get. A few people get—blackness, mistiness; they get a barrier to the process. Others, like you, get the personality. No big deal. In both cases, you get what you get . . ."

"What I want you to do during the first part of this day is to get clear what item you are choosing to get in touch with during the truth process. Now, the purpose of the truth process is not to make you *better*. It's an opportunity for you to recognize that you're always conceptualizing and learn to just *be* with your experience. I want you to choose some persistent, recurring item, some barrier we might call it. It might be an emotion, it might be a bodily sensation, it might be a point of view, it might be an action, a recurring action of yours which you experience persisting despite your efforts to change it. And I don't want you to take an item still in your belief system. Get in touch with it. Find its existence in your body, in actual experience. I don't want any of you romantic heroes to pick as your item 'injustice' or 'social deprivation' or some of you religious assholes to tell me your item is 'sin.' I want you to have good, solid, specific items: 'A pain in the right zorch,' 'a feeling of nausea associated with seeing my husband,' 'chattering teeth when I have to make a speech.' Yes, Kirsten?"

"I'm twenty-six years old and I think my item is the arthritis I've had in my hands and knees for several years. [She looks around a little.] Days like today will usually find me in bed with painfully swollen joints. My mother also has it. It's hereditary. Right now I'm in a lot of pain."

"Hereditary, you said?"

"Yes, my mother had it, has it now too." Her small body is slanted at an angle, her neck slightly bent forward, and the mike is held in her right hand. She is alert, nervous.

"*Where* do you feel pain, Kirsten?"

"In my left hand and shoulder."

"Where? *Exactly* where?"

She is puzzled a moment, looks around for help. "You mean, where in my left hand?"

"Exactly."

"In the left middle and ring fingers. Inside the knuckles. They're swollen."

"Describe the pain you experience."

"Describe the pain?"

"Yes."

She hesitates. "Well, it's like a fiery ache when I move my fingers. The fire is inside the knuckle, and every time I move my left shoulder, I have pain right in there. [She points to a spot on her shoulder.] It's, uh, like a small burning fire in the center of my shoulder [She flourishes a hand.], between the bones."

"It's *your* experience, you're the one who feels this shooting fire. Have I got it right?"

"Yes."

"Okay, that's your item. In the truth process, I'll ask you to get in touch with your arthritis and after a while see if it's associated with any images from the past. Thank you . . ."

"My item is anxiety," says Robert, who is now the sixth person to stand to try to clarify his "barrier."

"That's pretty vague, Robert," says the trainer, striding across the platform toward him. "When do you experience this anxiety?"

Robert stands tensely in silence for several seconds and then replies:

"All the time. I think I'm anxious all the time."

"BULLSHIT!" snaps the trainer. "Anything you think you're experiencing all the time is obviously a concept. I want to know a specific *place* and *time* when you really *experience* anxiety."

"Okay," says Robert rapidly. "When I go for an audition. I'm an actor and when I'm auditioning, before I go on, I'm in terror."

"All right, now we're getting closer. If you're going to observe and reexperience this anxiety, you've got to get in touch with its *elements*. I want to know what bodily sensations, what feelings, what points of view you experience when you're waiting for an audition."

"Tremendous tension. My whole body is tense."

"That's CRAP, Robert. When your whole body is tense it's called rigor mortis. You're dead. I want you to pin it down. First of all, where are you waiting for this audition?"

"What audition?"

"The specific actual audition during which you're sure you experienced anxiety."

"Oh . . . well, all right, I'm sitting in a theater seat on the left side of the theater about three rows back."

"Good. Are you sitting up?"

"No. I'm slumped way down. My knees are up against the seat in front of me."

"Fine. What bodily sensations are you experiencing?"

"Ah ... I'm grinding my teeth ... my stomach muscles are—"

"BULLSHIT! You wouldn't know a stomach muscle if I handed it to you on a platter. *Where* do you experience tight muscles?"

"Well, I'd say about ... a bit below the stomach actually."

"That's more crap!" barks the trainer, wheeling away from Robert and glaring out over the entire audience. "Look, you assholes, don't give me this stomach bit. Unless you're a physician none of you in here can locate within a foot the actual location of your stomach. If you want to locate a bodily sensation between your breasts and your genitals use the belly button. I have confidence *most* of you can locate your belly button. Go ahead, Robert."

"All right, then, I experience great tension just above and all around the belly button and in deep."

"Deepcreepsheepbeep. HOW FAR, DAMN IT? For all I know 'in deep' means your fuckin' backbone."

"In three inches ..."

"Okay, good. You've got your item. It's the tenseness in your mid-zorch when you're attending auditions ..."

"Zania?"

A slight, attractive blonde woman in her early thirties, neatly dressed and carefully coiffured, stands up. With her first words, her voice shows she is crying.

"I'm so afraid I ... I don't know what's happening.... [She sniffles.] It's just ... I'm ... afraid."

"What are you afraid of, Zania?" asks the trainer.

"I don't *know*. I don't know.... [Sobbing now] I'm just ... afraid ..."

"WHAT ARE YOU AFRAID OF?" asks Don, now striding down the aisle toward her.

Zania is sobbing uncontrollably, holding the mike in both hands and bowing her head into it.

"I'm . . . afraid . . . I don't know . . ."

"BULLSHIT, ZANIA, YOU KNOW! WHAT ARE YOU AFRAID OF?" the trainer shouts almost in her ear.

"MY HUSBAND! MY HUSBAND!" Zania suddenly shouts through her sobs.

"All right, your husband," says Don, now standing beside her and taking the microphone from her to hold it for her near her face. "Close your eyes and put your hands by your sides and go into your space. . . . Why are you afraid of your husband?"

"I'm just [She pauses, weeping softly.] afraid of him."

"Why are you afraid of him?" Don asks again.

"HE BEATS ME!" Again she explodes out her answer.

"Okay, he beats you. *When* does he beat you?"

"All the TIME!"

"*When* does he beat you? Where does he beat you? A specific place and time."

Zania sobs for several seconds, mumbles something that can't be understood, and then says very softly and very clearly:

"I'm pregnant . . ."

"You're pregnant. When is this? Now? When did this happen?"

"Eight years ago . . ."

"Where was he beating you? Bedroom? Living room?"

"In the living room."

"What are you doing?"

"I'm . . . curled up on the floor . . . by the couch. . . . HE'S KICKING ME!"

"Fine," says the trainer, holding the mike near her lowered face and looking at her neutrally. "What are you saying to him?"

"Nothing . . . I'm just crying. . . . I'm so afraid . . ."

"What are you *feeling*? Your body sensations?"

"It's fear ..."

"I know it's fear. Fear's a concept! What are your bodily sensations and feelings?"

"I'm all knotted up. A big ball of pain in my chest ... all of my muscles are tense ..."

"*All* your muscles aren't tense. *Which* muscles?"

"My hands, my ... abdominal muscles, my jaw ... it's so *unfair!*"

"Is he saying anything to you?"

"No ... he's just kicking me ... he calls me a worthless bitch.... He swears at me ... he's drunk. He's drunk ALL THE TIME!"

"And what do you say to him?"

"NOTHING! I just lie there ... he's drunk ... he's not himself ..."

"What would you *like* to say to him?"

"It's unfair ... it's so unfair ..."

"SAY IT TO HIM!"

"IT'S UNFAIR! YOU'VE NO RIGHT TO KICK ME! I'M CARRYING YOUR BABY!"

"Good. What else would you like to say to him?"

"I'M A GOOD WIFE! ... You've no right to beat me.... It's OUR BABY!"

"What's your posture then, your facial expression?"

"I'm all curled up, my knees are at my chin.... I want to protect the baby. I'm crying."

"Okay. What attitudes or points of view do you have?"

"It's unfair. It's so unfair. If only he'd change. If only he wouldn't drink."

"Why is he kicking you?"

"He's drunk.... He's not himself ..."

"Good. Why is he kicking you?"

"I don't know.... I LOVE HIM!"

"That's fine. Why is he kicking you, Zania?"

Zania stands, head lowered, sobbing for several seconds.

"... I don't know.... He just gets upset ..."

"WHY DOES HE KICK YOU, ZANIA?"

"HE DRINKS! I TELL HIM HE'S A DRUNKARD!"

"Okay, good. He beats you, you're lying there. What image from the past comes up? Take what you get."

"Nothing . . ."

"He's beating you. You're lying there curled up. What image from the past?"

"It's just mist . . . blackness . . ."

"What age comes to your mind? Don't think! Just take what comes."

"Six. I'm six years old . . ."

"Good. What images are you getting?"

"It's just . . . blackness. I don't remember."

"I don't *want* you to remember. Just look for images. Anything you get. Don't *think!*"

"It's just blackness!"

"Keep looking. . . . THERE! Right *there!* What did you get?!"

"I don't know . . . nothing."

"LOOK, Zania! You're six years old . . . you're being beaten . . . it's unfair . . . you're curled up . . . your knees are at your chin . . . he's swearing at you—"

"Oh!"

"WHAT'S THERE, ZANIA?"

"I . . . I'm lying on my bed. I'm crying . . ."

"Go on."

Zania begins to sob again so uncontrollably she doesn't speak.

"What's happening, Zania? Tell us what you see."

"I'm . . . crying . . . I'm curled up. . . . My father spanked me . . ."

"Where did he spank you? When? What did he say?"

"On the behind . . . on the bed . . . he's just left . . ."

"*Why* did he spank you?"

"IT'S UNFAIR! I didn't do anything. My father just gets mad."

"Why did he spank you?"

"I don't know.... He always spanks me.... He doesn't love me ... he hates me ..."

"Why does he hate you?"

"He just ... I'M NOT A BOY!" Zania explodes out and then breaks into loud sobbing.

"All right, you're in bed, curled up crying. What do you want to say to your father, Zania?"

"IT'S UNFAIR! I can't help it if I'm a girl! WHY DON'T YOU LOVE ME?"

"What are you feeling, Zania ... right now?"

"I'm ... just sad ... so sad ..."

"What bodily sensations do you have?"

"My eyes are burning ... my throat is sore ... a heaviness in my stomach ..."

"Where's the heaviness? What do you mean, 'heaviness'?"

"A huge ball of ... sensation, heavy sensation, like a basket-ball ... beginning at my belly button ... everywhere up to my heart."

"Okay. Thank you, Zania." The trainer hands her a tissue from an assistant. "Look, we've just scratched the surface of all this. Are you willing during the truth process coming up to just be there with your body, your emotions, your feelings, your images, and to complete any experiences that come up to you?"

"Yes ..."

"Don't try to understand them. Don't try to figure them out. Just take what comes and experience it out.... Okay?"

"Yes."

"All right. In a moment I'm going to ask you to open your eyes and return to the room and take your seat. Are you ready now to return to this room?"

"Yes."

"Okay. Open your eyes. Thank you, Zania."

There is loud applause as Don strides back up onto the platform and Zania, no longer crying, takes her seat, wiping her eyes with tissues. Several other trainees have been crying also and are signaling with raised hands their need for tissues. The atmosphere in the room is very heavy.

"NOW LOOK, YOU PEOPLE," the trainer booms out to the trainees. "I DON'T WANT ANY OF THE ASSHOLES AMONG YOU TO THINK YOU UNDERSTAND ZANIA. There's nothing to understand. I want you to *get* that. The purpose of your picking an item and examining it is NOT to understand it. It's to *experience* it, to get in touch with it. Find out where the stuckness is. I don't want any asshole Freuds to think because you find out you love your mother and hate your father that automatically all your problems will disappear. Understanding is the booby prize! Just take what you get and *experience* it ... complete your experience ..."

"All right, yes, John, stand up, take the mike."

John, an older man in his fifties, with gray hair and glasses, and wearing one of the few neckties seen in the room, stands at the far left side of the room.

"When I was a boy," he is saying with a dignified voice, "—this was many years ago—I suffered an unusual social trauma. It seems that—"

"HOLD IT! HOLD IT!" the trainer interrupts loudly. "You never experienced a social trauma in your whole fucking life."

"Oh, but I *did*," insists John firmly. "When I was six—"

"HOLD IT!" Don shouts again, coming off the platform toward John. "A social trauma is a concept, an idea, a generalization. It's not an actual experience. What *happened*, John?"

"Well, I cannot actually describe what happened," says John nervously. "I mean it was quite embarrassing ... a social trauma, in fact, and not something I wish to be explicit about on this occasion ..."

"WHAT THE FUCK ARE YOU TALKING ABOUT?"

"Beg pardon?"

"Look, John, why are you standing?"

"I wish to clarify my item."

"Fine. I got it. What's your item?"

"My item is an unusual social trauma which has been bothering me for years and—"

"HOLD IT! John ... look, John ... tell me what happened when you were six."

"I ... well ... you see ... actually in church on my sixth birthday I did a BM in my pants."

"AND YOU'VE BEEN CARRYING IT AROUND WITH YOU FOR FIFTY YEARS!"

(Loud and long laughter)

John is flushed and smiling.

"That's right. I never thought I would tell anyone. . . . Now I feel relieved of it."

(Laughter)

"John, what's your item?" asks the trainer, somehow not smiling.

"I don't know," John replies. "It's all gone. I'll have to make a new one."

Laughter again explodes out across the room in welcome relief from the heavier moments.

"Not in here, John," Don says, as he moves back up to the center of the platform. "This is not a church ..."

"So the elements of experience are bodily sensations—postures, facial expressions, points of view, feelings, emotions, and images of the past. If you stay in touch with one or more of these at least you can be sure you're alive. . . . Yes, Henrietta?"

A plump woman in her early forties, Henrietta, stands with a slight slump to her shoulders and speaks in a tremulous voice.

"I'm afraid I have the impression that I'm being left behind this morning," she says. "This item business has me thoroughly confused."

The trainer moves quickly off the platform and down the aisle toward her.

"You feel you're being left behind?" he asks her sharply.

"Yes . . ." she says uncertainly. "This item business . . ."

"WHEN WERE YOU LEFT BEHIND, HENRIETTA?" he suddenly shouts at her.

"I don't understand," she replies in consternation. "I only meant that intellectually."

"Close your eyes, Henrietta. Give me the mike. That's it. Put your hands at your sides."

"But I only meant—"

"I KNOW WHAT YOU MEANT! Now go into your space. . . . All right, Henrietta, *when were you left behind?*"

Suddenly Henrietta is sobbing, her shoulders shuddering, her face in her hands. An assistant rushes up with tissues.

"When were you left behind, Henrietta?" the trainer insists sharply.

"My . . . mother . . . ," Henrietta gets out between sobs, "my mother left me . . . with my grandmother when I was nine."

"What happened when you were nine?" the trainer insists, holding the mike up to Henrietta's tear-stained face.

"She . . . LEFT ME! . . . I told her I wanted to go with her . . . but she left me behind . . ."

"What happened, Henrietta?"

"My father had been institutionalized years before and suddenly my mother . . . said I had to live with grandmother. . . . But I didn't want to. I didn't *want* to!"

"Tell your mother that, Henrietta."

"DON'T LEAVE, MOMMY, DON'T LEAVE ME. I want to be with you. Please, Mommy, take me with you, I DON'T WANT TO BE LEFT BEHIND! . . ."

Henrietta is crying more softly and accepts the tissues from an assistant.

"Okay, Henrietta," the trainer says quietly. "I want you to tell me exactly where you were and what you were feeling when your mother was leaving you."

Henrietta wipes her nose and eyes, her head still bent down on her chest.

"I was in my grandmother's kitchen. My grandmother was trying to get me to eat cookies. I HATE COOKIES! There was a plateful on the table in front of me and my mother said, 'Nana will take good care of you.' I began to cry and my mother and Nana kept telling me it would be all right and I felt so rejected . . . so helpless . . ."

"What precisely were you feeling?" the trainer asks.

"Just numb, helpless, left behind . . ."

"Those are concepts, not feelings. What are your body sensations right now?"

"An ache . . . such an ache . . . under my heart—here, right *here*," says Henrietta, and she looks up defiantly at the trainer and bangs a tiny fist against her chest.

"Good. Anything else?"

Henrietta closes her eyes again and pauses, thinking.

"And . . . and tension in my neck and throat . . . I want to speak but I can't."

"Good. Where's that tension exactly?"

"Here," says Henrietta, pointing first at her throat and then at the back of her neck.

"Did you feel that tension or that ache before you stood up to tell me you were feeling left behind this morning in the training?"

Henrietta opens her eyes again and looks directly at the trainer as if considering what she had experienced then.

"Yes," she says. "Oh yes, I was, I was."

"All right, Henrietta, thank you. If you'd like, you can take as your item the ache in your chest and tension in your throat and neck associated with being left behind. Are you clear now that this could be your item?"

"Yes."

"You can choose something else if you'd like or you can choose this. You've only begun to reexperience that event. In the truth process later you can go into it more deeply. Thank you, Henrietta. [Applause]

"All right, next," says the trainer, returning to the platform. "Jack? Stand up."

Jack stands up near the back of the room.

"It's difficult to pinpoint," says Jack in thoughtful concentration. "I guess I'd have to say my item is boredom."

"Oh, Jesus, DON'T GIVE ME YOUR WORLD-WEARY CRAP! BOREDOM IS A CONCEPT! Get in touch with an actual situation, time, and place, and the actual bodily sensations, feelings, and so on that the situation produces."

"Ah! Right! Well, in here, as a matter of fact. Through most of the training I've been bored."

"Good. Now you're living. Think of one precise moment in the training in particular when you were bored."

"Okay. Let's see. When you talked about levels of . . . mmm . . . I'm not even sure I remember . . . levels of certainty, I think it was."

"Good. How were you sitting? What were your bodily sensations?"

"Right. Okay. Now I've got it. I get you now."

"That's terrific. Do you mind answering my questions?"

"Right. I was sitting forward with my head in my hands and experiencing a numbness in my brain."

"A numbness in your brain?"

"Yes."

"Look, Jack, no one ever experienced a numbness in the brain. Numbness means absence of feeling. How can you experience absence of feeling in a place that normally has no feeling?"

Jack looks neutrally at the trainer.

"Wrong word," he says after a while. "A heaviness in the brain."

"Brain's a concept too. Say 'head.' Where in the head?"

"Back two-thirds."

"Okay, Jack, you've got your item. A heaviness in the back two-thirds of your head whenever I'm speaking, right?"

"Right!" says Jack, smiling and looking very unbored.

(Applause)

"My barrier is my ego." Tom, the bearded, beaded fellow who has spoken before, takes the mike. "I've been working on detachment from my ego now for—"

"EGO!" asks the trainer, eyes widening in mock horror. "You have problems with your *ego*?"

"Well, yes," says Tom. "It seems to me that for anyone on the Path, the ego is the number one problem."

"Tom," begins the trainer with exaggerated patience. "Tom, locate your ego."

Tom stares back.

"Locate my ego?"

"Yes, locate your ego."

"I can't."

"Good. That solves that problem. You got another?"

"But how does it solve my problem?"

"If you can't find your fuckin' ego, then how can it be bothering you?"

"Well, it does."

"Tom," the trainer says, again in a soft, patient voice. "Are you haunted by ghosts?"

"No."

"Good. Are you haunted by ego?"

Tom stands silently.

"Ego is a concept," he says tentatively.

"EGO IS A CONCEPT!" Don shouts. "Yes. Ego is a concept. Now if you'd like to experience a recurring persistent barrier, I suggest you consider a specific situation, time, and place, which creates in you an uptightness, an ego-hangup or attachment or whatever you usually call it, and find out what you are actually experiencing. And I don't want any bullshit about ego. If you tell me that when you lose in a game of bridge you feel a pain in your left zorch, that's fine, but don't tell me losing at bridge gives you an ego problem."

"It's a tension in my abdomen."

"Okay, you're getting closer. Locate the sensation precisely and then in the truth process we'll see what other feelings, points of view, body posture, facial expressions are associated with it. Got it?"

"Got it. Thank you, Don."

(Applause)

"You people who've been into Zen and some Eastern things are all wrapped up in getting rid of what you call ego, you gotta get rid of ego. Next week we'll find out what the ego really is, but for now let me say that most of your fighting your ego are still in the trap of trying to change. You've got what you call an ego? Great! You've got an ego. You've also got a big nose and a bald spot. What is, is. If you've got an ego, ride with it, let it go. No more sense in trying to stamp out your ego than there is in trying to grow hair on your bald spot. You might be able to artificially cover up your ego or your bald spot with a bit of camouflage, but when the wind blows look what's there: bald spot and ego.

"But I sympathize with you, Tom. When I was first training to be a trainer I was really into Zen and a couple of other things and working like crazy on my ego. I'd been leading a graduate seminar for about two months when Werner asks me, 'Don, have you been experiencing any ego in your leading that seminar?'

"'Holy shit,' I said to myself, 'He's got me now. Sees right through me. Oh boy.'

"'Yeah, I guess a little bit, Werner,' I said aloud.

"'Come off it, Don,' Werner says right back to me. 'It's *all* ego. You stand up there glittering out ego like a five-hundred-watt bulb.'

"I laughed and said I guessed I really did enjoy being a seminar leader.

"'That's fine,' Werner said. 'If you accept what you call your ego and ride with it, it's okay. Just don't stand up there pretending there's not ego gratification.'

"And that's the way it is," Don concludes. "If you enjoy winning, enjoy winning. If you're detached from winning and losing then be detached from winning and losing. But remember, it's no more necessary to get rid of what you call your ego than it is to get rid of your bald spot: let them both shine forth. . . . HEY! Where are you going?"

Hank, a short, stout middle-aged man, has stood up and is walking down the center aisle toward the back of the room. The assistant Richard is standing at the end of the aisle to confront him and when the trainer shouts, Hank stops and turns.

"I'm leaving," he announces.

"No, you're not. Come back and take your seat."

"I've stood about as much of this nonsense as I can," Hank says, holding his ground. "You've already wasted one and a half days of my time insulting us, lecturing at us with trivial jargon, and making us put up with your not dealing intellectually with our rational objections. Well I'm done. I'm leaving. Right now I wish I could get all of us who feel that this is a colossal ripoff to come with me to the Better Business Bureau on Fifth Avenue. Who'd like to ride with me down there?"

"Sit down, Hank," the trainer says firmly. "We'll handle rides later."

(Laughter)

"But . . ."

"We handle rides to the Better Business Bureau at the end of the evening, Hank, not now. Remember, you agreed to keep your sole in the room and follow instructions."

"I'm done with your stupid agreements."

"They're not mine, Hank, they're yours. You had a chance to leave yesterday morning and *you* chose to stay, and you entered into the agreements when you chose to stay."

"Well, now I choose to break my agreement."

"Sit down, Hank. Think how much more stuff you can tell the Better Business Bureau if you hold out until midnight. Besides, if you break your agreement and leave now, then you'll have no case against us, since *you* broke *your* contract."

This statement is greeted with silence by both Hank and the

other trainees for several seconds, but then a gentle wave of laughter breaks across the room. Hank flushes.

"Okay," he says, and marches back to his seat.

"Let's thank Hank for sharing with us," says the trainer, taking a sip from his thermos, and the audience acknowledges Hank with applause . . .

"I just wish you wouldn't shout," Linda is saying mildly to the trainer, who has just finished shouting at someone else. Linda is a lovely woman with long dark hair, beautiful eyes, and a full figure.

"You don't like my shouting?" the trainer replies, edging over toward where she is standing in the second row.

"No, I don't like your shouting. It makes me nervous. I wish you would communicate to people in a gentler voice."

"WHY DON'T YOU LIKE SHOUTING, LINDA?" Don abruptly shouts at her from only ten feet away.

"DON'T SHOUT!" Linda screams back.

"WHY DON'T YOU LIKE SHOUTING?" Don shouts again, moving into the aisle to be even closer to her.

"STOP IT! STOP IT!" Linda screams furiously.

"Who shouted, Linda?" he asks her in a loud voice just below a shout.

She stares steadily at him with anger.

"Who shouted, Linda?" he repeats in a softer voice, taking the microphone from her hands and holding it near her face.

Her eyes drop, her shoulders slump.

"My father," she says in a low voice after a while.

"Thank you. Who did he shout at, Linda?"

"At everyone. He shouted at everyone . . ."

"I want you to close your eyes and go into your space. . . . I want you to tell me in association with your father's shouting what image do you get from the past? . . . There! Right there! What do you get?"

"Nothing . . . nothing. I don't remember . . ."

"I don't *want* you to remember. I just want you to tell me what you get from the past in association with your father's shouting ..."

"Nothing ... there's just blackness ..."

"All right, in association with your father's shouting what *age* are you? Don't think! JUST SPEAK!"

"DON'T SHOUT!"

"WHAT AGE!"

"FOUR! I'M FOUR! DON'T SHOUT!"

"All right. You're four years old, Linda, you're four years old. ... Your father is shouting ... *who is he shouting at?*"

"My mother, my mother," Linda replies softly. Her face is stony and hard.

"What's he saying, Linda?" the trainer asks. "Tell us what he's shouting at your mother."

"He's ... he's ... calling her ... a whore ... a worthless ... peasant ... whore ..."

"Good," says the trainer after a brief silence. "Why is he shouting?"

"He always ... shouts at her. He always calls her whore ... peasant. He was rich ... she was poor ... when they married ..."

"What do you want to tell your father?"

"I want to tell him not to shout ..."

"TELL HIM!"

"DON'T SHOUT!"

"TELL HIM!"

"I'M TELLING HIM. DON'T SHOUT! DON'T SHOUT AT MOMMY! YOU'RE NOT FAIR TO MOMMY! DON'T SHOUT!"

Linda's forehead is deeply furrowed with tension, her eyes tightly closed, her head held higher.

"What happened this time when you were four, Linda?" the trainer asks, his face stern and unsympathetic. For a long moment Linda just stands, her face twisted with tension, and when she answers it is in a whisper.

"He kicked her out when I was four. She disappeared. He shouted ... and she disappeared ..."

"All right, Linda, that's good.... You've gotten in touch with something important. We've only just got in contact with it, and are you willing to experience this thing out, to be with it and not resist it?"

"Yes," she whispers.

"In the truth process are you willing to take as your item the feelings you had then when you heard your father call your mother 'whore' and to really get in touch with those feelings?"

"... Yes."

"Okay. Soon I'll ask you to open your eyes and take your seat. First I want you to visualize the room in your mind.... Okay, open your eyes. [Applause]

"You know I don't want you assholes to think you're learning anything. I don't want you to start drawing conclusions. There are probably two hundred of you sitting in here right now saying to yourselves, 'Poor Linda, her daddy done her dirt and messed her whole life up.' That's *bullshit*, assholes, perfectly formed bullshit. Don't be taken in. Next Saturday you'll find out who *really* did Linda dirt, and it wasn't daddy. You'll find out who really screwed up Zania and it wasn't *her* daddy. You'll find out who *really* screwed up *your* life and it wasn't *your* daddy.... So just don't draw any brilliant conclusions. Whenever you have a thought, try to remember that you're an asshole and that any thought making an appearance in your mind is probably only another turd.

"Yes, Jerry?"

"I'm not sure how I should describe my item. I mean essentially it's a problem."

"Go ahead."

"The problem is that my wife has begun to complain a lot about my traveling. I mean I travel about twenty weeks a year. But she knew that when we got married. She knew it. But now, just lately, after four years, she's started really dumping on my traveling. She said last week: 'Me and the children just get used to having you around and then off you go. Maybe it would be better if you never came home.' [Some laughter] I mean I love my wife and I love the traveling too. But ... she loves me too, but she's suddenly ... now it's not all right for me to travel."

"Okay. Good. There are two things, Jerry. First let's look at your problem. Then we'll try to see what your item should be."

Don strides to the blackboard on the side nearest where Jerry is standing in the second row right.

"Actually, there are *two* problems. One for your wife. One for you. But since your wife's problem comes first let's look at hers first. How might your wife word *her* problem?"

"She'd say something like: 'I don't like your traveling.' "

"That's not a problem. If she doesn't like your traveling, she gets you to stop it and that's it."

"Yeah, but she loves me and she knows I need to travel for my job."

"Great! Now we got a problem. 'I don't like Jerry's traveling but I love him and know he needs to travel to support the family.' Good enough?"

"Yeah, that's it."

"Fine."

Don draws a vertical line down the center of the blackboard and writes the first half of the wife's sentence (I DON'T LIKE JERRY'S TRAVELING) on the left, the word BUT in the center, and the other two parts of her sentence on the right (I LOVE HIM and HE NEEDS TO TRAVEL AND ENJOYS IT).

"Now," the trainer says, turning to the audience, "where's the problem?"

"On the board?" Jerry replies quizzically.

"Where on the board?"

"She doesn't like my traveling ..."

"No. We already concluded that that statement in itself didn't present a problem."

"The whole thing."

"No. That's not narrowing it enough. Is her loving you a problem?"

"Not usually."

(Laughter)

"Is your need to travel to earn income a problem?"

"Not in itself."

"Then where's the problem? Anybody," asks the trainer, turning to the other trainees. "Where's the problem?"

Several people shout out the suggestion that it's in the word *but*.

"Yes!" the trainer agrees loudly. "In the word *but*. Look, if I write, 'I have homework to do tonight,' is that a problem?"

"No."

"If I write the word *and* after that have I got a problem?"

"No."

"Good. And if I add the sentence, 'I like going to the movies,' have I got a problem?"

"No."

"NO! All I've got is the statement 'I like going to the movies and I have to do homework tonight.' No big deal. No problem. Now look what happens if I change the word *and* to the word *but*. Now the statement reads 'I like going to the movies but I have to do homework tonight.' Now we got a problem. You know what the problem consists of? The word *but*. Our lives are filled with contradictory desires every second of every day and we experience only *some* of the contradictions as problems only some of the time. Every now and then we in effect *choose* to experience a contradiction as a problem. For four years Jerry's wife lived apparently peacefully with Jerry's traveling. She probably didn't enjoy it at any time, but she didn't consider it a problem. Now she does.

"A lot of you in this room would like to eat dinner, and you're all stuck in the training until I release you. [There are groans, both real and mocking.] Some of you experience this as a big-deal problem. Others don't. Most everyone is hungry and everyone is now stuck in this room; only some of you make a problem of it. The rest of you simply live with it: 'I'm hungry *and* I can't eat now.'

"Okay. So your *wife* experiences a problem. What should she do about it?"

Jerry considers this for several moments.

"Get a divorce?" he asks with a frown.

(Laughter)

"EXACTLY!" says the trainer. "That's exactly how normal assholes solve problems. THEY 'SOLVE' THEM! And you know what? Having 'solved' this problem, she has now sixteen new ones that make your traveling seem like peanuts.

"No. What should she do about her problem of Jerry's traveling?" the trainer asks, turning to all the trainees.

"Have him get a different job," someone suggests.

"Great. Jerry gets a new job near home and guess what? Jerry now has the problem, 'I love traveling but my wife makes me work near home,' and she's now got the problem, 'Jerry's miserable, but I refuse to let him travel so much.' Beautiful progress. By Jesus, give us enough time and we'll solve this one yet with divorce. Bill?"

"She should learn to live with it," suggests Bill firmly.

"Oh yeah: learn to live with a problem! Isn't that a mature answer? I love mature answers. You got a lion loose in your house? Learn to live with it. . . . You got an alcoholic husband who beats you? Learn to live with it.

"No, Bill, phrased that way, you got a guaranteed martyr, and the biggest pains in the ass, the biggest problem-creators in the whole known universe, are martyrs." The trainer strides over to one corner of his platform.

"*What can Jerry's wife do about her problem?*" he asks.

"Experience it!" shouts someone.

"YES! *Experience* it. . . . Experience it. If she fully experiences her resentment of his traveling—and resentment, by the way, is actually a mild dislike which you are resisting and thus managing to build up into what we call resentment—then her resentment may disappear and she'll be left with a dislike of his traveling and without a problem. Or if she fully experiences it, it'll disappear and she'll suddenly know what's *really* bothering her."

"How does your solution differ from my suggestion that she learn to live with her problem?" Bill asks. "It seems to me fully experiencing a lion in your living room isn't too wise a solution."

"There's a big difference between learning to live with a problem—which implies trying to ignore it, and that's a form of resistance—and experiencing fully what we're experiencing, whether it be resentment of a husband's traveling or fear of having a lion in the house. Someone who says 'I *hate* my husband's traveling, I can't stand it, but I put up with it for the sake of the children,' is living with her problem and is a royal pain in the ass. So is someone petrified with fear who announces they've learned to live with the lion in their house. What we want is for you to get in touch with the situation and with the emotions generated by the problem. When you do that, surprise! your problem will clear up just in the process of living, and, surprise!—you'll probably uncover a more basic one underneath.

"Look," says Don, moving away from Jerry and addressing the entire group. "Human beings normally deal with a problem by ignoring it or by trying to solve it. Both of these represent resistance and in both cases another problem is created overlaying the first.

"In *est* we witness problems and when they disappear, lo and behold, the one hiding behind them, a more basic one, appears. Experiencing problems fully is like peeling the layers of an onion. Normal problem-solving and problem-avoiding is like *adding* skins to the onion. In here we'll guarantee you better and bigger problems: new ones, the ones you've been hiding from since you were six. And the *weight* of your problems will get less and less as the skins of the onion are peeled, instead of getting heavier as it does with normal problem-solving."

The trainer pauses and takes a long slow sip from his metal thermos while reading a note that Richard has brought up to him. Then he sets down thermos and note and resumes:

"Notice that Linda had a problem with my shouting. She fully experienced it. Her problem with *my* shouting disappeared. Now she's got maybe a bigger problem: how does she *really* feel about daddy?

"Henrietta had a problem with feeling left behind in the training. Could I have solved it by *helping* her, by going slower and repeating what I'd said before? No. Her problem about the pace of the training simply disappeared when she really examined her experience. She peeled the layer of onion skin and got closer to the core.

"We don't know what Jerry's wife will find if she fully experiences her resentment of Jerry's being away. But it will be some sort of more basic upset which occurred in the past. I know half you assholes in here think his wife has a legitimate beef, a legitimate problem, and that's because you're the same sort of mechanical problem-creators as she is. Half the people in the world are utterly convinced that if they could just be together with their lover more often their relationship would be all right. You know what the other half of the world is convinced of? The other half is utterly convinced that if they could only spend more time *away* from their lover their relationship would be all right. And both halves of the world are assholes. UNTIL YOU EXPERIENCE YOUR EXPERIENCE, UNTIL YOU FULLY WITNESS YOUR PROBLEM, YOUR PROBLEM WILL PERSIST FOREVER! You may add a new layer to the onion, change the shape or form of your problem, and the only way you're ever going to begin to get to basics is to do what we've been doing in this room today: don't lie, get in touch with your experience, and take what you get . . .

"Now, Jerry, you're still standing there. What's your problem?"

(Laughter)

"My problem is my wife's problem."

"Oh yeah, right. Your problem is 'I love my wife but I can't stand her nagging me about my traveling.' Right?"

"Yeah, that's the way it is."

"Good. You've just heard me give you clues for ten minutes. Tell me, what should you do?"

Jerry stands indecisively, shifting his weight from foot to foot and swaying the mike.

"I guess find out why her nagging bothers me . . ."

"That's good, Jerry. That's almost it. Get in touch with your experience when you're being nagged. What you experience then, the bodily sensations and so on, that's your item."

"Thank you, Don."

(Applause)

"Nancy?"

"I think you're totally unfair about that wife's problem," the tall, pretty woman named Nancy says vehemently. "You're implying that all problems are just something from the past that's bugging us. I think a woman trapped in a lousy marriage with a husband who is away half the time, and probably a bore when he *is* around, has got a *real* problem in the here and now."

"Absolutely," Don replies, "but that wasn't the situation that was described to me by Jerry."

"All right, then, say *I'm* stuck in a lousy marriage. Do you expect me to sit around examining my lousy husband for the rest of my life?"

"NO!" the trainer shouts. "That's not what we've been *saying*. Your problem is not your *husband*, it's your own *stuckness*, your own failure to leave. If you get really in touch with your stuckness you'll find . . . we don't know what . . . that you really love him and he's *not* lousy, or maybe you'll get in touch with the source of the barrier to leaving him and when you experience it out, you'll leave. In either case your problem of experiencing yourself as stuck in a lousy marriage will disappear."

Nancy stands attentive and silent for a while.

"I see," she says, still obviously considering what has been said. "While I'm up," she says, after another moment, "I think I'd like to comment that there are a lot of male chauvinist pigs in this room."

(Laughter, and some applause)

"A male chauvinist pig, Nancy, is an asshole human stuck in a belief system about what women are or should be. Just leave 'em to us, Nancy, and by Sunday we'll have them all letting you grease their automobiles ..."

And much later, we at last begin the "truth process." After the intense emotional confrontations and breakdowns, it is for some a release to be able to stack the chairs at the side of the room and lie on the floor and "go into our space." But for most the tension in the room has been building. Each trainee has been living with his or her "item" for six or seven hours and witnessing others breaking through their barriers to dramatic past events that often seem to lie at the base of the barrier. Will this happen to us? Since the most common item chosen by the trainees is fear, there is a good deal of fear in the room as the process begins. There are some 250 trainees lying on the floor, a half dozen sitting in chairs, and a dozen assistants present to hand out tissues or vomit bags where needed.

And again we locate spaces in our bodies, ease the tension in our faces, breathe deeply and R E L A A A X; again we listen to the long, tranquil affirmation of life read by the trainer, and we play for a few moments on our beach. This long process of quieting the yamayama and resistance of the mind takes twenty or thirty minutes, and then the trainer asks us to begin to experience our items.

We are asked to create a specific situation in which the persistent, recurring barrier occurred and then to *experience* the item. What bodily sensations do we experience? Where? How far in? How strong are they? What feelings do we experience? What emotions do we experience? *Experience* them ...

Several people in the room have begun to cry, their sobbing distracting some of the other trainees from concentration on their own experience and the trainer's instructions, but the process goes on.

What body postures do we associate with our item? What

facial expressions? What points of view? What considerations? What decisions? The trainer has us look at each of these aspects of experience several times before going on to the next. Crying and groaning and moaning are more audible in the room now.

"What images of the past are associated with your item? Good. Take what you get.... What images from the past? Fine! Take what you get.... What images from the past are associated with your item? ... Great! Take what you get ..." And on and on and on and on and on ...

It seems now that almost the entire roomful of people are crying, moaning, groaning, sobbing, screaming, shouting, writhing. "Stop it! Stop it!" "No! No! No!" "I didn't do it! I didn't do it!" "Please ..." "Help!" "Daddy, daddy, daddy ..." The groans, the crying, the shouts reinforce each other; the emotion pours out of the trainees. For some, the uninhibited hysterics of others becomes a barrier: they freeze and lose contact with their own experience.

... A half hour later the trainer brings the group back to their beach, then slowly back into the world of the hotel room with the garish drapes and stolid assistants and wet-eyed, tissue-wielding trainees. The process is over. It is time for a dinner break. Whatever we got, we got. What we didn't get, we didn't get. For the moment, isolated in our vivid individual experience of our individual barrier, we wander absentmindedly out of the hotel to have a meal most of us no longer hunger for and to talk to our friends with whom most of us no longer feel like talking.

"Now we're going to show you about fear. We're going to assist you in experiencing all your phoniness, all your acts, all your bullshit. Each one of you, as part of a row of twenty-five, is going to come to the front of the room and stand and face the entire rest of the audience. All I want you to do is to stand up here and be here. I don't want you to look cool. I don't want you to have a sexy smile. I don't want you to be Joe Friendly. I don't want you to be dignified. I don't want you to be relaxed. I want you to come up here and just *be*. And those still in the audience, I want you to be aware of what's going on with you. Now as you sit pretending to be with the people up front facing you, you're actually busy as a bee preparing your own act. That's what the danger process is all about: getting you in touch with your fuckin' acts. Getting you to experience your failure to just *be*. Getting you to see that you're so scared that people might see who you *really are* that you have to play a role for people. *est* isn't interested in roles; it wants you to get in touch with who you are and just *be* who you are.

"All right. Second row, two center sections, stand up! Take off your sweaters and jackets. Turn to your right and march up onto the platform. Let's GO!"

The people in the second row stand up, and several remove sweaters and jackets. They all begin to shuffle off to their right, then down the aisle, then up and across the platform. As they pass in front of the other trainees, most look guilty, embarrassed, or frightened; if it weren't for the neat, urban modes of dress, this shambling group of fearful adults would resemble prisoners of war being marched before a firing squad. Finally, each comes to a halt and turns to face the audience; many look as if they see guns aiming at them.

One girl stares in terror above the heads of the audience; a portly man stares with a sickly smile at the floor; an immaculately dressed middle-aged woman grins fully at the audience in general, her right cheek twitching. A slim, smooth-complexioned blonde girl in her early twenties, wearing a revealingly sheer white blouse, does not look at anyone, but stares stiffly at the opposite wall. Several people have trouble finding a place for their hands.

"WIPE THAT STUPID SMILE OFF YOUR FACE! YOU ASSHOLE!"

Since three or four people have stupid smiles and probably another half dozen *think* they might have stupid smiles, the shouted command of the trainer stuns many into examining their faces. The woman with the frozen grin never wavers; it's as if she didn't hear. The trainer walks over in front of her.

"Okay, Marcy, get rid of your stupid smile and just be here with us."

Marcy's smile remains; that it doesn't alter makes it seem even more frozen and artificial.

"You've been hiding behind that stupid smile for twenty years, Marcy, WIPE IT OFF. GET RID OF IT! WE DON'T WANT YOUR PHONINESS ANYMORE. WE WANT YOU!"

Like a statue that has been nudged by a careless passerby, Marcy's whole body seems to teeter once or twice but the smile remains as rigid as ever.

"I can't," she says in a small voice through her fixed social grin.

"WIPE IT OFF. That bullshit act has been running your life. Just *be* here."

"I can't," whispers the statue.

"Look, Marcy. What are you experiencing right now?"

". . . I don't know."

"EXACTLY! YOU'RE SO SCARED YOU DON'T EVEN KNOW YOU'RE SCARED."

Marcy's frozen smile is now complemented by tears forming in her eyes, one flowing down her left cheek.

"Come here, Marcy," says the trainer, and he takes her by the hand out of line and off the platform, over to the right side of the line, facing it.

"Look at Diane there, Marcy. She's so scared she can't even look at the audience. You see that?"

"Yes," says Marcy, nearly inaudibly.

"Look at the audience, Diane," the trainer says in a gentle voice to the sexy, frozen-looking woman in the sheer blouse. Blinking rapidly, Diane looks down at the audience and smiles nervously.

"Thank you, Diane. Now look at the audience and be with the audience and don't smile. . . . Thank you. Okay, Marcy, now look at Larry there. Does he look happy and relaxed?"

"No," says Marcy after a short pause.

"He's scared."

"Yes."

"What's he scared of?"

"I don't know."

"What are you scared of, Larry?"

"Little nervous I guess."

"YOU'RE SCARED SHITLESS, LARRY! Now, Marcy, look at Jerome. Is he scared?"

". . . No. He seems okay."

"Are you scared, Jerome?"

"I don't think so."

"Why aren't you scared, Jerome?"

"I don't know. I guess there's nothing to be afraid of."

"Is he being stupid, Marcy? Is he stupid not to be scared?"

"No . . ."

"Is he smiling?"

"No."

"Are *you* smiling?"

For a moment Marcy, who still has her frozen smile, manages to frown, cry, and smile all at once.

"Probably. I mean, yes."

"Okay, I want you to get back in line and look at somebody in the front row, and I want you to concentrate on experiencing your smile. Feel the muscles in your face, in your lips, in your forehead. Fully experience your smile. If it stays, it stays. If it disappears, it disappears."

Marcy takes her place back in the line and after a few minutes, eight stony-faced assistants march down a side aisle and up across the platform to assume positions nose to nose with eight of the trainees. Diane, the lovely blonde with the cool face and see-through blouse, is one of those whom an assistant chooses to "be" with nose-to-nose, and after five minutes her cool face is wet with tears. The portly man who was staring at the floor begins to breathe in heavy gagging gasps but manages to maintain his eye contact. After ten minutes— through most of the time the trainer is berating everyone to get off his act and just *be*—the assistants march away and a couple of minutes later the first twenty-five trainees are permitted to sit.

The next line to stand before the rest is not quite so dramatically fearful as the first, but in this one a man begins to cry. In the fourth "lineup" a woman faints, and an assistant standing behind her, obviously prepared for such an occasion, catches her and lowers her to the platform, immediately reassuming his robotlike position at attention behind the line. Don comes over to stand near her and says, in an absolutely neutral voice, "Look at her—she'll do anything, even faint, in order to avoid being here with us. Get up, Elaine. The instructions are for you to *stand* and just *be* with the other trainees. Don't give us your damsel-in-distress act. Just stand up and *be*."

Elaine, a middle-aged woman wearing a purple pants suit, lies grotesquely on her back in almost the exact center of the platform, with a dozen standing trainees stretched out on each side. And, amazingly, she continues to lie there as the assistants march up to confront selected trainees, as they leave again, even while the other twenty-four trainees return to their seats—twelve of them detouring around her prostrate body.

The fifth group of trainees marches up and takes its position facing the others and still Elaine lies there in the center of the platform. The trainer continues exhorting the others to loosen up and just be. He seems to have forgotten all about Elaine, whose presence even the other trainees are beginning not to notice.

When the sixth group is about ready to leave, the trainer goes up and whispers something in Elaine's ear. Then, a half minute later, he tells the sixth line that he's about to excuse them and adds:

"Elaine, this is your last chance. I want you to stand up now."

Elaine groans and slowly rolls over onto her stomach, then gets to her hands and knees and finally stands. She looks dazedly at the audience.

"Fine. All right, you can all go back to your seats." And off they all march, Elaine included.

At the conclusion of the danger process, a trainee asks what Don whispered to Elaine to get her to undo her faint.

"I didn't tell her 'truth,'" Don replies. "I wasn't reasonable. I just said something I knew would work. Elaine? Do you want to share what I whispered?"

There is a silence and then a very soft "no" from the direction of Elaine.

"You see, Richard, Elaine doesn't want to share what I whispered because her getting up when she did, her *hearing* what I whispered, exposed her fainting as the phony act it was. I don't mean she didn't really faint. I mean that she was free to unchoose her faint at any time after hitting the floor, and she knew it and I knew it. So I whispered something that made her decide her act wasn't worth continuing."

"What was it?" Richard asks.

"Elaine will tell you next weekend," says the trainer blandly . . .

It is the last process of the night and we are all lying on the floor with our eyes closed. We have located our spaces and relaxed and played on our beaches, and now we are being instructed to become actors and actresses and pretend to be filled with fear, to be terrified of the person lying next to us.

We fake it a bit (that's what the instructions are) and moan a little. Then we are told to extend our fear to the people on all four sides of us—they are dangerous and fill us with fear. Someone screams and several trainees groan and writhe . . . Now everyone on our whole side of the room is dangerous and frightening . . . More screams; a "No! No!" Everyone in the whole room is out to kill us . . . The whole city is our enemy and fills us with fear . . . Everybody on earth is after us, they are *all* our enemies, they *all* frighten us. After a slow, repetitious buildup the whole room is filled with writhing, groaning, moaning, screaming, shrieking, crying—some acted, and some very real.

And at the very height of the dramatized fear the trainer quiets us enough so that his voice can be heard again over the din:

"And you know," he is telling us, "the thing you ought to know is that the person lying beside you who you were afraid of? He is deathly afraid of *you*. And the truth is—the amazing truth is that everyone in this *room* is afraid, screaming, moaning, afraid of *you*. [Laughter is heard.] And finally, yes, you've got it, everyone on this whole planet that frightened you, everyone is actually deathly afraid of *you*. They're all afraid of you, *everybody*, and they always have been and always will be. Those people you never dare look at on elevators—they're afraid to look at *you*. [Laughter] ... Those people whose eyes you don't meet when you're passing people in the street, they're fucking scared shitless of *you*! ... And that boss who called you into the office the other day, he was frightened as hell, of *you*. ... The doorman, the waitress, the desk clerk, the policeman, yes, the *policeman*, they're all afraid of you ...

"So when you go out into the streets of the city tonight I want you to be careful. If you were to say 'boo' to the elevator man he'd probably faint. ... And don't be too hard on your boss next time you see him. Remember, he's scared. ... But also remember that everyone you meet, the whole planet, is afraid of *you*, just the way asshole you was afraid of them. It's as if it were all the cruel joke of some crazy mechanic who made four billion toy robots and programmed them all to be deathly afraid of each other ..."

And soon the first weekend of the training is over. The trainees burst out into the streets of the city like the hordes of Genghis Khan, ravishing men and maidens with looks and conquering whole nations with stares—in any case, being as fearless as robots programmed to fear ever get.

3

DAY THREE
"Who Done Me Dirt?"

I am locked in a cage I build
Myself, caught by cops
I create each day, condemned by judges
Who preside in me, dragged
To my cell by my own two arms,
Jail and jailer and jailed
All one, imprisoned in self by my
Self alone, in the circle of self I call
My own, encircled circles all
My own.

We have met the Creator and He is Us.

"Something amazing has happened . . . is happening . . . amazing. This is the first time I've shared, the only time I've said anything into a microphone, because . . . I stutter. I mean I *have* stuttered or rather did stutter for seventeen years—always since I was eight years old. It was really . . . I see now it was really my racket. It ran my whole life. . . . People would *have* to listen to me, just to hear if I *might* be saying something important. But . . . well, now I'm not stuttering.

"Last Sunday night during the truth process I went into my barrier of stuttering and the feelings I have just before I begin to speak and I got right into those feelings and when Don asked me to go back to an early event associated with stuttering I was suddenly about four years old and lying on the ground and I knew I'd just been hit by a car and someone's voice—it may have been my mother's—kept saying 'Don't say anything! Don't say anything!' I didn't reexperience the actual being hit by the car but rather the lying there on the road. My left leg ached and I felt gravel in my back and heard that voice. I don't know what that memory has to do with stuttering. According to my mother I didn't start stuttering until I was seven or eight.

"But anyway, that night after the training I was going to take a taxi home alone but noticed a woman who was sharing a ride to the Upper West Side where I live. I went up to her and said, 'Hey, can I get into that group with you that's going uptown?' and she said 'Sure.'

"It was only when I was sitting in the car with them all that I realized that I was talking without stuttering. And—it certainly is weird, to say the least—I haven't stuttered since."

The audience interrupts Loretta before she sits with long, spontaneous applause.

"Just one more thing, I guess," says Loretta after the applause ends. Her face is flushed and happy. "These last three days I keep expecting someone to come up to me who's known me as a stutterer for many years and say, 'Come off it, Loretta, quit pretending you don't stutter.' "

(Applause)

We are in the mid-training seminar, which lasts for a little over three hours on the Wednesday evening between the two weekends. Much of it consists of the trainees sharing what has been or has not been happening in their lives . . .

Sven: "I thought the first weekend was interesting but that I *personally* hadn't gotten much out of it. I mean it was good for some of the trainees, but my life just didn't need it. This morning at breakfast as I put a plate of scrambled eggs in front of my wife she stared up at me and said something like 'Another weekend of *est* and I can retire.' 'Huh?' I said. And she pointed out that in the three days since the first weekend I had made breakfast all three mornings, which matched my previous output of breakfasts for the whole year!"

Doug: "I . . . I'm very nervous, frightened really, but I want to speak. . . . I took as my item my fear . . . my fear in association with getting close to people . . . psychologically close. . . . And after the process was over—the truth process—my fear didn't disappear. And during that last process Sunday night— when . . . when we were all supposed to be actors pretending fear—well, the fear for me was real. I was terrified. I screamed once for help and . . . well, I *meant* it. And every day since the weekend I've occasionally been overwhelmed with fear attacks for no reason at all. I'll be arranging papers on my desk or just finishing a conversation with some secretary and suddenly be flooded with such anxiety I have to sit down. It's as if my disease of fear were spreading as the result of the truth process rather than getting better . . ."

"Just stay with it, Doug," comments Don when Doug has finished. "DON'T FIGHT IT! Just let it come full force, be with it, observe it, weigh it. What's happened is that you've peeled away a layer of onion problem and gotten closer to the core. Each time your fear comes just say to yourself, 'Hey, how interesting, here comes my fear flood again. I wonder how big it'll be this time.' DON'T FIGHT IT. Just go with it. . . . Thank you. [Applause] Marcy?"

Marcy, the woman with the frozen smile last Sunday night, stands up. Her face, though it smiles briefly, seems this evening more relaxed.

"On Sunday I didn't think standing up in front of people would be a problem. I mean I've had to handle groups for several years in my women's clubs. I walked up onto the platform with my row and I stood and looked at the audience. Or I thought I was looking at the audience. I don't remember feeling anything or seeing anything or thinking anything. I vaguely heard Don shouting at somebody. Then I noticed him standing in front of me and I thought, Oh, he must have been attracted by my warm smile. [Laughter] Then I realized he was asking me to stop smiling. I didn't feel anything. I felt frozen. I couldn't tell whether I was smiling or not.

" 'Wipe it off!' I heard him yell from far away. 'Get rid of it! We don't want your phoniness anymore!'

"I honestly didn't know what he was talking about. I did realize that I was smiling but I was too frozen to do anything about it. He kept shouting or talking to me and then dragged me out to look at the others. They looked scared. When I saw how scared one man looked I felt, for the first time, a great rush of fear flow through my *own* body. I mean I *felt* fear, I *experienced* my fear of people for the first time in my life. Don kept asking me questions and I suppose I kept answering but it wasn't until he let me get back in line that I found I could actually feel my facial muscles. I tried smiling and unsmiling and noticed for the first time someone in the audience—a man, looking at me from the audience—it was you, Ken. As soon as I noticed him I felt my face lock into that smile. He kept looking at me—his face was absolutely unsmiling but it some-how communicated warmth or okayness or acceptance any-way. When I managed to wipe the smile off my face, Ken's expression didn't change. When the smile snapped back on he still just looked at me. When I noticed that, a tremendous wave of relief passed through me, something seemed to be released: I could smile or not smile and it was okay. It was then that I stopped smiling and began to cry. I felt so sad about all the time I'd wasted with my phony smiliness and how much fear I must be carrying around. It seemed so sad. And it was so good that someone could look at me and like me whether I smiled or not. Or, actually, look at me and not be taken in by my smile, not *care* whether I smiled or not . . ."

Annabelle: "Both during that second day and afterwards I felt brief periods of disorientation. I mean not real disorienta-tion—I always knew where I was and who I was with, but for instance I noticed that I would forget the names of people—not my children, but my friends—and once, even my husband! I would eventually recall their names but it was like briefly being buried in a state of semiconsciousness or being in a deep meditative or trancelike state. It frightened me, and I wondered again about that 'brainwashing' business I had read about in one of the magazine articles about *est*.

"I should also share that I was extremely efficient and energetic and have written more letters in the last three days than I had in a month, but I was also irritable and authoritative with my children—I'm not usually. I was amazed to get so much done so quickly and easily, and that made me think about the 'brainwashing' too. I wondered whether I'd been hypnotized or something. I have the impression that I must have gone very thoroughly into several of the meditative states and didn't quite get myself reoriented totally from my inner space. Eventually everything has gotten back to normal again ... although that too I suppose might be part of the brainwashing."

"HOLD IT!" Don shouts as Annabelle begins to sit. "Let's get clear about this brainwashing nonsense, Annabelle. You've heard at least a dozen people share this morning. How many have described their experience as being similar to yours?"

"Well," says Annabelle, standing slump-shouldered and uncertain. "Not many. None, actually."

"You're damn right, none," Don says. "And what kind of brainwashing is it that manages to give twelve people twelve entirely different experiences?"

"I guess that's not the way it works, is it?"

"NO! That's not the way *brainwashing* works. It's the way *est* works. We're interested in creating the space where *you* can learn to be *you*, just *be* yourself. And that's all. We don't have any theory about how you *ought* to be. There is no such thing as the *est* personality; there's only more aliveness, more joy, more love, and more self-expression. Do you get that?"

"Yes," Annabelle says, standing straighter. "I see that my ... disorientation had nothing to do with what that article was talking about."

"Good. Now we don't know what it is your mind is trying to hide from that's causing it to disorient you, but you just stick with it, stay in touch with exactly what you're experiencing when you think you're being disoriented, and take what you get. Thank you, Annabelle. [Applause]

"Okay, Diane?"

Diane, dressed this evening more casually and less provocatively than three days before, stands up. After taking the microphone, she remains staring down at it as if collecting her thoughts. She speaks slowly but firmly.

"During the truth process last weekend I got in touch with . . . I took as my item my failure to enjoy sex with men. I'm living with a man now whom I think I love but I have to completely fake it when we make love. I don't really *feel* anything. When Don asked us to contact an image from the past I got the time when I was ten years old and my uncle molested me. I've remembered this incident ever since it occurred—it wasn't something I had repressed. I was playing on my uncle's lap when my parents were out and he began doing dirty things with his hands and then making me do dirty things with mine. When I—"

"Hold it, Diane," Don interrupts. " 'Dirty things' is your belief system, your concept, it's something you added then and are adding now to what actually occurred. Just tell us what occurred."

Diane stares at Don at first without replying.

"I was only ten years old!" she says.

"I got that," says Don. "And your uncle touched your right elbow, is that right?"

"No! He touched me . . . between the legs."

"Good. I got it. Go on."

"Well," says Diane, now a little flushed. "He molested me and later I realized what I had done was wrong. My mother—"

"I'm sorry, Diane," interrupts Don again. "This coming weekend when we talk about reality and 'Who did it?' you'll understand why I want you to look now at *who* is making what you and your uncle did 'dirty' or 'wrong.' "

"Everybody does. It was *dirty*," says Diane.

"You choose to experience it as dirty," says Don, standing on the platform opposite Diane. "Look, in a graduate seminar a woman shared that for four years she had committed incest with her father and she felt terrible about it. There was incest and there was her feeling terrible about it. Immediately after that woman finished sharing another woman stood up and said, 'I just realized listening to this woman how much I loved my father and part of me wished my father had committed incest with me. It almost seems like it would have been wonderful.'

"Now it's not that one woman is right and the other one wrong. What I want you to get is that the same physical event can be *experienced* as dirty or wonderful."

"All right," says Diane, looking, if anything, annoyed at the interruption of her story. "Anyway, ever ... ever since ...," she stops and stares at the microphone again, thinking. "Anyway, during the danger process I was very self-conscious because I realized that my act for years has been to be very sexy, to dress sexy, and then ... usually ... decide that men were dirty because ... because they found me sexy and wanted sex. For me it's very hard just to *be* anyplace, just to *be* with people, I ... I have to always *present* myself, be attractive, be desirable.... It was very sad."

When Diane abruptly sits, the trainees applaud.

"Okay, thank you, Diane," says Don. "Who else wants to share? Jed? Go ahead."

Jed, a teen-ager in patched blue jeans and a tee shirt with a marijuana-leaf motif, stands and takes the mike.

"I thought that last process about everybody being afraid of everybody else was just great. When I went out of the hotel I said 'boo' to the doorman and, boy, did he look nervous, and then I sort of stared wide-eyed at the first few guys passing and they walked way around me, I mean *way* around me, and I said 'boo' to a couple of other people and one started running. [Laughter] But the really groovy thing happened when I was heading down the subway steps and I was walking next to this tall, skinny older man in a nice expensive-looking coat and I said 'boo' and he looks back at me without any expression at all at first and then he looks real fierce and says 'BOO' so loud I jumped, and as we went to get our tokens he smiled and said to me, 'I already took the training.'"

(Laughter and applause)

And the sharing goes on. Several trainees report that their energy levels have increased remarkably, others share how they enjoyed the last process, several talk about their problems or their successes during the truth process. A few report that nothing seems to be happening.

During this mid-training session, the *est* staff member in charge of the Graduate Division in our city comes up and tells us about the graduate seminar series available and in particular about the Be Here Now seminar series especially available for our group beginning two weeks after the conclusion of our training. Barbara stands up and complains that we shouldn't have to think about paying for a graduate course when we don't even know whether we like the undergraduate course, and Hank complains about training time being taken up with someone trying to sell us more *est*. Many other trainees ask questions about the seminar series and indicate their desire to enroll.

Early in the mid-training seminar there is a meditationlike process; at the end there is a long process in which the trainee is asked to expand his awareness out first into the whole room, then out into the city, to the state, over the whole planet, and finally out into the entire universe; and at 10:30 P.M., having been serenely dissipated over several galaxies and gently returned to the room, we are released until the second weekend.

The man who strides to the platform Saturday morning at a little after nine is shorter than Don, almost squat, with muscular arms and a thick neck. His hair is dark and full, and his face, were it not for its resolutely neutral expression, would be pudgily pleasant. He is wearing neatly pressed pants and a tan long-sleeved open-neck shirt. He looks over the trainees from behind the small lectern where he has placed his notebook, and then, moving with surprising ease and grace for so compact a man, he comes to the front of the platform. The trainees are looking at him with interest, with resentment that the trainer is different, with pleasure that the trainer is different, with curiosity.

"GOOD MORNING," he says loudly, "MY NAME IS MICHAEL REED. I AM YOUR TRAINER FOR THIS SECOND WEEKEND."

He pauses and looks from right to left.

"MY NAME IS NOT DON MALLORY. I WAS NOT YOUR TRAINER FOR THE FIRST WEEKEND." He walks effortlessly off to his left. "I know a lot of you wish that I *were* Don. A lot of you may feel that just as you've finally decided that maybe Don wasn't an arrogant fascist bastard, *est* brings in a new guy who obviously is a fascist bastard. [Laughter]

"I want you all to let go of Don. Werner has trained the trainers so that whatever personalities we may have get gently obliterated while we're doing the training. The only difference between Don and Michael during the training is that one of us is six feet and one of us is five feet nine, and one wears DON and one wears MICHAEL. We both do either the first or the second weekend interchangeably. The only thing you have to worry about is keeping your sole in the room and taking what you get ...

"Today we're going to spend much of the time trying to get in touch with 'reality'—a worthy enterprise you'll agree—and then trying to answer the question of 'Who did it?' 'Who is responsible for what happens to us?' But before we do that let's begin with some sharing. Let's find out what's been happening since you were last all together. Who'd like to begin? Yes, Kirsten?"

"I just wanted to share that my hereditary arthritis hasn't disappeared," says Kirsten rapidly, looking nervous. "I really worked on it during the truth process last Sunday but it hasn't changed much at all. I just wanted you all to know. Thank you."

(Applause)

"Hank?" says the trainer. "Take the mike."

"I tried to walk out last Sunday," Hank says loudly into the mike, "but Don talked me out of it. I haven't decided yet what I'm going to do today, but somebody told me, Richard told me, that I'd get a chance this morning to get my money back. Is that so?"

"Sure, Hank," Michael replies amiably. "You just stay with this sharing for a while and in an hour or two I'm going to ask everyone here to choose again either to be here or to get out. We don't want people wasting chairs sitting here thinking they're trapped. We tell you what's gonna happen, ask you to choose to stay, to follow instructions and keep the agreements, *or* to choose to get out—with your full money back, half an *est* training for free, a real bargain. And you go through life telling people how worthless *est* is—*you* know, you went through half of it free. So you'll get a chance to leave in an hour or two. But no one leaves before or after that moment . . ."

"Thank you," says Hank, sitting.

(Applause)

"Celia? Stand up," says the trainer.

Celia is a small woman in her early twenties, neither noticeably attractive or unattractive, with straight brown hair.

"I've been trying to do what Don said about observing rather than resisting," she says in a soft, clear voice. "In my case it's my . . . sexual impulses. . . . I went out last Wednesday night after the mid-training with a man I met in this training and while eating dinner in the restaurant I began to tingle all over and feel funny . . . and realized that I wanted to go to his apartment or to mine and have him make love to me. This may seem groovy to some of you, but I tend to get this feeling with almost *every* man I'm with, no matter what he's doing or saying, or in some cases no matter how ... gross he looks.

"In the past I've tried to ... sometimes to resist this feeling, suppress it. What happens is that I become sort of paralyzed. I don't talk. I don't even move unless urged to by the man, and usually, if he wants me, he takes me, and if he doesn't, he disappears, probably wondering what kind of a zombie I am. Of course, when I have sex I'm not always a zombie. Sometimes I am, sometimes I lie there just as paralyzed as I get in the first place, but sometimes I come out of it and go into a kind of frenzy. But most men don't like that either. At least after a while. It frightens them. Anyway no man seems to find me someone he wants around for very long ..."

The room is very still as Celia goes on in her soft, barely audible voice.

"So I thought I wouldn't try to resist my ... desire, I'll try to ... I mean I'll observe it, just let it be. I felt things can't get any worse than they already are ...

"So in the restaurant Wednesday night when the tingling feeling hit me I started automatically first to resist it and I became paralyzed. Then I remembered to look, to witness it. Actually, what I first observed wasn't my sexual desire but the paralysis, the numbness. I tried to change the paralysis back to the tingling and that didn't work at all, the paralysis just got stronger, I got *more* numb and rigid. When I felt this happening I began to panic and tried to observe harder and harder and the paralysis and panic just got even stronger. I guess I wasn't really observing, I was resisting and trying to disappear it. Then I heard the man I was with saying, 'What's the matter? What's happening to you?' and he looked kinda worried.

"I told him that I was feeling a sort of anxiety attack and that I was trying to disappear it by just being with it, but it wasn't working. Well, of course, I wasn't really sharing honestly with him but it was sharing more than I usually do or ever had before with a man, and he began saying it was persisting because I was *trying* to disappear it. He began asking me to describe to him everything I was feeling. So I did. I located tensions and numbness all over the place and after about five minutes of locating dozens of bodily sensations connected with my paralysis and panic I began to feel the tingling again.... [Celia laughs nervously, and the audience emits a rippling sigh of sympathetic laughter.]

"Well ... he ... then I described to him all my tingles—actually it turns out that's not all that was happening when I got really in touch with my body—anyway, all of my sensations from my toes to my nipples to my earlobes. I was really looking at them. After ten minutes they were all gone. I was experiencing a tension in my abdomen and a smiley feeling in my face, but that was all. And I ended up telling him all about what was really going on—about my sex problem, about what I've shared with you right now—and when that was done the only feeling I had left was the smiley feeling in my face ..."

When Celia pauses in her narration, still standing, a few of the trainees begin to applaud, and they are joined by the others until long, loud applause flows from the audience, many of whom are smiling in shared triumph.

"But wait a minute!" Celia says after the room begins to quiet. "Wait ... I'm not done. I mean I really enjoyed being with this guy, but ... what happened is that he kissed me good night and for a while in my room alone I felt wonderful, and the next day I felt horrible. Because here was the first man in two years that I really *should* have felt like ... making love to and what happens? Nothing! No tingling, no desire at all. A nice good-night kiss and nothing! For him just a ... I don't know, warmth, I guess. What worries me is that when I observed like Don says, things disappeared all right—as long as I wasn't *trying* to disappear them, as long as I was just really being with them—but after things have disappeared I'm left with ... nothing!"

(Silence)

"And nothing is frightening, isn't it, Celia?" Michael says, moving to the left corner of the platform to be near where she is standing in the second row.

"It's horrible!"

"ANYTHING," Michael goes on loudly to all of the trainees. "Anything—anxiety, anger, fear, compulsive lust, depression, hatred, guilt, bitterness—to the mind ANYTHING that it hooks up with survival is better than *nothing*. Because, remember, *nothing* is that space one has to go through to get from nonexperience to experience. If you feel the same thing for every man you're with it's obvious, isn't it, Celia, that YOU'RE NOT EXPERIENCING ANY OF THE MEN. You're going through life playing your compulsive tapes, your compulsive acts. For you the button is simply a man, any man. I don't care how many frenzies you think you've gone through, you probably haven't BEEN with a man in your whole fucking adult life! Until last Wednesday night . . ."

(Silence)

"But why didn't I *feel* anything for him after I shared what was happening with him?"

"You got what you got. Your tape must still be telling you that you ought to love every man you meet. Also, Celia, you tell us you felt warmth . . ."

"Yes . . ."

"Most alive people come to share with hundreds of people. They may feel strong physical attraction for only a tiny handful of these, and feel what you call *warmth* and what others might call love for the rest. Feeling *warmth* for a man in that situation is what was *real* for you. Just because it doesn't fit your *belief* about how you *ought* to feel lust shouldn't be a problem."

Celia stands there in silence and then smiles.

"I got it. Thank you, Michael."

(Long applause)

"Okay, who's next? Over there. Stand up, is it Ronald?"

"Yes. I have a confession to make, Michael," Ronald says. He is neatly dressed in a checkered sports coat and open-necked blue shirt. "I wasn't able to keep the agreement about drugs. I tried. I couldn't go to sleep. The night before last I took two sleeping pills. Before that I hadn't slept much for two nights. ... It was really getting to me." He sits down and applause follows.

"Thank you, Ronald," says Michael. "You've opened up the space for others now to share their broken agreements. Anyone else? Yes, Tina?"

"I smoked a joint with an old friend at a concert Tuesday."

"Thank you. [Applause] Frank?"

"I don't know if I've broken an agreement or not," he begins.

"Well, if you don't know," says Michael, "we can be sure you have. Go on, Frank."

"I didn't take a drink or pills or smoke anything I shouldn't have, but I told a friend about the training in some detail. I shared with her what was going on."

"Sharing your experience with someone is one of the things *est* is all about. To share your experience is to make it real. On the other hand, you *can* share irresponsibly by the retelling of the intimate sharing of other people's experience in this room or by trying to *explain est* and giving inaccurate data. The important thing to get in your sharing with other people is that *est* is an *experience*. It's very hard to describe the training, but you can describe your *experience* of it. As for thinking you may have broken an agreement—if there are any maybes or sort ofs or possibles in there, you undoubtedly did, Frank, and that goes for the rest of you. As a matter of fact let's see now, how many of you think you broke an agreement sometime since the training started? Stand up. Any more?"

Gradually more than half the trainees stand amidst self-conscious laughter and groans.

"You might as well own up now and get rid of it. Don't spend the next six hours wondering whether you ought to have stood up and confessed. If you think you might have, you more than likely did."

Several more rise; two-thirds of the trainees are now standing.

"Fine. Now we see why the world doesn't work. Very few

people are willing to be responsible for keeping their agreements. Okay, sit down, thank you.... The rest of you who
didn't stand up, don't sit there feeling righteous, clinging to
your goody two-shoes because you kept your agreements. Get
off it! For all we know some of you are as stuck in *keeping*
agreements as all those who stood are in breaking them. . . .
All right, Lester?"

Tossing his long hair away from his face, Lester stands and
takes the mike.

"I don't have any trouble keeping important agreements," he
says firmly, "but I'm damned if I'm going to bust my ass to
keep trivial agreements."

"Oh yeah," says Michael, putting down his thermos with an
abrupt, almost violent motion. "How many times have we
heard that one? WAKE UP, LESTER! Every time in your
whole fuckin' life you've felt like breaking an agreement, THE
AGREEMENT HAS AUTOMATICALLY SEEMED AT
THAT MOMENT TRIVIAL! That's how the mind *works*! If
someone owes you twenty bucks that's a fuckin' important
agreement, right? But if *you* owe twenty bucks, surprise!, it's a
trivial agreement."

(Laughter)

"That's not true, I—"

"IT'S ALWAYS TRUE! It may not be true with you about
twenty bucks, but the fact is that the mind will evaluate the
importance of an agreement on the basis of how much it feels
like keeping it. Do you get that?"

"Oh, well, sure, I guess I get that all right . . ."

"What is reality?" Michael asks much later, after the sharing is
over and he has given the trainees an opportunity to leave if
they want. (Only one trainee, a man named Alan, has done
so.) "Yes, Robert?"

"Reality is mind."

"Good. Reality is mind. What is reality? Jane?"

"Reality is things and thoughts."

"Fine . . ."

"Reality is everything we sense," suggests another trainee.

"Reality is matter and energy . . ."

"Reality is consciousness . . ."

Reality is everything perceived . . . spiritual energy . . . space, matter, and form . . . the physical universe . . . a pain in the ass . . . an electrochemical amalgam of energy . . . God . . . one's own experience . . . and so on.

"Well, let's see," says Michael, after considering twenty such suggestions. "What *is* reality? Let's take an archetypal situation. You are standing on the corner of Fifth Avenue and you take three steps out into the street against the traffic light when a bus is speeding along at you at thirty miles an hour. At the last instant you glance up at the bus. Is the bus real?"

Several voices reply affirmatively.

"You're *damn right it's real!* You better believe it. Okay, you look at the bus, and you say to yourself, 'Ah, here comes a bit of reality.' Now, do you also say to yourself, 'Here comes a bit of mind'?"

Several people shout no's but one trainee shouts yes.

"YES?" shouts the trainer. "You asshole, since when has anyone gotten run over by a piece of mind?" He pauses and glares at the offending trainee. "Okay," he goes on, "do you say to yourself, 'Here comes spirit'? . . . No . . . Do you say to yourself, 'Oh wow, here comes God at thirty miles an hour'? . . . No . . . That's *reality* bearing down on you, and those things aren't really what we mean by reality. I mean, what *is* there about that bus bearing down on us that makes us *know* it's real? Yes, Helen?"

"We can *feel* it," says Helen.

"That's not true," Michael responds. "While you're standing there you haven't *felt* it and yet that bus is still *real.* Whether or not you can feel a thing is not a test for reality. How do we know that bus is real? Jorge?"

"It will knock me down."

"*How* will it knock you down?"

"Bam-boom. I'm down."

"But what is there about the bus which causes it to knock you down?"

"It's there."

"I know it's there. But what is there about that bus that lets me know that it's there, that it's real? Bob?"

"It's physical matter."

"It's PHYSICAL! The test for reality is *physicalness*. What is *real* is *physical*! ..."

"All right," Michael is saying an hour later, a light layer of perspiration showing on his forehead beneath his thick dark hair. He has been interacting vigorously with the trainees on the subject of reality and has met resistance from several. "Let's see what we've learned so far about the way people talk about reality.

"First, it's *physical*. We don't call something real unless it's physical. Physicalness manifests itself in time, distance, and form. Things that are physical have form, they exist in time, and they cover or occupy a distance.

"We can say that something like the Easter bunny *exists*, but it isn't *real*. An imaginary Easter bunny has no location or distance and doesn't exist in time.

"Secondly, the substance of physicalness is *measurability*. That is to say, time, form, and distance all necessitate the ability to measure, and when something is measurable it simply means it has a beginning, a middle, and an end.

"Hold your questions for a minute, Richard." Michael interrupts himself to quiet a vigorously raised hand. "I want to complete this recapitulation.

"Okay. Thirdly, the substance of measurability is *agreement*. For something to be measurable it must have a beginning. And all beginnings follow an end which is preceded by a middle. The exact end of this blackboard here is the *beginning* of the

space between the blackboard and the door at the back of the
room, and that space has a middle which is, let's say, where
Jason is sitting out there. And that middle may be the beginning of the top of Jason's head, which is also the end of the
space between the ceiling and the top of his head, and so on,
everything being a beginning of something, a middle of something and an end. Everything in the universe is in *agreement*:
its beginnings absolutely depend on the ends of other things
and extend into their middles. Everything in the universe flows
into everything else—it's all one—beginnings, middles, and
ends—all in agreement.

"This blackboard is *real* because of its physicalness—it has
form, it exists in time, it has location, distance, and it is measurable: it has a beginning, middle, and end. Are you clear on
what we've said thus far? Yes, Lester?"

"I still don't see why we have to say reality is physical,"
Lester says, continuing an objection he has made earlier. "As
far as I can see the only thing that exists is mind, is consciousness. Berkeley and Hume said the same thing. How is that
blackboard or that bus we were talking about any more real
than my experiencing thoughts of Raquel Welch?"

"Well, don't forget your thoughts of Raquel Welch are real,
Lester. They have form, they exist in time and have distance.
It's only that your thoughts of Raquel don't have the substance
that a bus does. You may get physically run over by a bus and
you may be physically run by thoughts of Raquel."

"Then you agree," says Lester. "They both exist in my consciousness?"

"No!" shouts Michael. "Your thoughts of Raquel Welch are
real but there's another reality, namely Raquel herself, and you
can be damned sure there's a difference. So too with the *real*
bus and your real thought of a bus."

"There is no bus except in my consciousness," insists Lester.

"I know that's *your* theory!" Michael responds sharply. "I'm
happy you've studied Berkeley and Hume. Your theory is that
if I knock you unconscious and lay you down on Fifth Avenue

in front of a bus and you get run over, that the bus isn't real because it didn't enter your consciousness."

"For *me*, it would never have been real," agrees Lester.

"I don't give a shit whether you think it's real for you or not. Whether you think something is real or not doesn't have anything at all to do with whether it actually *is* real. The bus that ran you over would seem very real to your wife and wouldn't seem real to you. But in any case it *is real*."

"No. It just means we have different realities."

"Look, Lester, do you get that for most everyone it makes sense to say that if twenty people go out in front of something that most of us call a bus and all twenty get run over, that maybe, just maybe, it might be convenient to consider that bus *real* because of its repeatedly demonstrated physicalness?"

"Oh, yeah, I see that."

"Good. Another example: let's say we create a hologram of a blackboard between these two blackboards—you know, an electronically created image of a blackboard. For everyone entering this room all three blackboards *seem* real, but only two of them are physical, measurable, are real blackboards. The middle one turns out to be a real hologram. What's real for a person doesn't necessarily have anything to do with what is, in fact, real."

"Okay," says Lester, "but what about something like, unh, like the existence of say, an invasion from Mars. Orson Welles once made a radio program that made a lot of people think we were being invaded from Mars. Their thoughts of an invasion scared them just as much as the invasion might have. For them it was real."

"NO, ASSHOLE!" Michael shouts, and he comes to the edge of the platform near Lester. "Their thoughts are real and they let themselves be run by their thoughts. But when people checked in the streets it was found the invasion was *not* real.

"Look, Lester, one of the things you're stuck with is the interim test to reality. While physicalness—measurability—is our ultimate test for what is real, there is an interim test that we often have to apply. In the case of the Orson Welles radio program the listeners applied the interim test: anything a radio announcer says is happening must be happening. They couldn't or didn't physically test for the presence of Martians; they accepted the authority of the radio voice.

"Let's say I announce to all of you that in an hour we're going to have to shift from this hotel to another one fifteen blocks away. I then announce that you'll all line up and leave, and to take us the fifteen blocks we'll all be boarding elephants that are waiting for us on the street outside. Elephants ...

"Now here in the room you have to use an interim test to determine the reality of the elephants. What is it? What do you use to decide whether there are real elephants waiting for you downstairs? Yes, Bob?"

"It's ridiculous."

"If I said there were buses waiting?"

"That would be reasonable. I'd probably believe you."

"So what's the test?"

"Whether what you say makes sense, whether it's reasonable or not."

"Yes, REASONABLENESS," says Michael. "In general we use as an interim test of reality whether it seems *reasonable* or not. An authority is just one form of reasonableness. Others might be whether we think something is likely or not, or whether a consensus of the people we consult thinks it's reasonable or not, whether it seems natural and proper, whether it's intrinsically believable or not, and so on. Now the next question is: what is the essence of all of these elements of reasonableness?"

"Whether I *agree* that you're an authority or not," says Barbara. "Whether I agree that it's reasonable that it's real."

"Yes, agreement. We have to agree with the consensus, we have to agree that it's natural for snow to fall in Utah in December, for buses to exist in Tokyo. But remember, our agreement on the interim test doesn't mean that the snow actually fell in Utah or that there are buses in Tokyo. Only physicalness can ultimately verify that. In any case, agreement is thus basic to both physicalness, our primary estimate of what is real, and to reasonableness, our secondary or interim test of what is real. . . . Yes, Brad?"

"But it seems to me . . ."

And on it goes about the nature of what is real. We trainees shift in our chairs, get drawn into the discussion for a while and then tune out as the trainer goes back and forth over the points, illustrating them, refuting objections, answering questions, and slowly plowing forward through the argument. Just before an afternoon break, he brings five trainees up on the stage, lining up four of them facing in the same direction, chests touching backs, with the fifth trainee standing two feet behind the other four. The trainer then abruptly shoves the first person in line, causing the tightly packed four to topple backward like a row of dominoes into the arms of the fifth.

"From the point of view of the *fourth* person in line," says Michael after the five trainees have resumed their seats, "why did he fall backwards into the arms of the fifth man?"

"The third man fell backwards into him," suggests a trainee.

"All right. Good. The third man *causes* the *effect* of his falling backwards into the fifth. He experiences himself as the effect of number three. What about number three? How does he view the event?"

"Number two did it!" shouts someone.

"He's the effect of number two," says someone else.

"Yes. Number two's backward motion *causes* the *effect* of number three's falling backwards, which is seen as *cause* of the *effect* of number four's falling. What about number two?"

"Number one is cause," suggests a voice.

"Good. Number one *causes* the *effect* of number two's falling which is the *cause* of the *effect* of number three's falling which is the *cause* of the *effect* number four's falling. . . . But who *really* did it?"

"You did!" shout several voices in reply.

"Right! *I* shoved Ben, which was the *cause* of the *effect* Ben's toppling backwards, which *effect* was the *cause* of number two's falling, and so on. Cause-effect, cause-effect, cause-effect, or actually, cause, effect, effect, effect, effect, effect.

"Very good. But wait a minute. My shoving Ben was the *effect* of Werner's instructions, right?"

After a brief silence several affirmative answers are heard.

"And Werner's instructions in this process were the *effect* of his viewing his father shove his mother when he was four years old. And his father's shoving his mother at that time was the *effect* of her having just called him lazy which was the *effect* of her having overheard her father say that men should always be busy. And her father's saying that men should always be busy was the *effect* of *his* father's spanking him once when he was . . .

"Effect, effect, effect, effect, effect, effect, effect, effect, effect, effect, effect, effect . . ." Michael turns to us at the conclusion of his monotonous recital.

"In this type of analysis it's *all* effect. There *never is* a cause. And this is the type of analysis you've been using all your lives. It's the one that goes with our reality. After all, it's 'scientific,' right? You experience yourselves as the *effect* of what someone else does to you, and that someone else experiences *himself* as the effect of something in his past, which was the *effect* of someone else, and SO ON FOREVER. Effect, effect, effect, effect, effect, effect, effect, effect, effect, effect.

"We have a simple name for this type of superficial causal analysis of effect, effect, effect. We call it 'FALSE CAUSE,' and it's what you've been letting run your lives. After the break, we'll find out who *really* did it . . ."

"We are now going to answer the ultimate question: 'Who did it?' " says Michael after we have returned from a brief thirty-minute break to relieve ourselves, get a drink, and generally unwind. "Answering the ultimate question—not bad for two hundred fifty dollars. And when we've answered it the truth shall make you free. Most likely the truth shall first make you pissed off, but later, perhaps, you'll experience your freedom. To begin our search for 'Who did it?' or 'How do we escape the reality of false cause?' we must look at what must be the nature of unreality. What is unreality? What is unreality? George?"

"Everything."

(Laughter)

"Terrence?"

"Imagination."

"Brad?"

"Thoughts."

Fantasy . . . beliefs . . . concepts . . . consciousness . . . mind . . . feelings . . . God . . . heating bills . . . spirit . . . illusions . . . and so on.

"Okay. Thank you. Before deciding among these, the first thing we can say for sure is that unreality must not be any of the things reality is. If reality is physical, then *un*reality must be *not* physical. Right?"

(There is no response.)

"RIGHT!? WAKE UP OUT THERE. RIGHT?"

"RIGHT!" now shout a dozen voices.

"If reality is measurable, then unreality is not measurable. Right?"

"Right!" comes the reply from many trainees.

"If reality is sometimes determined by reasonableness, then unreality cannot be estimated by reasonableness, right?"

"Right!"

"And if reality ultimately depends on agreement, unreality must *not* depend on agreement, right?"

"Right."

"Unreality must not be dependent on authority or consensus, or appropriateness or naturalness or any of those parts of reasonableness, right?"

"Right!"

"And if reality is ultimately dependent on concepts, then unreality must not be dependent on concepts . . .

"Okay then, let's see what we've got. We've got unreality as something which is *not* physical, is *not* measurable, is *not* determined by reasonableness, authority, or consensus, and is *not* dependent on agreement or concepts. Can you thing of anything, *anything* that fits this description?"

Michael steps away from the left blackboard where he has been pointing to the various characteristics he has listed of reality and unreality. He looks over the now silent trainees.

"What is not physical, not measurable, not reasonable, and not dependent on agreement or concepts?"

"Mind," suggests someone.

"Consciousness," shouts a trainee from the back.

"No," says the trainer. "You haven't got it. You're giving me concepts. It's not dependent on reason, concepts, or agreement."

"Thoughts," says a woman in the front row.

"Imagination," a man calls out.

"Experience," says someone else.

"Yes, EXPERIENCE!" shouts the trainer. "Experience is not physical, can't be measured, is not determined by reasonableness, and doesn't depend on agreement. Unreality is *experience*. Unreality is experience . . . not your feelings, not your thoughts, not your evaluations about it, not your analysis . . . your experience."

He pauses to let this sink in, looking first at the board, where he has written the word EXPERIENCE on the side of UNREALITY, and then back at the trainees.

"And wait a minute, we're not finished. If reality is effect, effect, effect, effect, then unreality must be cause, cause, cause, cause, the very source of all things. And of course our experience is the *source*, as a few of you argued earlier . . .

"So what do we have? On our left, 'reality,' which is physical, measurable, and based on agreement and which necessitates a world of effect, effect, effect, effect; and on our right, 'unreality,' which is experience—not physical, not measurable, and not based on agreement, and which we must acknowledge as the source or cause of all things . . ."

Again he pauses to look first at the board and then back to the trainees.

"Anything wrong here?"

He waits, but for many moments there are no answers. Finally a voice comes from the back row:

"Yeah," says Mitch. "One problem: experience is the most real thing I know. What the hell is it doing over there on the unreal side?"

The trainer acts almost as if he didn't hear Mitch, simply staring around at the trainees.

"YES!" he shouts, and wheels back to the blackboard. "We have a minor problem: experience is the most real thing we know. It's the source of everything. It is absolutely basic to everything. It is *real*.

"And on the other side we have what most people call 'reality,' which is entirely dependent on *agreement, entirely* dependent on agreement. If we get enough people to agree that the world is flat, bingo!, we got a real flat world. If physicists agree that the atom is the ultimate element of matter, then the atom is the real ultimate element of matter. Of course, when they then agree that the electron is the ultimate element, then reality changes. And of course, later they'll agree that the electron is *not* the ultimate element . . . it's a positron, or a piece of antimatter, or something else—it all depends on whether it's a weekday or a weekend.

"You turkeys!" Michael shouts at us. "We got ourselves one *giant* of a minor problem: what everyone calls *real* is really *illusion,* is really *un*real. And what everyone calls *unreality* is actually the most *real* thing we know. The only problem we have up on the board is that what we've labeled 'reality' is actually 'unreality,' and what we labeled 'unreality' is 'reality.' "

Michael stares out at us for a moment and then goes to the blackboard and draws a thick line through the word REALITY

and prints over it UNREALITY, and draws another line through
UNREALITY on the right and prints over it the word REALITY.
When he has finished he bounces back to the front of the
platform.

"But let me warn you right now," he goes on loudly, "don't
let this get out of this room ... because they'll cancel your
vote. I mean you start going around telling people that physicists spend all their time playing with illusions and they'll lock
you up. A *physicist* won't be bothered, he *knows* that his whole
profession is based on ths intelligent playing with agreed-upon
unrealities, but everybody else will cancel your vote.

"And try telling people that the only real thing is your experience. Lots of luck. No, we'll have to stick to the code
words society accepts. When we talk about the unreal physical
universe we'll have to call it by its code word: 'reality.' And
when we talk about our real experiences of the training we'll
have to call it 'unreality.' After all, according to society the
'real' training must be something we can measure, something
typed up in this notebook maybe, something we can all agree
upon ..."

Michael pauses with a sardonic expression on his face and
sits down in one of the upholstered chairs. "All right, Henrietta?"

"You mean you're now telling us the physical universe is
unreal?"

"What we call the physical universe is entirely based on
agreement. An atom—the once-basic unit of the physical universe—is simply an agreement among physicists. Nowadays,
physicists are agreeing on the existence of more and more
particles they haven't *seen*. 'Okay, Charlie,' one physicist says
to another, 'something must be causing that phenomenon.
Let's call it a positron and see what characteristics we can find
for it.' 'Righto, Wally,' says Charlie. 'Only I wish just once we
could call one of our new particles a Charlitron.' Sometimes
physicists find it convenient to pretend that light is waves;
other times it seems to work to pretend that light is moving
particles. They're not interested in what light *really* is. They

know that they can never know what light *really* is because light can't really be anything except what they experience. In the world of unreality in which they know they operate, light will always be what they choose to agree it is. And nothing more ...

"Yes, Henrietta, the physical universe is unreal, but don't tell anyone that's what you think, 'cause they'll cancel your vote."

Light laughter flows across the room as Henrietta stands nervously with the mike.

"But if we walk out in front of a bus we'll get hit," she says. "You said we would."

(Laughter)

"Right," Michael responds. "No doubt about it, the unreal physical universe is *solid*, it can kill. Our experience is the ultimate reality, but you better believe that that agreement of a bus coming at you, whatever it is in each person's experience, is certainly solid. A 'bus' is an agreement; it's unreal, and it can kill. Got it?"

"I thought so," says Henrietta, sitting.

(Laughter)

"Yes. Elaine? Stand up."

"It seems to me that this is all very interesting but I don't see how it answers the question of 'Who did it?' You promised us to answer that."

"Very true," says Michael, moving effortlessly back to the center of the platform behind his small lectern. "We still haven't found out who did it. However, it should be a little easier knowing what's real and unreal instead of operating in the world of illusion, in the world of effect effect effect ..."

"The answer's so simple I'm a little embarrassed to have to suggest it. *Experience* is real, right?"

"Yes," she replies.

"Well, who is the source or cause of your experience?"

Elaine stands erect and dignified but doesn't answer until ten seconds have elapsed.

"Well ...," she begins tentatively. "Some of the things in my experience are caused by some things or people and others by other."

"NO! ALL OF YOUR EXPERIENCE HAS ONE SOURCE AND ONE SOURCE ONLY."

". . . *One* source?" asks Elaine uncertainly.

"One source," the trainer replies mildly, ignoring the dozens of raised hands around the room. "Who or what is the source of all your experience?"

". . . Well, me," answers Elaine softly.

"YES, YOU!" Michael shouts. "Not your mommy, not your husband, not me, not your Oedipus complex, YOU!"

"But I'm not the source of *everything* I experience. When I get hit by a bus, the bus is a partial source of my experience."

"That bus is an *agreement* and you have to agree that that hunk of matter is a bus before you can experience getting hit by a bus."

"But I'll get killed whether I agree that it's a bus or not!"

"You'll get killed all right. But *your* experience will be determined by what agreements you've entered into about the unreal physical universe we inhabit. *You* are the source of those agreements and of your subsequent experience."

"Well, it seems a little abstract . . . ," says Elaine as she sits to light applause.

"OF COURSE IT SEEMS ABSTRACT! You don't want to admit that you're responsible for your experience because if you did, you'd have to give up all your rackets and games which totally depend on your pretending that *other* people are to blame for what happens to you.

"If reality exists only by agreement, then each one of you is responsible for his particular 'reality.' We each create our own experience. You can't name anything for which you yourself are not responsible. Kirsten? Take the mike."

Kirsten takes the microphone with impatience and speaks rapidly.

"You seem to be saying that the sharp pains in my hands and shoulder from hereditary arthritis are *my fault*."

"We're not talking about *blame*, we're talking about *responsibility*."

"Well, I'm certainly not going to take responsibility for the burning sensations in my hands. My mother has them too. They're hereditary."

"It's *your* experience, you're the one who feels this burning pain, right?"

"Yes." She looks directly at the trainer, intently puzzled.

"And who is the source of this experience of pain?"

She stares perplexed and does not answer. "I am," she says finally, then, checking, "You mean me?" She points a hand to her chest.

"*You* are the source of your arthritis, you are the source of the experience of that burning fire in your left knuckle. Nobody handed it to you. No one else can experience it for you. There isn't anyone else in here or out there who is the source of that burning-fire sensation in your left knuckle. Are you listening, Kirsten? *You're it! You're responsible! You're the source*, the cause of your pain." He turns to the rest of us. Kirsten passes the mike to the robotlike assistant.

"And that goes for the rest of you arthritics, ulcers, and hypertensives, and the lot of you with colds or headaches or whatever pain or ache you've made. *It's all yours.* You're the source of your own experience. When you begin to get that and can begin to accept responsibility for every experience you have, then your life will begin to work.

"You 'think' [He makes quotation marks with his fingers.] that you're the way you are because your father or your mother did this or that to you, or your wife or husband or your boss or whoever the hell else you blame for your life not working. But that's being at effect, effect, effect. I GOT NEWS FOR YOU! If your life doesn't work, guess who's doing it to you. Any guesses?" He pauses in his walking to look over his shoulder at his victimized audience. "That's right, it's *you*," he adds. Someone raises a hand in the silence.

A young man with bushy black hair and thick glasses stands

up and accepts the mike. "Well, what about God?!" There is exasperation and anger in his voice.

"What do you mean, 'Well, what about God?' How the hell did she get in here? What do you know about God? Any of you? Who's God? Don't give me your religious shit. Are you gonna tell me *God* did it to you? LIKE HELL SHE DID."

"I mean," the young man goes on, irritated, "that it could be our lives are all planned and written out for us and what happens to us in this life is the karma we're working out now from our past lives. There is no accident. It's all preordained."

"Like a TV dinner, huh?" He stands a few feet from the bushy-haired Cliff. "Look, Cliff, what do you know about God? I bet you wouldn't recognize God if She stepped on your toes! The only real thing in your life is your experience. Beyond that is either blackness or else the illusory realm of belief and reasonableness. You don't *know* anything about God."

"I *know* God exists. I've felt it. I've *experienced* it, to use your own words."

"You have experienced Her, huh. Describe the experience of God to us, Cliff."

Cliff looks around a minute and then says, "You're deliberately trying to provoke me. All right, I'll tell you. I've *experienced* moments of bliss while meditating and felt a union with the universe. If you haven't felt it, you don't know what I'm talking about."

"I acknowledge your experience, Cliff. I have no problems with that. What conclusions do you draw from your experience?"

"God exists," Cliff replies. "God is all-powerful and all-knowing. Our lives may be preordained."

"That's wonderful," the trainer says, turning to the other trainees. "Do you assholes *see* what Cliff just did? He took a perfectly valid experience and tacked onto it a perfectly irrelevant belief. I'll tell you what, Cliff," he continues, turning back to Cliff, "you keep on *believing*. You keep right on having your life not work by *believing* God did it to you. When are you gonna stop laying the blame on God's doorstep?"

"I'm not laying the blame on God's doorstep! All I'm trying to say is that whatever direction our lives take may be already decided whether it's good or bad. I'm not blaming anyone!"

"You're so fucked up you don't see that what you're saying is, 'If my life doesn't work, it's because it's been predetermined by God to not work.' And you throw up your arms, sit back, and complain and bitch and wait for a magical moment of union with the universe so you can forget about what's happening right now! So you can turn off your experience!" He walks around on the platform looking at all of us and back at Cliff. "That's okay. There are lots of zombies around to keep you company. And I've got another piece of news for you." He threatens us like a teacher, and we wait for the exam to come. "Every time you turn off your experience and don't take responsibility for it, you sacrifice your aliveness. You also get a repeat performance. You get stuck repeating your stuff."

Cliff, who has sat down, now wants the mike back again and is acknowledged with a nod. "I get the impression," he says, "that no matter what we say, we can't win in here." He sits down again.

"That's right. I don't get paid to lose. Let me put it another way for you. No matter what you say right now, I'm gonna win, but you can't lose—in the end. Yes, Kirsten."

"I think I need a paper bag and some tissues."

The assistants quietly hand her what she needs. She sits nervously but does not get sick.

"All right," says the trainer. "Barbara?"

"Well, I'm sorry," says Barbara, a large-boned, attractively dressed woman in her late twenties. "I've followed you all this way but I find that idea of total responsibility ridiculous. Two weeks ago, while I was at my job, my apartment was broken into and I was ripped off of a brand-new stereo system, my TV, and some valuable clothes. And I assure you, I didn't cause my apartment to be robbed."

"You certainly did," says the trainer on his way to the back lectern for a drink from his thermos.

"But *I* didn't rob my apartment."

"Who did?"

"I don't know the thief!" says Barbara, standing with one hand on her hip and looking annoyed.

"What makes you think your apartment was robbed?"

"I came home and my stereo was gone!"

"Maybe I borrowed it."

(Laughter)

"My apartment was robbed and *I* am *not* responsible."

"You tell me you experienced that your apartment was robbed and I say you created that experience."

"But I didn't. I kept extra locks on the doors, I told my doorman—"

"Do you take responsibility for buying the stereo system?"

"Yes."

"Do you take responsibility for buying the TV and the expensive clothes?"

"Sure, but I didn't steal them."

"Do you take responsibility for renting the apartment you're in?"

"Yes."

"Do you take responsibility for taking a job which leaves the apartment vacant all day?"

"So what?"

"Do you?"

"Yes."

"Do you take responsibility for not having created friends who might have stayed in the apartment most of the time?"

"Maybe, but—"

"Whose idea is it that because you come home and find things missing from your apartment that you were robbed?"

"*My* idea!"

"Precisely."

"Damn it," says Barbara irritably. "Precisely what!?"

"Precisely you created the idea that you were robbed."

"But I didn't *cause* the robbery."

"There *was* no robbery unless you created it. If your stereo was stolen you did it."

"You're out of your mind!"

"That's what *est* is all about," says Michael nonchalantly, and then he takes a step toward Barbara and shouts.

"GET OUT OF YOUR MIND, BARBARA! YOU'RE THINKING IN CLICHÉS AND LETTING OTHER PEOPLE DICTATE REALITY when you actually create it yourself!"

"Don't shout," she responds nervously.

"I shout when I shout, Barbara, and when I don't shout, I don't shout," he replies quietly. "You created the robbery. Seems absurd, doesn't it?"

"Yes."

"Barbara robbed her own apartment. Seems absurd, doesn't it, assholes?"

(Nervous laughter, a few yes's. Someone shouts, "*Damn* absurd.")

"Fine," says Michael, and then he continues in a low, serious voice.

"Once upon a time there was an old Zen master named Nonoko who lived alone in a hut in the woods. One night while Nonoko was sitting in meditation a powerful stranger came to the door and, brandishing a sword, asked Nonoko for all his money. Nonoko continued to count his breaths while saying to the stranger, 'All my money is on the shelf behind the books. Take all you need but leave me ten yen. I need to pay my taxes this week.'

"The stranger went to the shelf and removed all the money except ten yen. He also took a lovely urn on the shelf.

" 'Be careful how you carry that urn,' said Nonoko. 'It can easily crack.'

"The stranger looked once more around the small barren room and began to leave.

" 'You have forgotten to say thank you,' said Nonoko.

"The stranger said thank you and left.

"The next day the whole village was in an uproar. Half a dozen people claimed they'd been robbed. When a friend noted that Nonoko's urn was missing, he asked Nonoko if he too had been a victim of the thief.

" 'Oh no,' said Nonoko. 'I loaned the urn to a stranger, along with some money. He said thank you and left. He was pleasant enough but careless with his sword.' "

(Silence)

"Nonoko chose *not* to have his apartment robbed," the trainer comments after a while.

(Silence)

"The Sufis tell a different story on the same subject," he goes on quietly. "A rich Moslem went to the mosque after a party and of course had to remove his very expensive boots and leave them with the hundreds of other pairs of footwear outside the mosque. When he emerged later after prayer the expensive boots were gone.

" 'How could I be so thoughtless,' he said to a friend. 'By foolishly wearing such expensive boots to the mosque I have been the occasion of some poor man's taking them and believing that he's stealing. I would gladly have given them but instead I am responsible for creating a thief.' "

(Silence)

Someone coughs.

(Silence)

"Who robbed your apartment, Barbara?" Michael asks.

(Silence)

"I didn't leave my stereo outside a mosque," she finally says.

(Laughter)

"No, you didn't."

(Silence)

"But I see what you mean."

"What do I mean, Barbara?"

Barbara frowns in serious concentration. "I bought some

expensive things," she says slowly. "One day ... the expensive things disappeared.... And that's all. Thank you, Michael," she concludes, and sits.

(Long applause)

"You people may wonder later on why, when *est* graduates applaud a trainer or seminar leader, he or she applauds back. But it's simple. The trainer knows that *you* and you alone create the trainer in your universe and if you then come to like him and admire him he's *your* creation and *you* deserve the credit.

"But so, too, assholes, if you experience me as an arrogant fascist bastard [Laughter], guess who created me? . . Yeah ..."

(Laughter and applause)

"You are each the sole source of your own experience, and thus TOTALLY RESPONSIBLE FOR EVERYTHING YOU EX-PERIENCE. When you get that, you're going to have to give up ninety percent of the bullshit that's running your lives. Yes, Hank?"

"Look," says burly Hank, looking quite irritated, "I get that I'm responsible for everything I do. I see that. But when I get mugged, there's no way I'm gonna accept responsibility for getting mugged."

"Who's the source of your experience, Hank?"

"In this case, it would be the mugger."

"The mugger would take over your mind?"

"My mind and my wallet!"

(Laughter)

"Do you take responsibility for getting out of bed that morning?"

"Sure."

"For being on that street?"

"Yes."

"For seeing a man with a gun in his hand?"

"For *seeing* him?"

"Yes, seeing the mugger."

"Take responsibility for seeing him?"

"Yes."

"Well," says Hank. "I would certainly see him."

"If you had at that moment no eyes, no ears, nose, or sensations in the skin, you wouldn't experience this mugger, would you?"

"My wallet would!"

"But with no senses you would never know whether your wallet was missing or not. Do you get that you are responsible for seeing a man with a real gun asking for your money?"

"Okay, I get that."

"That you are responsible for being at that street at that hour with money that might be stolen?"

"Okay, I get that."

"That you *chose* not to risk your life by resisting this man and that you *chose* to give up your wallet?"

"When a guy says give me your money with a gun in his hand, there's no choice."

"Did you choose to be at that place at that time?"

"Yeah, but I didn't choose to have that guy show up."

"You saw him, didn't you?"

"Sure."

"You take responsibility for seeing him, don't you?"

"For seeing him, yeah."

"Then get it: EVERYTHING THAT YOU EXPERIENCE DOESN'T EXIST UNLESS YOU EXPERIENCE IT."

"That mugger's still alive."

"That day walking beside you is a being from Mars. The being from Mars has ears which hear only ultrasonic sound, eyes which react only to light emissions of very high frequencies, and no other senses. After you've been mugged he would probably turn to you and say, 'I say, did you notice the groovy radiation that blob was emitting?' [Laughter]

"EVERYTHING A LIVING CREATURE EXPERIENCES

IS CREATED UNIQUELY BY THAT LIVING CREATURE
WHO IS THE SOLE SOURCE OF THAT EXPERIENCE."

"But somebody would be out there!"

"One theory is that STIMULI are out there," says Michael
amiably. "Billions every millisecond. But how you experience
them is your contribution to the universe."

"But I didn't *choose* to be mugged."

"NOBODY chose for you. You and you alone have created
the way you experience things."

". . . Huh."

"Did you choose, seeing the man approach, to lend him a
hundred bucks?"

"NO!"

"WAKE UP, HANK!"

"I don't get it."

"There would be eight million people in New York City that
day. Maybe twenty would be mugged. The others, all 7,999,-
980 of them, would manage to avoid it. You manage to get
mugged."

"Huh."

"Thank you."

(Applause)

"Fred. Take the mike."

"Okay. So I see where we create our experience. Big deal.
Cats create their experience. Dogs create theirs. Right?"

"Right, Fred."

"My wife gets cancer. I experience her getting cancer. That
makes me *responsible*?"

"Right, Fred."

"That's bullshit! How the hell am *I* responsible for my wife's
getting cancer?"

"You're responsible for creating the experience of your wife's
manifesting behavior which you choose to call, by agreement
with others, a disease called cancer."

"But I didn't *cause* the cancer."

"Look, Fred, I get that what I'm saying is hard for you to fit into your belief system. You've worked hard for forty years to create your belief system and though I get that right now you're being as open-minded as you can be, for forty years you've believed that *things happen out there* and that you, *passive, innocent bystander*, keep getting RUN OVER—by cars, buses, stock-market crashes, neurotic friends, and cancer. I get that. Everyone in this room has lived with that same belief system. ME, INNOCENT; REALITY OUT THERE, GUILTY.

"BUT THAT BELIEF SYSTEM DOESN'T WORK! IT'S ONE REASON WHY YOUR LIFE DOESN'T WORK. *The reality that counts is your experience, and you are the sole creator of your experience.* Marcia? Thank you, Fred. [Applause; inaudible voice] Take the mike, Marcia."

"I'm sorry, but I think you're just playing with words. The way words are normally used, that man's wife got cancer—her cancer was caused by something, but it certainly wasn't Fred."

"I acknowledge that."

"And most people would find it meaningless to say Fred created his wife's cancer."

"I get that. It's true that certain physical changes take place in the wife which we know Fred didn't create and which are nowadays labeled 'cancer.' But do you get that Fred's *experience* of her cancer, Fred's *reality*, may be incredibly different from someone else's? A few individuals seem able to die of cancer joyfully—that's right, to experience cancer joyfully—while most of us don't. And if you, Marcia, experience Fred's wife's cancer as a depressing, horrible thing, you ought to know that it's *you* who create it that way, it's you who create the particular case of cancer which you experience."

(Silence)

"Wow," says Marcia finally. "I'm beginning to see what you're driving at."

"Certain Indian tribes see a man who goes around singing to himself and announcing he talks to God and accept him as a holy man and let him roam free. We label him a schizophrenic and lock him up. We CREATE that man a schizophrenic. The Iroquois Indians create him a holy man. Somebody else might create him the Messiah. Whatever it is an individual creates in his experience he is responsible for."

"I'm beginning to get it," says Marcia. "But aren't there some things—space, time, atoms, say, the differences between a man and woman—which are *real*, for everybody?"

"Sure, they're real all right, but labels and the experience of those realities will always be different. You can't name one aspect of space or time or one difference between man and woman that people would experience the same, even just the people in this room."

"Well I could, but I'd be too embarrassed to say it."

(Laughter)

"Say it."

"Well . . . a man has a penis and a woman doesn't."

"Do you all agree to that?"

(Three or four audible no's)

"Next?"

"Wow," says Marcia. "They must have seen some men I haven't seen."

(Laughter)

"You're damn right they have. EVERY FUCKIN' MAN THEY'VE SEEN IS TOTALLY DIFFERENT FROM EVERY MAN YOU'VE SEEN."

(Silence)

"I get that now," says Marcia slowly. "Still, you are on the platform and I am not. Everyone here agrees with that."

"Oh yeah?" says Michael. "Does everyone agree that I'm on the platform?"

Several trainees shout no vigorously.

"Where am I, Marcia?" the trainer asks, taking a single step toward her and staring intently.

"Still on the platform," she says, frowning.

"Where am I, Marcia?" he asks again.

Marcia stares back at him, confused. She glances quickly off to her right for a moment as if for help.

"You're up there on the platform."

"Look at your *experience*, Marcia," says the trainer. "Am I there?"

"Yes, well, the way I see it anyway, you're on the platform."

"Ah," says Michael, "the way *you* see it. Uh-huh. Where am I, Marcia?"

She stares at him. "I . . . in my experience?"

"Yes! And if I'm in your experience, who created me?"

"*I* did."

"Shame on you! [Laughter]

"YES! You create me. You create me every second you choose to create me in your experience. Do you now, Marcia, accept responsibility for choosing to create me and let me be on this platform and let *you* be here in the room *not* on the platform?"

". . . Yes, I do."

"Do you accept responsibility for creating Fred's wife's cancer?"

(Silence)

"Yes, I do."

"Thank you. [Applause]

"David."

"You're still playing with words," says David firmly. "Marcia may accept responsibility but I bet she's not going to pay the hospital bills."

"I get that."

"So there's a difference between accepting responsibility for creating anger in one's self or anxiety—that I understand and agree is important—and this other thing of creating soldiers in Vietnam or cancer in somebody's wife."

"You're right, David, there is."

(Silence)

"So they're not the same," says David, surprised at the agreement.

"They're not the same, David. Anxiety is anxiety and somebody else's cancer is somebody else's cancer. For *some* people, somebody else's cancer is more frightening than their own anxiety. For you, your anxiety is important and Fred's wife's cancer isn't. I get that. I get that some of the things you create you create as extremely important to you and others you create to seem trivial or irrelevant. All I'm saying—you shouldn't believe me of course—is that you create them all."

"I'll think about it," says David, frowning as he sits.

(Applause)

"Robbie?"

"You can't have it both ways, Michael," says Robbie, a young black man. "On the one hand you keep telling us not to believe what you're saying but on the other you're stating very loudly and authoritatively a lot of ideas which if we agree with we have to believe."

"NO! You DON'T have to believe them. You don't have to agree with them. All I ask you to do is EXAMINE YOUR EXPERIENCE and see if you don't experience the WORK-ABILITY of certain points of view Werner has developed. If you can't experience your reality with these notions, just *believing* them is no improvement over whatever set of beliefs you have now. BELIEFS DON'T WORK."

"But, look," says Robbie. "I work in this electronics firm in Queens and I got a boss who's a one-hundred-percent nut. He doesn't appreciate anything *anyone* does. Now how am *I* responsible for him?"

"You think you've got a lousy boss?"

"I *know* I've got a lousy boss," says Robbie, smiling.

"How many of you other turkeys are stuck with lousy bosses?" asks Michael.

At least fifty or sixty hands seem to be raised, and nervous laughter flows across the room. Michael simply stands and shakes his head slowly.

"You want to know why things don't work out there?" he asks suddenly. "Because you don't *want* them to work out there! If things *worked* in your office then your boss would get the credit and you know your boss is an asshole and doesn't deserve any credit. You're damned if *you're* going to do a good job in an unjust world. No, sir!

"You know, you people are crazy. Your boss isn't doing any good work because *he* knows *his* boss doesn't deserve it, and you're goofing off because of your boss, and that asshole of a secretary of yours—I wonder why she doesn't work harder?

"IF THE JOB ISN'T GETTING DONE TAKE THE RESPONSIBILITY TO SEE THAT IT DOES GET DONE! I don't care who gets the credit; *you're* going to benefit from doing good work no matter who gets the external credit. And if you begin to take responsibility for creating your bastard boss —bingo! you're going to find your boss changing.

"Let me tell you a story. I once worked in the public relations office of Burroughs Corporation, and my boss never smiled, never gave me the slightest encouragement, and for about a year I'd given up and was doing as little as I could and still hold my job. Then I took the training and I thought the idea that I created my shitass boss was ridiculous. Still, after about a month I decided—just for a lark, a game it was—to pretend that I could make the whole office work. That it wasn't Burroughs Corporation it was My Corporation: Reed Corporation.

"So I worked hard. When someone wasn't doing his job, I did it, and often in a way that I didn't think anyone would realize that I was doing it. I was sort of a saboteur who in the dead of night *fixed* machines instead of wrecking them.

"You know, within three months, both my boss and my secretary seemed to be working twice as hard as I'd ever seen them work before and my boss and I were having martinis together at lunch three or four times a week. He still didn't praise me, didn't smile much, but boy, did we get things done."

"But my working harder," says Robbie, after a long hesitation, "isn't going to make my boss any less of a nut."

"Maybe not," says Michael. "But it'll make *you* less of a nut. You'll end up getting more cheese and that's what it's all about."

"Oh yeah, I can dig that. Yeah, I get that. But are you telling us we all gotta work harder even if we don't like the system we're working in?"

"There's nothing you *have* to do. We're simply trying to answer the question who's responsible for you doing a good job. Is it your boss?"

"... No."

"Who is it?"

"Me."

"Fine. All I want you to see, to experience, is that you experience your boss as a nut who doesn't appreciate anyone *and* you are responsible for your work on the job. Don't blame nutty or corrupt or lazy bosses because you *choose* to do a lousy job. WAKE UP OUT THERE! YOU are cause in the matter and don't you forget it ..."

The question of "Who did it?" has been answered; the "truth" makes some people free, but, as Michael hinted, it makes others pissed off.

The remainder of this third day of the training—and only half the day has passed—consists of four long processes, all intensely interesting to experience and the first coming as a welcome break from the heaviness of dealing with one's own responsibility for the universe.

In it the trainer offers the opportunity for all the trainees to make asses of themselves. The process consists of the trainees acting out a series of brief ridiculous roles, each of which requires shouting and gesturing strongly, often in ways contrary to our self-imposed, socially accepted roles. It seems somewhat paradoxical that, having just learned to take full responsibility for our lives, our first act should be to create ourselves as fools. For some, it is a marvelous chance to let go. For others it is more difficult than was the danger process, for we are being asked to abandon our acts, our dignity, our seriousness, our properness. In two of the most difficult roles, women are asked to play the role of a loud, stupid, blustering drunk, and men are asked to play a "cute" ten-year-old girl reciting a silly flirtatious poem about herself: the women being asked to be aggressively masculine, the men pertly feminine. In all the roles the trainees are asked to evaluate those performing to determine whether they have really gotten into the role or whether they are stuck and unable to let their bodies go in full expression.

"Gimme a WHISKEY!" shout twenty-five women in unison in front of the audience, and then, addressing an imaginary piano player in the imaginary western bar, "PLAY ME A TUNE ON THAT THERE PEEANNY, BROKEN NOSE!" ... "My name ain't Broken Nose," the women reply to themselves, and then, in the role of the drunk, they swing a roundhouse right: Pow! ... "Well, it is NOW!" they shout in conclusion, and the watching trainees laugh and applaud.

But the trainer immediately singles out five women who have been inhibited in their performances.

"I warned you," he says. "The way to show you want to star and do it all alone on stage is to *not* let yourselves go and really do it."

Michael carefully rehearses the lines again for them, acting them out himself in exaggerated fashion, and then the five women go through another performance.

"Gimme a WHISKEY!" the five shout, or rather four, because one of them, Lillian, a pretty dark-haired woman, is more wooden than a puppet. The five play out the whole role a second time, and all but Lillian are returned with applause to their seats.

"Oh, no," whispers Lillian, when she realizes she has been singled out to perform alone.

"I want you to really throw yourself into it this time," says Michael.

"I can't do it," says Lillian in a soft voice. "It's ... too ... I can't do it." She is glancing from the floor to the back of the room with a frightened look.

"Nothing but other asses out there," says Michael. "Just let go of your old act and get into this one."

"No, please, I can't do it. Let me sit," pleads Lillian, and she starts off the platform. Michael confronts her, his voice firm but with a soft insistence:

"No sense going through the rest of your life with that barrier, Lillian. It's run your life long enough. I want you to get off it. Let me hear you scream."

"I can't," she says softly from the edge of the platform, looking at him with a brief terrified glance.

"I just want you to shout," Michael says. "Just shout."

"I can't," Lillian whispers, tears forming in her eyes.

"SHOUT!" shouts Michael.

"I *can't*!" says Lillian more loudly.

"You dumb bitch, SHOUT!" shouts Michael.

"I CAN'T!" Lillian says loudly.

"WHAT?" asks Michael, putting his hand to his ear as if he can't hear.

"I can't," Lillian says quietly.

"Come off it, Lillian. You almost shouted a second ago. Tell me, do you have a husband?"

"Yes."

"Good. Have you ever shouted at him?"

Lillian looks squarely at the trainer and flushes fully.

"Yes," she whispers. "But not in public," she announces loudly.

"Okay, great. Tell everyone loudly, 'Not in public.'"

"Not in public!" Lillian says loudly.

"LOUDER!"

"NOT IN PUBLIC!"

"LOUDER!"

"*NOT IN PUBLIC!!*" Lillian screams.

(Laughter and applause)

"Okay, great," says Michael. "Now I want you to look me straight in the eye and say in your toughest voice, 'Gimme a WHISKEY!'"

Lillian, flushed now and smiling, looks him straight in the eye and says, "Gimme a whiskey."

"LOUDER!"

"GIMME A WHISKEY!"

"Okay, fine, Lillian, thank you." Michael escorts her off the platform to loud applause.

"Okay, men, your turn . . . ," and twenty-five men are soon on the platform reciting in high-pitched voices how they have "Ten little fingers, ten little toes, long wavy hair and a turned-up nose, big brown eyes and a cute little figure. Stay away boys, till I get bigger!"

In the second lineup of twenty-five men, a young man named Terry, who looks as if he might be a linebacker for the Pittsburgh Steelers, has trouble wiggling his hips when he talks about his "cute little figure," and Michael singles him out for assistance.

"I can't do this shit," Terry announces, looking very uncomfortable when he discovers himself alone on the stage with Michael, who, six inches shorter, looks dwarfed.

"Nothing to it, Terry," Michael responds. "Every man has a little girl in him somewhere, and if he's got a barrier to expressing it he's got an area of stuckness. Every heterosexual has a homosexual element in him someplace, and every homosexual has a repressed heterosexual inside. You've seen me and twenty-four other guys do it twice, and we all seem to have survived. Just let go."

Michael recites again in a high-pitched voice the silly little poem and wiggles his hips when describing his "cute little figure," and then asks Terry to do it again.

Terry struggles through it a second time, forgetting most of the lines and showing less movement than a statue. When he is done there is a total silence as Michael stands surveying the situation.

"Okay, Terry, let's simplify it a bit," says Michael. "I want you to say in a fake high-pitched voice, 'I've got a turned-up nose,' and with one hand make a little gesture showing the shape of a turned-up nose."

"I can't do it," says Terry sullenly.

"Let me hear you say 'I've got a turned-up nose'!"

After a long hesitation, Terry says, "I've got a turned-up nose," in a deep, sullen, masculine voice, and the audience laughs.

"Shuttup, you turkeys," Michael barks out at the trainees. "It'll be your turn next and some of you probably can't even say 'ten little fingers.' Okay, Terry, say it again only in a softer, more feminine, more girlish voice."

"I don't feel like it," says Terry gloomily.

"I get that, Terry. None of the other men felt like it either, but they were *men* enough to do it anyway. Do you get that, Terry? If you're worried about your manhood the surest way to make *us* worry about it is not to be able to be a little girl. A full human, a full man, can be *both* masculine and feminine."

"I'm not worried about my manhood," grumbles Terry.

"Great. I'm going to do this stupid little poem recited by this ten-year-old girl all dressed in frilly white and then *you* do it, okay?"

"I'll try," says Terry.

"I don't want you to *try*," says Michael. "I want you to *do* it."

"Okay."

Michael again goes through the act, and when he's finished Terry does it again, poorly, but with more movement than before. The other trainees applaud lightly.

"Not bad, Terry," says Michael. "You're showing talent. Look, you're a good-looking man, right?"

"Maybe," says Terry, still looking glum.

"Now I want you to pretend that you're a sexy woman who wants to seduce you. She walks across the room like this ... [Michael's compact body oozes across a few feet of platform in hip-swaying sexiness.] and says to you in a Mae West sort of voice, 'Hiya, Big Boy, come up and *see* me some time.' [Laughter and applause for Michael] Now, can you do that?"

"Maybe."

"Fine. Go ahead. Pretend the lectern is *you*."

Terry stands a moment in concentration and then sways

across the platform and, in a genuinely throaty Mae West voice, completes the role in fine fashion. He is rewarded with loud applause.

"That's great," says Michael, as Terry, smiling, returns to his seat with the other trainees. "And remember, all of you out there, male and female and in between, whenever you're feeling bored with yourself as you usually are, there's always Mae West some place deep down inside you waiting to get out . . ."

In the second long process we stack all our chairs against the walls and spread out throughout the room on the floor. Eyes closed, we are guided in creating for ourselves a "center," a safe space anywhere in the world where we can retreat and simply be with ourselves. Each of us is asked to find a favorite spot, in the woods, by the sea, on a mountain, where we would like to create our one-room center. We actually act out for ourselves in pantomime the building of the structure with our hands, using materials of our own choosing, so that its walls, windows, doors, and furnishings will be real for us. The trainer instructs us to construct inside the center a desk and two chairs; a magic wish button; a telephone that permits us to talk to anyone in the world; a television screen; a digital clock that permits us to view any event at any time in the past; a stage where we can bring people to life; an "abilities cabinet" where we can hang the "suits" which, when donned, give us mastery of any ability we would like to have; and other items that will permit us to get in touch with aspects of ourselves perhaps rarely contacted and to reexperience past experiences. Our center becomes for the remainder of the training a useful space for the trainees to begin to experience the creation of their own experience.

This night the trainees are asked to bring into our center two people, one male and one female, whom we wish to be in close touch with, and to create each person from head to foot with our hands as a sculptor might. After the naked body is created then it is to be clothed and finally to be brought to real life and talked to and escorted to a seat in our center. When the process is over there is the long-awaited break for a very late dinner . . .

Under the chairs as the trainees return are little bundles of fruit—a cherry tomato, a lemon wedge, and a strawberry. There is also a smooth black stone, a small block of wood, a cube of metal, and a daisy. Toys! The atmosphere becomes lighter. There are small smiles and giggles here and there. For a while, bearing the awesome pressure of a harangue, or reacting to someone else's tragic life story, or having to handle one's own "mistakes" in life can be put aside. In spite of the nice discovery of the innocuous things under the chair, the threat exists that even this is going to be made into one of those emotional probes under one's armored hide. Inevitably, the instructions come, precise, thorough, one at a time.

The trainees are instructed to pick up one item at a time, smell it, lick it, rub it against our faces, check its temperature, texture, form, size, color, weight. Observe how it reflects light; how many seeds are there; taste it outside, finally inside. Its multiple qualities and distinctions are carefully pointed out and "experienced."

"Notice the daisy has a round center that consists of a hundred tiny stamen, and it has an 'eye' in the very center. Take it apart and examine one of the stamen. . . . See how the leaves of the daisy are jagged and pointed. . . . What do you see on the leaves?" Finally we get to the delicious strawberry and notice the many hard little seeds; how the inside tastes different from the outside; how its color inside varies from outside. "Notice how rough it is against your skin . . ."

This event is delightful. Most trainees are following exact instructions; a few go just so far and then eat the fruit without waiting any longer. It tastes especially good after so many injunctions against eating in the room.

Later, a final process develops out of this attention to the properties of these objects. Spread out on the floor of the ballroom, we go into our space, eyes closed, and create our center. One by one we imagine and get inside each of the seven objects, culminating in our creating an immense strawberry, its heavy top side down, which we begin climbing. This seems a little precarious, for the strawberry is thirty feet high; but the trainees are told they can use mountain-climbing equipment and begin digging in for good footholds.

Once at the top, we cut open a hole and climb down inside the open passageway that runs through the center of most of the length of the strawberry. Down we go into the pulp, eventually eating our way out the side near the bottom.

Our last creation of the night is to climb our sixty-foot-high daisy and, after spending ten minutes using the petals and core as a trampoline, slide down the length of the stem to the floor.

When the trainer brings us eventually out of our centers and out of our created worlds into the one we create of him and the hotel room, we all feel very good: either high or relaxed. And our good spirits aren't even dampened when Michael reminds us that tomorrow is the big day, tomorrow is the "anatomy of the mind," tomorrow we will "get it." Having just spent a lovely sensuous hour living inside a stone, a tomato, a strawberry, and other unusual domiciles, "getting it" seems strangely unimportant—until tomorrow.

4

DAY FOUR
"Getting It," or
At Last ... Nothing

"I come, O Master, to seek Enlighten-
ment," announced the Seeker.
"Goody-goody gumdrop for you," replied
the Master.

When the Zen monk Kuleki finally "got
it," he said to himself:
"After almost forty years I seem, at last,
to be ready to be a nobody. What a long
journey! What a lot of trouble! Especially
considering that I was there all the time."

"For me the interesting part of creating the center," says Stuart, the old man who says he's afraid of death, "came when I
nonchalantly decided to create as my 'friend' one of the major
characters of a novel I'm working on." It is the last day of the
training and Stuart, red-faced and wrinkled, but looking better
than he did when he last stood, is one of the first trainees to
share about the previous night's processes. "When the door of
that magic cabinet you asked us to use began to lower, the
head was revealed first and I was surprised to see that it wasn't
the character's head but my own, only younger," continues
Stuart in a firm voice. "The hair was darker and my skin was
blotchy. But the body that began appearing wasn't my body.
It was huge, a big, husky, solid body totally unlike my own but

like *another* character in a novel I wrote decades ago. I started creating this body with my hands as you directed and realized when I got to the thighs that the body was gigantic, the thighs two feet thick, and this body was *growing* even as I molded it with my hands. When I finished he was about twelve feet tall. When I pushed a button to dress him, lo and behold he was wearing a black tuxedo—totally out of character. It was baffling.

"The female friend that I next created was not surprising until her clothes turned out to be a maid's or waitress's black uniform. When I had brought them both to life in my center I asked the woman why she was wearing the maid's uniform and she said, 'Don't you remember? We're here to serve you.' It was only then that I saw the giant's tuxedo as a waiter's uniform and looking again at him I saw he was growing again—like the strawberry I suppose—and was now thirty feet high. I said to him 'Do you realize you're growing?' and after he answered yes I asked him why. 'I am here to give you power,' he said, and the woman said she was here to give me feminine wiliness. I must confess I was thrilled by this. It's not every day one is given such gifts. But she was growing smaller! Before I knew it she was less than six inches high and I had to pick her up in my hand to ask her what was happening. She said it was all more convenient this way and the next thing I knew she jumped into my mouth and I swallowed her!"

Stuart paused and cleared his throat and looked around brightly at the trainees sitting nearest him.

"I know this must all sound absurd," he went on. "I don't ever remember in my whole life, not with alcohol or drugs or the simple gift of the muses, ever having my imagination flow out of control in the way it did last night . . .

"Well, to conclude. I turned to the giant, who, by the way, was still growing, and asked him, 'Can either of you help me to handle death?' And the giant man replied: 'You will handle death as you have handled us . . .'

"I didn't understand what he meant by that but before I

could question him further Michael began instructing us to come out of our centers and my giant friend disappeared, dematerialized."

Stuart pauses again and his wrinkled, serious face blooms into a radiant and mischievous smile.

"Last night after I got home I lay in bed trying to comprehend what my archetypal power source meant by saying that I'd handle death as I handled them.... It made no sense to me. I fell asleep—without drinking I should note—and it still made no sense. Then this morning as we were waiting to enter the ballroom I was talking to a young man named Frank and I shared with him what I have just now shared with everyone, and as soon as I got to the point of saying it made no sense to me, it made complete sense. I 'got it' as you would say, Michael. I got that I will handle death as I handled my giant and my wily woman: I will create my death.... I will create my own death as I do everything ... and it will be as mysterious and beautiful and as uniquely mine as is everything else. And it will be good ..."

"First of all," starts Eileen, who has a breathy sound-quality to her voice and a hand that never ceases rotating around her monologue, "I would never climb a strawberry. I'd be afraid it might topple over or something, but when you told us to throw a rope up and begin climbing I went on and somewhat unwillingly decided this was in the imagination anyway, and if I were to get benefit from it I had to follow instructions. It was as safe as most of these processes, I guess, at least for me. So up I went and at the top I cut that hole and climbed down in. And then it got really terrific. I could really vividly imagine being there ... the hard, rocklike seeds like footballs, the soft reddish fruit underneath my feet—it seemed a little like digging my feet into flesh.... I don't think I ever knew what a strawberry was like before this. It really came alive for me."

"... When I went into my center," says Catherine with a frown of concentration on her face, "and started creating my boyfriend, it started turning out its own way—just like what happened to Stuart—and it became my brother. My brother died in Vietnam, so I was upset when he began to materialize. I didn't want to deal with him, with someone dead especially. I kept trying to dematerialize him and create my boyfriend, but each time my brother kept coming back. Finally I got so upset, I began crying and just watched my brother materialize. When he was all there, I began hugging him and crying and telling him I missed him and was so sorry I wouldn't see him again. He hugged me back and told me that he was all right and not to worry about him anymore, and live my life, that everything was okay with him. I told him how upset I had been, and he told me that was okay, but now I should see that he was all right and be done with that part of my life and go on and be happy. Finally we said good-bye. It was warm and friendly and I felt suddenly lighter, that it really was all right.

"When we received the notice that my brother was killed, I was very upset internally. I was shocked. I really hadn't accepted it, you know. It was too close to me, the death. I couldn't cry. I didn't want to believe it. I think I wanted to pretend it wasn't so and he would come back from the war, even though I *knew* it would never happen. I feel tremendously lighter now and for the first time my brother's death is real for me and it really is all right . . ."

". . . What I remember most," says Ann, an attractive, graying woman, "is not liking the smothering womblike effect of being inside *any* of the objects, especially the tomato and the strawberry. I felt trapped. I thought we would never get out of any of them. In the strawberry I even made several attempts to get out before you told us to and even brought myself out twice to get air. I'm not really claustrophobic. That is, I ride elevators and go into dark halls and rooms and don't have jitters or whatever happens to people who don't like being in such places. But I thought you took forever getting us out of those objects. It was the worst process so far . . ."

"No, Ann, don't sit down," says Michael. "Take the mike again."

"I just wanted to share about being in the objects . . ."

"Close your eyes and go into your space."

"But I . . . But I . . ." Ann looks disturbed that she is about to be a subject, but then closes her eyes and lets Michael take the mike and hold it for her.

"Just be in your space, Ann," says Michael. "All right. I want you to go back in time. Are you willing to do that?"

"Yes . . ."

"Go back to the day of your birth. Take what you get . . ."

Ann remains silent.

"What do you get?" asks Michael.

"Well, I can't say I can be that infant again. It was too long ago . . ."

"NO. YOU'RE THINKING. DON'T THINK. I want you to go back to your birth, you're inside the womb, it's dark and warm . . . just take what comes."

Ann hesitates, her eyes closed, head bent down toward the mike.

"Well," she begins. "There are metal hospital beds, pale green, and very large windows. The hospital is an old house rather than a modern brick building. My mother is young—"

"NO," interrupts Michael. "You're thinking again, or remembering. Just *look*. I want you to go back to that time in your mother's womb just before birth . . ."

"I just get blackness . . . nothing."

"You're inside your mother . . . surrounded by warm walls . . ."

"Just blackness . . . nothing . . ."

"It's tight . . . warm confinement . . . soft but pressing, pressing."

Ann stands a long time with her head bent, not speaking. Then her body shudders. "Oh," she says, "I want to get out! . . . I need air. . . . I want to breathe. . . . Let me out. . . . I feel terribly frustrated. I can't get out. . . . I keep trying. . . . I feel like I'm going to smother. Oh! that hurts. I can't get out. I don't like it. . . ." She opens her eyes and stares out absently.

"Close your eyes again, Ann. Go back into your space. You're struggling to get out, you're pushing . . ." Michael is standing next to her, holding the mike, listening. The other trainees are quiet, interested. Ann is silent a long time . . .

"I'm pushing. . . . It's so hard. . . . It's taking forever. . . . There's a wall, it's closed, the opening is closed. . . . I push harder. . . . I'm being squeezed so much! . . . It's so slow. . . . I'm moving. . . . The opening is unblocking a little, I'm breathing! . . . How wonderful. . . . What a release!" She sighs and is silent.

"Okay, Ann, when you're ready, come out of your space, back into this room, re-create the chairs, the drapes, the people, and open your eyes."

"Wait a minute," she says now with eyes open. "I just remembered something. About fifteen years ago when I asked my mother what time I was born she told me about ten to one in the early morning. She told me she kept crossing her legs tight to hold me back all the previous evening. I was shocked. She might have hurt me! She said she didn't know any better and crossing her legs stopped the contractions and the pain. I felt when she told me that I might have been born a day earlier and my whole life might be different. . . . Do you suppose," she suddenly asks Michael, "that I hated going into those objects and have often resented my mother for . . . for confining me during my childhood and adolescence because of . . . of that birth?"

"I don't suppose anything," Michael replies. "You experienced what you experienced. What you did was reexperience the experience of birth. Don't try to understand it. Just take what you get."

"Thank you, Michael," says Ann, and she sits to the long applause of the trainees.

"Elaine?"

"Well," says Elaine, looking nervously at no one in particular and speaking in a tremulous voice. "I'm very nervous now.

This is very difficult for me. . . . I, ah, I never thought Don's prediction would come true. I mean I never thought I'd be standing up today to share what he whispered to me last Sunday to get me to undo my faint." Elaine looks around a bit at the other trainees and smiles hesitantly. "In fact, all week I was resenting him both for what he said and also for his daring to predict what I would do. I think the only reason I returned to the training this weekend at all was to prove the trainer wrong." Elaine hesitates and frowns. "I still think it was wrong of him to whisper what he did, but . . . it worked. I ended my faint. That really bothered me all week. I thought my faint was genuine and yet I heard what he said and I got up . . .

"Then yesterday afternoon I got it. I mean that business about our creating our own experience really meant a lot to me. And the trainer's saying last weekend that I'd do anything to avoid just being with people—that suddenly made sense too. I don't normally faint, of course, but I usually manage to have some sort of business to do, reading or sewing or telephoning. I really see now how I created my own fainting."

Elaine stops talking and hands the mike back toward the assistant.

"What did he *say* to you?" some other trainee shouts at Elaine.

"Don't stop now!" says another voice.

"Oh!" says Elaine. "That. Well, he's not here. . . . Maybe I shouldn't repeat it . . ."

"You can repeat it," says Michael. "All trainers' whispers are carefully programmed in the training manual by Werner."

"Not this one, I hope!" Elaine exclaims with a look of genuine shock. "After I'd been lying there for what my friend tells me was almost twenty minutes, I suddenly heard Don whispering in my ear. . . . Well, I'm not sure I can . . . He whispered in my ear, 'Okay, Elaine, the play's over. The next time I ask you to get up if you don't get up, one of the assistants is going to lie down on top of you and pretend to hump you.'

"Thirty seconds later," concludes Elaine, "he said out loud,

'All right, Elaine, it's time to get up,' and suddenly I regained consciousness ..."

(Laughter and applause)

"Today we are going to do the anatomy of the mind," says the trainer, moving back and forth slowly and easily before the trainees. "Today is the last day of your training and in one sense everything that's happened in the first three days can be forgotten. You can let it go. Today we do the anatomy of the mind, and when we're done your mind is going to sizzle and hiss and shake and tremble and resist resist resist resist resist and then, in most cases, gently explode. Or, it won't explode. Listen to the anatomy of the mind and take what you get, and in any case, you'll get it. You can no more *not* get it than a fish can not get water.

"Last night we asked, 'What *is* the mind?' and you all had a chance to suggest answers. They were all good answers, all were useful for one purpose or another, all showed insight into one or another feature of the mind, and this morning I'd like to ask you to let them go. Just let them go. I'd like to ask you to wipe the slate clean and be open to the anatomy of the mind that we will develop here this morning. I want you to feel free to ask questions about these notions, I want you to ask questions, but if you remain stuck in trying to be *right* about *your* notion of the mind it'll take longer for us to reach the end. We know already that your particular notion of the mind is the *right* one, but we also know that for some reason your notion doesn't work.

"What is the mind? That's the first question we'd like to ask. What *is* the mind?

"The mind is a linear arrangement of multisensory total records of successive moments of now. The mind is a linear arrangement ... of multisensory total records ... of successive moments of now. Let's see what this means. First of all, the mind is a linear arrangement of records. We can visualize this as a stack of tapes or records, arranged one on top of the other or one after another, as if threaded on a long invisible string. Each of these tapes or records is a complete or *total* record of a specific experience—successive moments of now. These records are multisensory: they contain not only visual and auditory experience but also the complete experience of the other senses as well—touch, smell, taste, thoughts, feelings, images, and so on.

"This means that each of our minds has records of millions of different experiences from our past. Some event that occurred at a specific time and place years ago may be recorded completely and be present in our stacks even though we have had no conscious memory of this event since it occurred. The complete multisensory record of the event may be there. What an individual saw, heard, smelled, touched, felt, and thought during a small segment of successive moments of now is available on a record. For example, in Marie's mind there may be a tape or record of her birthday party in 1964: her mother cooking a chocolate layer cake, the radio playing the Beatles' 'I Want to Hold Your Hand,' the sniffles from her cold, her thoughts about what her presents are going to be. That record may have been in her mind all this time without it once consciously influencing her behavior or surfacing as what she might call memory.

"The mind is a linear arrangement of such records, which are multisensory and total, and are records of successive moments of now.

"This answers the first important question about the anatomy of the mind. Yes, Richard?"

Richard, a plump, jolly-looking man in his late twenties and wearing a heavy blue turtleneck sweater, stands up in the center of the second row.

"I'm a doctor of dentistry and in *Science* magazine a few months ago I read about some research by a brain surgeon in Canada who said that whenever he touched an electrode to a part of the brain the patient, who was under a local anaesthesia but conscious, would experience some event completely that happened years ago. It apparently was like a tape playing —just like you're saying now. The electrode stimulation would activate something that seemed to constitute the complete record—the patient could remember the smallest details even though the details hadn't been in his conscious mind since the thing happened twenty or so years before. And there seemed to be thousands of these records—the doctor never knew what the patient would come up with when he probed with the electrode . . ."

Richard stops speaking and remains standing.

"Do you have a question?" the trainer asks.

"I guess not," says Richard. "I guess I'm just a little amazed that two months after reading that article, *est* should suddenly give me a definition of the mind that is really far out except that this Canadian guy apparently found the same thing."

"All right, Richard," says the trainer. "But remember, your brain surgeon was studying the *brain* and we're talking about the *mind.* The two aren't the same. Yes, John?"

(Applause for Richard as he sits)

John, an older man in his fifties, stands up in the last row.

"You mean that everything that's ever happened to us is sitting there in the mind?" he asks.

"That's not what I said, John. The individual *records* are complete, are total. Everything Marie experienced in that kitchen on that birthday in 1964 is there: the color of the floor, the dishes in the sink, whether her mother wore an apron or not, what the disc jockey said after the Beatles' song was over. The stacks of the mind contain multisensory *total* records— that we know. We didn't say that all the records are there. In fact you already know that they aren't. Remember, when an experience is completely experienced it disappears. I mean totally disappears. Out of the stack it goes. It's as if somebody borrowed the record and then never returned it."

"But you mean it's possible that I could remember vividly the moment I was born?"

"Memory is a different concept. However, it's true that most people have a multisensory total record of the moment of their birth."

"I see," says John, and he sits as the other trainees applaud.

"Yes, Barbara?" says the trainer, pointing to another raised hand.

"But does that mean all I am is a bunch of records?"

"No, Barbara, we're not talking about *you*, right now, we're talking about the *mind*. We're answering the question 'What is the mind?' "

"Oh," Barbara responds. "But I'd call what you're talking about the brain."

"Fine. I get that. But we're talking about the mind and I asked you to let go of how you think about the mind and listen to this. Okay?"

"Okay, fine . . ."

(Applause)

"The next question we have to answer is this: what is the *purpose* of the mind, or more accurately, what is the design function of this linear arrangement of total records? What is the purpose of the mind? Yes, Phyllis?"

"I'd say the purpose is to acquire information so that we can make valid decisions."

"Well, Phyllis, I'm afraid that's not it," says Michael. "The mind has millions of records of labels of beer cans, of the weather, the taste of a peanut, which clearly seem to be of no assistance in decision-making whatsoever. Yes, Peter?"

"It has no purpose," says Peter. "It just is."

"No, that's not true either. It's got a purpose all right. Yes, Rick."

"Ah'd say the purpose of the mind is just to help us save our asses, just to suh*vive*."

"Yes, SURVIVAL!" Michael agrees loudly. "That's not only the first purpose of the mind, it's the *only* purpose of the mind."

"But how can a mind have *any* purpose?" asks Nancy. "It's not a person."

"I told you," says the trainer. "We're really talking about the design function of the mind. The design function of the mind is survival, the survival of the being, as Rick said, but also of anything which the being considers itself to be."

"Then you mean," says Nancy, "that the being, namely the human, developed the mind as a sort of tool to aid survival?"

"That's right," replies Michael.

"Is it like Darwin's theory of evolution? Is it that the mind develops the way it develops through some sort of natural selection in order to help the being survive?"

"That could be," says Michael, "but there's more to it than that. The purpose of the mind is the survival of the being, *and*, don't forget this, anything which the *being* identifies itself with or considers itself to be."

"What do you mean by that?" asks Nancy.

"I mean that if you, for example, identify your being with your husband then your mind would send you into a burning building to death if your husband was trapped inside. Darwin can't explain that. Unless we acknowledge that the mind's purpose extends beyond the survival of the being we can't explain why people rush into burning buildings, go off to war, commit suicide. On those occasions the mind must think it can survive only by doing something which incidentally *kills the body*."

"Mmmmm. But when people fight in wars—I don't know how that . . . how the mind thinks being out on the front line is necessary for survival."

"The purpose of the mind is the survival of the being or of anything which the being considers itself to be. Now if George over there beside you comes to consider himself a good American and a brave man, look what happens. We ask George who he is, and he'll say—among other things—he's a good American and a brave man. Would George like to survive if he's a traitor to his country? 'Never!' says George. Does George want to be a coward? 'Never!' says George. He identifies himself not with his body but with his country and with his bravery. Next thing you know George is on the front lines getting his ass shot up. The mind is still working for the survival of what the being identifies with as necessary for the survival of the being."

"Okay, thank you."

(Applause)

"Some of you people are old enough to remember the old Jack Benny radio programs. Jack played the role of a complete miser. Money was everything to him. Probably the most famous single joke on his radio show occurs when a mugger comes up to Jack on the street and we hear the mugger say: 'Your money or your life!' And for the next fifteen seconds there is complete silence. And finally we hear Jack say, 'Well ...' [Laughter]

"In that case Jack's being doesn't know whether it considers itself money or a body, and thus poor Jack can't make up his mind. Someone may rush into a burning building to save the family jewels. Someone else to save a manuscript he's worked on for years. A third person will rush in to save a child. And most of us will rush out. [Laughter] And we won't rush back in for money, manuscript, jewels, or in many cases, our spouse or our kids. In those cases the being identifies his survival first with his own body and not with his manuscript or kid.

"It's not that one guy is brave and another guy a coward. It's just that in one case the being thinks he is nothing without his children or his money and in the other the being thinks he's nothing without his body! Yes, Bill?"

"But then what you're doing now is to bring in abstract things like bravery or country or being a writer and I don't quite see how the being comes to identify itself with these more abstract ... I mean actually identify its survival with these more ... these other things."

"Okay. Good. That question takes us on to another important point I'd like to make. You can sit down and I'll answer you. Thank you. [Applause]

"You've all heard of the ego?" the trainer goes on. "Big troublemaker. The Hindus and Buddhists have written thirty trillion words about the problems of the ego. You people into Eastern religions have probably been sweating away for years trying to reduce your ego, control your ego. You've probably also spent a lot of time wondering what the fuck it *is*.

"What the ego is, is quite simple, and when we see it, we'll see why it's caused so much trouble. We'll also see why the mind has such a helluva time trying to figure out *what* the ego is.

"The EGO is what we call the state of affairs when the being comes to identify itself with the mind. Look. The being is a little square here on the left-hand side of the board. The mind is a stack of records here on the right. The being thinks it *is* the mind. Presto!—the being becomes a part of the mind, gets inside the old stack of records. When that happens you've got *ego*.

"Let's see what happens when the being comes to identify itself with the mind, what the consequences are.

"If you think you *are* your mind, and the purpose of the mind is the survival of the being and of everything the being thinks it *is*, then, automatically, what does the purpose of the mind become? . . . Well?"

"The survival of the ego?" suggests one trainee.

"Partly, partly."

"The purpose becomes to save the being?" suggests another.

"No. PAY ATTENTION! Where did we get all these assholes? At this rate, we'll have to rent this hotel for two more days."

"The mind's purpose becomes the survival of the mind!" shouts someone.

"YES. YES!" the trainer shouts back. "If the purpose of the mind is the survival of what the being thinks it is, and the being thinks it's the mind, then the mind's purpose becomes ITS OWN SURVIVAL.

"And with that little switch human beings got problems. We call the problems, or rather the state of affairs where the being gets incorporated into the mind, 'ego.'

"Because now the purpose of the mind becomes the survival of the mind itself, the survival of the records, the *tapes*, of the *points of view* of the mind, of the *decisions* of the mind, of the *thoughts*, of the conclusions and *beliefs* of the mind. Now the mind has a vested interest in all these. What it does to try to survive is to try to keep itself intact, replay the same tapes, prove itself right. That becomes now the purpose of the mind: to survive by again and again proving itself right.

"As you people sit out there listening to me you think you're trying to understand me, to understand what the mind is. BULLSHIT! What your minds want to do is to *survive*, and to keep itself surviving the mind is only interested in getting its tapes reconfirmed. You know what understanding is? The mind makes you feel you understand something when the mind gets to play one of its old tapes. 'Oh,' you say, 'now I understand that the mind is a tape recorder.' What that means is that the mind has found a place in its belief system where our definition of mind fits in and the mind can survive.

"Of course, when I start saying things that threaten the survival of the mind then zzzzt, hiss, bowang!—the mind begins to do all it can to *avoid* dealing with the new material. It runs away from the training data the way you and I run away from a burning building, and for the same reason: SURVIVAL!

"So if the mind's purpose is to keep itself intact, what do you think it makes you look for out in the world? Yes, Bill?"

"It makes us look for other similar minds."

"Good. Diane?"

"It makes us look for books that have our beliefs in them."

"That's good. What else? What sort of things does the mind try to do to keep itself intact? Jason?"

"It's always trying to justify itself."

"YES! It's always trying to justify itself. What else? Lorraine."

"Well, it seems to me the mind would always be seeking consensus with others."

"Good. What's another word for consensus?"

"Popular opinion?"

"Yes. What's another word. Anyone?"

"Agreement," someone shouts.

"Yes. AGREEMENT!" echoes the trainer loudly. "The mind is always looking for *agreement*. I bet two-thirds of you signed up for the training only *after* reassuring yourselves that *est* was probably exactly what you've been thinking all along for years. [Nervous laughter] Surprise! [Louder laughter and applause] We've *not* been telling you what you've always been thinking and that's one reason your minds are giving you such a hard time.

"THE MIND WANTS AGREEMENT IN ORDER TO SURVIVE. It wants reconfirmation of its point of view, of its *decisions*, of its *conclusions*. It wants to keep proving itself right.

"Some of you eggheads out there have read your Nietzsche, supposed to be a great philosopher, one of the very greatest. He wrote a lot of books about how the mind will do anything to dominate, anything to prove itself right. He was sort of a master detective going around smelling out how people would develop religions so that poor people would feel right in their poverty, how philosophers would develop philosophies to prove right what they felt like doing anyway, how writers would write books whose secret purpose was to justify themselves. Nietzsche's will to power isn't a lot of Nazis goose-stepping around to build up their thigh muscles, it's about how all the world's religions, all the philosophies, all the great books, all of 'em, are just the mind's way of trying to prove itself right and dominate others. The mind doesn't want cheese, it wants to keep playing the survival tape of going up the fourth tunnel . . . *all* minds, including Nietzsche's . . ."

"All right, then," Michael says much later, after spending half an hour getting Lester to understand the consequences of the being's identifying itself with the mind. "Let me summarize where we've been so far and then go on to the next point." Michael points to the blackboard to the left where many of the phrases he is about to repeat are written out.

"The mind is a linear arrangement of multisensory total records of successive moments of now. Its purpose, its design function, is survival: the survival of the being and anything which the being considers itself to be. When the being identifies itself with its mind, we call this state of affairs the ego, and it means that the mind's purpose becomes the survival of the mind itself. For the mind to survive, it tries to keep itself intact, it seeks agreement and tries to avoid disagreement. It wants to dominate and avoid domination, it wants to justify its points of view, conclusions, decisions, and avoid invalidation. It wants to be right. Running through it all, over it all, is the unending effort of the mind to prove itself right." Michael strides away from the board to the front of the platform.

"Okay, the next question we have to answer is how the mind is constructed. Originally I drew the mind on the board as a single large *stack* of tapes, but now we've got to refine this model and see whether all the tapes belong to one category or to more than one category.

"At the simplest level we discover that there are basically two different stacks of tapes. Every recorded event—every tape—is either one that involves the *survival* of the mind or one that does not. Remember, the mind's design function is survival and anything it records which is necessary for its survival is a hell of a lot more important than, say, the date that Columbus discovered America. I'm not saying you'll remember the event better, I'm saying that any tape the mind perceives as containing data necessary for its survival is in a different category from a tape not perceived as necessary for survival. Because if the mind thinks that that tape is necessary for survival it's going to *play it whenever it thinks it's threatened*. Whenever something in the environment makes it think it's threatened, it's going to play that tape.

"So there are essentially two stacks of records. One stack we'll label 'necessary for survival.'" Michael draws the two stacks on the blackboard. "The second we'll label '*un*necessary for survival.'

"Now the records in the stack labeled 'necessary for survival' can be divided into three different categories depending on which type of survival experience they record.

"The first, the *basic* threat to survival which gets recorded and filed in the 'necessary for survival' stack, consists of an experience involving pain, impact, relative unconsciousness, plus, of course, threat to survival. And by *relative* unconsciousness I mean anything from full unconsciousness as in sleep to the sort of semiconsciousness we experience when under extreme pain, or when under a partial anaesthesia.

"We call such an experience a number one experience. It involves pain, often impact, relative unconsciousness, and threat to survival.

"Here's an example. Little Joanie is four years old. She's playing in the park with her older brother, Jim, age seven, and her mother. Their dog, a cocker spaniel named Horace, is there too. When they go to leave the park, her brother Jim suddenly grabs a toy sailboat she happened to have with her and runs away, dashing down the ten concrete steps that lead away from the park. She runs after him beginning to cry, and the cocker spaniel Horace runs after her, barking. The dog gets tangled up in her feet a couple of steps from the top of the steps and she falls, banging her knees, scratching her elbows, and finally banging her head on the last bit of cement at the bottom. She's stunned into semiconsciousness and has just had a full number one experience: pain, impact, relative unconsciousness, and threat to survival of the being.

"As she was falling her mother looked back and yelled 'Joanie! Joanie!' and the dog barked.

"When she began to recover a bit of consciousness she was lying in the grass at the bottom of the steps crying, her mother was leaning over her with sunlight reflecting off her glasses, the dog was licking her face, and her brother Jimmy was saying, 'She's not hurt, she's not hurt.'

"Her mother picks her up and makes Jimmy give her her toy

sailboat which she hugs to herself while being carried home. Her head aches and her stomach is churning while her mother takes her home, puts her in bed, gives her some M&M's, and tells her to go to sleep and everything will be all right. She falls asleep and wakes up an hour later feeling okay and fully conscious. End of number one experience.

"Can someone name another example of a number one experience? Chuck?"

"A child that gets hit by a car."

"Perfect. A child that gets hit by a car. Threat to survival. Pain. Impact. And certainly unconsciousness. Another example. Ricardo?"

"Falling from a tree."

"Fine. Another good one. Boy twenty feet up slips or a branch breaks and down he goes: threat to survival, then pain, then relative unconsciousness. Great! Another number one experience. Fred?"

"When I was six years old, I was riding my bike and a big truck came up behind me and beeped his horn and when I turned to look I thought he was going to hit me and panicked. I lost control of the bike and crashed into a tree. Was that a number one experience?"

"Was there pain?"

"Oh yeah, I forgot. I got the wind knocked out of me against the tree. But I didn't hit my head."

"But there was pain?"

"Yes."

"And if you had the wind knocked out of you there was probably relative unconsciousness, right?"

"Oh yeah, I seemed to wake up looking up at the sunlight through the leaves of the tree."

"Great, Fred. You got a humdinger number one. Thank you. [Applause]

"Now tell me, anybody, what is the *earliest* number one experience you can think of?"

"Getting dropped as a baby," shouts someone.

"Birth," shout several others.

"Yes, BIRTH! There you are lying in heaven, food getting pumped in all day long, perfect temperature, all noises muffled, softest spot in the universe, don't even have to bother to breathe, when whoomp! An earthquake begins. A fuckin' earthquake. The walls of the universe start pressing you down down down into the narrowest passageway imaginable, I mean the guy who invented this passageway obviously never tried it himself. Your head gets squeezed, and squeezed and squeezed, and then some asshole in a white suit grabs your head with his hands or with some silver tongs and drags you out into the coldest air this side of the Arctic. The same fool in the white suit begins beating you on the rear end and you start breathing and crying, and you hear your mother moaning. Next thing you know somebody snip snip cuts off part of you near the stomach and suddenly for life you're stuck with a belly button, and, if you're a boy and everybody's sadistic, they also snip snip you a little lower down.

"In short, I think it's safe to say that birth is experienced as a *threat to survival,* as containing pain and impact, and it certainly takes place in a state of relative unconsciousness. Every fuckin' one of us *begins* life with a royal number one experience ...

"Okay, are we all clear on what a number one experience is? Good. It's time now to look at what Werner calls a number two experience. This is one in which the mind experiences a sudden shocking loss accompanied by strong emotion, usually negative. The easiest examples are the sudden deaths—to a child all deaths are sudden and unexpected—of a father or mother or brother. If the loss is connected by the mind with a number one experience then the shocking experience may seem to others trivial, whereas to the person involved it is important.

"For example, when Joanie is seven years old, she walks out of her house to go to school one day. After she has carefully crossed the street she suddenly hears a horn honk and the screech of brakes. She turns around and sees her dog, Horace, who has been following her, hit by the car, run over by the front wheel. Horace drags himself a few feet toward her and then dies in the gutter next to a crushed beer can.

"Now notice, there's no threat to her own survival here and no pain. This is not a number one experience.

"But all of a sudden her dog has been transformed from a tail-wagging cocker spaniel into a limp smashed bloody corpse. It is a shocking sudden loss—especially since her cocker spaniel is associated in her mind with her *survival* from an earlier experience. Remember, Horace licked her face after her fall down the steps and that's associated by her mind with her *survival* of the threat from the fall.

"Joanie cries out, rushes to Horace's side, puts her hand on him, and gets it covered with blood. She begins to cry hysterically. Her mother comes out and yells 'Joanie! Joanie!' and picks her up, carries her away from the dead dog, gives her some candy, and tells her to lie down and rest. Joanie cries for half an hour and falls asleep. End of classic number two experience. Any questions, or can you suggest some other number two experiences? Bob?"

"If Joanie lost her toy sailboat—let's say it sank in a pond and couldn't be recovered—would that be a number two experience?"

"Well, it might be, Bob," the trainer replies as he goes to his thermos for a drink. "Or it might be a number three experience. A number three is simply any experience which the mind associates with either a number one or number two experience. The toy boat is definitely associated in Joanie's mind with her survival: remember, she cuddled the sailboat while being carried back to the house after falling. Now let's say at the pond she's having an argument with her brother and is really mad, and he pushes her. She starts crying and he says, 'Oh, you're not hurt!' and then they notice the sailboat has disappeared. The shocking loss and strong emotion make it a number two experience. Isaac?"

"Did you say a number three experience is one associated with any number one or number two experience?"

"Yes."

"Does that mean that seeing a man in a white suit could be a number three experience? You know, from the birth?"

"Exactly, Isaac. You've got it. What would be some of the other things that might trigger a number three experience in anyone born in a hospital in the normal way? Anyone can answer this."

"Nurses," suggests someone.

"Good, what else?"

"Surgical gloves."

"Right!"

"Lights."

"Yes, even light and lights. What else?"

"A woman moaning."

"Great!"

"The forceps."

"Good."

"The doctor's hands."

"Right. What else?"

"Getting spanked."

"Getting spanked. Yes."

"Explosive breathing."

"Yes, explosive breathing. Good."

"Having one's penis cut."

(Laughter)

"That's right," says the trainer, smiling. "Whenever a man has his penis cut with a knife he feels a threat to his survival."

(Laughter)

"The color of the walls."

"Fine. Okay, you've got the idea. Now, normally a number three experience works like this. Let's say Joanie is now nineteen and really into dating men. One day she goes on a picnic with Walter, her favorite man, big and rugged even if he does wear glasses. After a good lunch they lie down and begin necking in the grass. Walter squeezes her too hard and she says, 'Ouch, that hurts!' and Walter says, 'Oh come on, you're not hurt,' and at that moment the sun glints off his glasses.

"She's lying in the grass, her side hurts where he squeezed her, sun is glinting off glasses, and a male is telling her it doesn't hurt. She suddenly finds she has a headache and her stomach is upset. She has to leave. A number three experience. Bob?"

"I don't quite understand how the mind is working in these cases. Does her head ache because it ached after she fell down the steps?"

"That's right, Bob. The mind has a special logic all its own. The logic of the mind is this: every element of a given event is the same as every other element except sometimes. Let's say that in the event of the falling down the steps there are, say, twenty chief elements. From the logic of the mind A equals B equals C equals D equals E equals F equals G equals H equals I equals J equals K equals L equals M and so on, except sometimes. What happened at Joanie's picnic with Walter is that G, the grass, S, the sun, H, Walter's telling her it doesn't hurt, and P, her pain in the side, are all stimulated by her experience and these in turn produce C and A, churning in stomach and ache in the head. Another time, that seemingly identical experience of lying in the grass might stimulate the response of her wanting to cry or getting a strong urge to eat M&M's or maybe have Walter lick her face. [Laughter]

"Don't laugh. That's how the mind works. She may end up *marrying* Walter because for some reason she loves the way he licks her. [Laughter]

"Actually, of course, she's marrying her dog Horace. [Laughter] Don't laugh. How many of you have married dogs? [Laughter]

"... Okay, Robert?"

"But the way you're talking about the mind's logic," says Robert, "it seems we don't have any control over our thoughts. What about our free will? What about decisions we make?"

"All right, Robert, to answer that question I want you to try

a little experiment with me, okay? Are you willing, just standing the way you are now, to do a little experiment?"

"Sure," says Robert.

"Fine. What I want you to do is bring your right hand up
and hold it horizontally in front of your face, like this. Okay?
Good. Now, in a little while I'm going to count out loud to
three and after I say 'three' I want you to watch your experience, and decide either to raise your hand several inches or to
lower your hand. Any questions? Fine, now raise your hand to
the horizontal position in front of your face. Good. One ...
two ... three."

Robert hesitates about two seconds and then his hand falls
to his side.

"Okay. To make sure you really *experience* what takes place
in your mind, I'd like you to do it again. Remember, watch
your experiences and choose to raise or lower your hand after
I've counted to three. One ... two ... three."

Again Robert stands motionless a few seconds, and then his
hand falls.

"Okay. What happened?" Michael asks.

"The first time after you said 'one two three' nothing happened. I mean no thoughts, no feelings, no movement. Then I
thought I gotta do something. Then I decided I'd lower it and
it fell."

"All right, Robert, that's good, and I'd like you to clarify
your experience for us just a bit. At first no thoughts go
through the mind. Right?"

"A complete blank."

"Then what?"

"I thought I gotta do something because—"

"Hold it! What was the exact thought?"

"Well, it was 'I gotta do something.' That's what it was."

"It flashed into your consciousness?"

"Yeah."

"Good, then what?"

"Then the thought came that I'll lower it, and my hand went
down."

"What happened the second time?"

"The second time was really strange. I decided before you said 'three' that I was going to raise my hand because the first time I'd lowered it. You said 'one two three' and for about a second nothing happened. Then I said to myself, 'I don't *feel* like raising it.' Another couple of seconds went by with nothing and then I thought I'm going to raise it anyway. Two more seconds passed and the damn hand went down!"

(Laughter)

"Okay, Robert, you asked about our having control over our thoughts and decisions we make. Is your question answered?"

Robert stares at Michael and shakes his head slowly. "I guess I didn't have much control then, but . . . but I must be free to choose . . . something."

"Oh yeah," says Michael. "At the end of the day we go into choice and it'll be quite clear what you're free to choose."

"Okay, thanks."

(Applause)

"Go ahead, Jason."

"Look, I find all of this fascinating, but I resent the fact that it seems to me you've stolen most of the whole tapes business from scientology."

"I get that, Jason. And there are six people who think we stole the good stuff from Zen, and eleven who think we robbed gestalt therapy, and two who know we got something from Silva Mind Control. You name it and Werner stole it. [Laughter] Alexander Graham Bell stole everything he put into his telephone, but so what, he invented something which as a whole was entirely new. Do you have a question about the anatomy of the mind?"

"Well, yes, I do. In scientology, which I studied for six years, Ron Hubbard demonstrates that our minds are filled with these number one and number two experiences—scientology calls them *engrams*. And last weekend that truth process was an amazing thing for getting rid of an engram. Scientology entirely agrees with this anatomy of the mind."

"How do you know, Jason? We may be only halfway through the anatomy of the mind."

"Well," says Jason. "It agrees so far anyway. The question I have is the same one that has come to bother me in scientology. Before the break you gave us an example of Joanie being upset lying in the grass with her boyfriend. And later you said that *all* upsets actually come from number one or number two experiences."

"No. I said they all come ultimately from some number one experience."

"Okay, then, all upsets come from number one experiences. My question is, do you mean to say that if I see a man killed in an automobile accident and get upset I'm actually getting upset from something in my past?"

"Of course."

"All the *time?*"

"Absolutely. What's the big fuss about a man getting run over? You people watched children getting bombed in Vietnam on Walter Cronkite for five fuckin' years. How many of you were upset at seeing it? [A few hands go up.]

"You see. Other people's deaths are not in themselves a threat to survival. They don't in themselves upset us."

"And you mean that when we, say, argue with our wives, and get upset, that that too is actually a past number one experience getting triggered?"

"OF COURSE IT IS! Why get upset because you're chatting with some woman? You notice you could argue with one woman about radical feminism and not get upset at all. Argue with your wife and you get upset. It's quite simple, your wife is actually your dog. [Laughter] More exactly, or rather more usually, your wife is probably your mother. And you can be *damned* sure your mother is in at least *one* major number one experience."

"But you mean *every* upset is actually the mind playing a tape from some past upset?"

"Some past number one experience. Right. I mean, *look* at

the fuckin' stupid trivial things that upset us. I shout at you trainees. Most of you aren't bothered by this at all. But a large number of you get a little upset *every* time I shout. Why? Because your mother or father shouted during some number one traumatic experience in the past. You remember last weekend a woman complained to Don about his shouting and he traced it back to her father shouting at her mother? Nothing about upsets is the way you think it is. One man gets upset in a traffic jam and another guy falls asleep. One woman swoons at the sight of blood and another secretly wants to drink it. One person fears snakes and others don't. The *only* truly upsetting things are threats to survival. All our upsets are related back to threats to survival associated with pain and relative unconsciousness. . . . Anything else? Good. [Applause] Richard?"

"In the book I read about *est*," says Richard, the dentist, with precise intonation, "it seemed that the training involves on this fourth day an intellectual analysis of the mind which concludes that the mind is essentially a machine. Now it seems to me—"

"Oh, you've read a *book* about *est*?" asks Michael, moving to the front of the platform.

"Yes. It was a good book with many intelligent criticisms, especially of *est*'s analysis of the mind. In fact the book made me more interested in taking the training. Now what it said—"

"Richard," interrupts the trainer mildly, "you've read a book about *est*. So have dozens of others. Three-quarters of the people in here have read articles about *est*. Great! But this training is an *experience*, not a book. If Werner thought he could do the same thing in a book he'd do it. Instead of working eighteen hours a day, he could relax at home and rake in the royalties. You've read a book and you've got all the answers. Great! *est* doesn't have any answers. You've read a book and you know all the intelligent criticism of *est*'s intellectual belief. *est* doesn't have any beliefs. You've read a book and you know what I'm going to say before I say it. Great! It doesn't make a damn bit of difference. We could let all you turkeys read every printed word of the training rap before you took the training and you know what would happen? Everything that's been happening. This training isn't answers, ideas. IT'S EXPERIENCE! IT'S EXPERIENCE HERE AND NOW IN THIS ROOM! Werner once said that the trainer could read from the telephone book off and on for four days and still the trainees would get it. It's the EXPERIENCE of *being* in *this* room, with *these* people, and getting what you get! That's the training.

"Now when you start telling me what you read in a book, you're trying to stop being in this room. You're trying to take a training you read about in some book. That's fine. That's fine. But why pay two hundred and fifty dollars to take a training you already think you took in a book? Pretty stupid. I want you to be here now with THIS training. I want you to experience *your* experience, not some author's. Got it?"

"Well, I understand your point, I suppose," says Richard, frowning. "But am I supposed to suppress all my criticisms that come from books?"

"No! *Experience* them. Take what you get. But don't sit there with your book about *est* nicely enclosed in your silver box, peeking at it every now and then to see how *wrong this* training is. [Laughter] Raise all the objections and questions you want; just make sure they're *yours*."

"Okay," says Richard, "can I still ask a question?"

"If it's *yours*, yes. Go ahead."

"Well," begins Richard, "I have the feeling you're talking way out of touch with reality. I mean whatever happened to all the creative aspects of the mind? Where do imagination, uh, artistic creativity, original thought, problem solving, where do these things fit into this stew?"

"Thank you, Richard. That's a good question. The stack here on the left, which contains only records that the mind interprets as necessary for survival, operates solely on stimulus-response, stimulus-response, stimulus-response, solely on an illogic of identities. This stack operates quite *mechanically*, quite automatically, quite moronically as a matter of fact. Let's say a rabbit is nibbling at grass, hears a bird cry, a branch snap, suddenly feels a sharp pain in his shoulder and hears a loud 'bang.' The rabbit runs like hell. The next time the rabbit is eating and hears a bird cry and a branch snap, guess what? He feels a twinge of pain in his shoulder and runs like hell. Always. That's how the survival mind works. Everything is like everything else except sometimes.

"Now the creative problem-solving features of man would seem to exist in one of two places—either in the other stack of records *or* in the spaces created when records are erased by being fully experienced.

"For example, John worried that if he erased his recording of how to get back home from the hotel by totally experiencing his experiences, he'd be lost forever.

"Not so. We know that if he fully experiences all his experiences related to getting from here to his home, he could still set out from this hotel tonight and drive right home. In the open spaces created by his erased records the 'problem' of how to get home would get solved, ex nihilo, it might seem."

Richard stands silently for several seconds, the trainer looking at him.

"But what *does* solve it? I mean saying something gets done by nothing isn't really an explanation, is it?"

"No, it's not," says Michael. "Any explanation I gave you would have to fit in with your mind's demands and whatever the 'nothing' is, it sure as hell isn't mind."

"But what is imagination? What is creativity? Where do they come in?"

"They never left. They've always been there."

"I don't get it."

"That's fine, Richard. Remember if your mind felt it understood it, it would probably only mean that it was having one of its tapes replayed. Thank you. Yes, Ronald."

(Applause for Richard)

"Can the records in the stacks necessary for survival be erased like the others?"

"Of course! *Any* experience fully experienced disappears. The truth process a week ago involved for many of you the re-creating of an experience and in some cases its disappearance. Upsets in the present are inevitably number three experiences: something happens which triggers a number one or two experience, ultimately a number one experience. Now, to eliminate these upsets we'd have to eliminate either the number one, or the connection between the one and the present stimuli."

"So theoretically, someone could experience out everything in his stacks and be pure open space?"

"In theory it would seem that way. But we'll see later on that there are certain barriers which make this something of an impossibility ..."

"Now, Elsa, I want you to do me a favor. Are you willing to share with me and the other trainees whatever comes up for you when I ask you a question? There's nothing tricky about this, it won't be embarrassing."

"All right," says Elsa, standing in the front row.

"Come up here on the platform, why don't you, and sit in this chair."

Elsa comes up and seats herself in one of the two uphol-stered chairs. She is a small and pretty woman, neatly dressed in a white blouse and slacks.

"Fine. Close your eyes and go into your space.... Good. Now in a moment I am going to name a date and I want you to share with us whatever you get. Whatever images, words, or feelings you get. Do you understand?"

"Uh-huh," says Elsa.

"Good. All right, the year 1807."

Elsa is silent for perhaps ten seconds.

"I get ... uh ... ships in the water. I ... I'm in a small ... rowboat rowing away from one of the ships ... a burning ship."

"Fine. What else?"

"I'm . . . there are two other men rowing with me, and my hand really hurts. It burns. It's hard to hold the left oar. And the water in the bottom of the rowboat is freezing my feet . . ."

"Anything else about the ships?"

"We're rowing away from there and I can see some men running around the deck of the one that's burning. I think there's somebody hurt lying behind me in our rowboat . . ."

"Fine. Anything else?"

"Yes," says Elsa, smiling. "I have to go to the bathroom."

"You mean you or the you in the boat?"

"The me in the boat. I'm fine."

"Thank you, Elsa. [Applause]

"All right. Look. What's this all about? Elsa is a reincarnated English sailor from some nineteenth-century war? No. No way to know that. Did she have her imagination stimulated and get all this stuff from history books? No way to know that. Could have all come from history books, but what's a history book for Elsa except just another record? Is it that in Elsa's stack of records, events exist not only from her own life but also from other people's lives back in the past? Again, no way to know. Like the other two, it's a possibility. In all the cases, though, it's a record from Elsa's mind. . . . It's *all* just records.

"Okay now. There's one little aspect of the mind I haven't told you about. Every one of us has come out of one cell formed at the moment of our conception, and that cell was formed from one cell from our father and one from our mother. And since the cell from our mother contains in effect a cellular inheritance from *her* father and mother, then we have one from our grandmother and grandfather. We all know this. We all know a boy may be the spit and image, not of his father, but of his grandfather. But, of course, that cellular inheritance we got from our grandfather also contains a cellular inheritance from *his* father and *his* mother and so on back forever. For all *you* know, you may not look like your father or grandfather but be the spit and image of your great-great-

great-great-great-grandfather. Or your great-great-great-great-great-great-grandmother, for that matter. The fact is that every one of us has a cellular inheritance from *every single past ancestor* and that every one of us, *ultimately*, is related to everyone else.

"Nothing new here. Nothing far out. It just means that it's *possible*, that's all I say, *possible* that Elsa, and every one of us, is carrying around tapes in our stack which were made *before* we were born. In any case, even if it's imagination, you must acknowledge that most human beings will immediately create in some detail a specific event when the mind is triggered by a specific date.

"The ancient yogis of India claimed they traced these memories back some three hundred and fifty trillion years. Before that, nothing. Take it or leave it, it's not important. It's just one of those phenomena we throw out to keep your minds in touch with how little they ever consciously know . . ."

"We're coming near the end of our anatomy of the mind and I want you all to be clear about what we've said.

"The mind is a linear arrangement of multisensory total records of successive moments of now. Its purpose is the survival of the being or of anything the being identifies with its survival. Since the being in fact inevitably identifies his being with his mind, the purpose of the mind becomes the survival of the mind: the survival of the tapes, the points of view, the decisions, the beliefs, the rightness of the mind. The mind thus seeks always for agreement and to avoid disagreement, always to be right and avoid being wrong, to dominate and avoid domination, to justify itself and avoid invalidation.

"The construction of the mind involves two stacks, one containing records of experiences necessary for survival, a second containing records *not* necessary to survival. Those experiences in the first stack are divided into three classes. Number ones are experiences involving pain, threat to survival, and relative unconsciousness. Number twos are experiences of loss or shocking loss associated with the number ones and involving strong emotion. Number threes are experiences triggered by important elements from either number ones or number twos.

"The second stack contains experiences not necessary for survival, experiences such as a child might have playing with his toys or walking when nothing in the environment is such as to make the experience a number three experience.

"The logic of the mind is that of illogical identity. For the mind A equals B equals C equals D equals E except sometimes not. The mind is an associative machine which associates one thing or event with every other thing within that event. Thus, our Joanie may associate the licking of her face by a dog with the pleasure of *her recovery* from her fall down the steps *or* with the pain and upset of the fall. We can never be sure which identity the mind will make.

The final question we must now ask is what is the extent of the mind? What are the relative sizes of the two stacks of tapes? Let's now look at this question.

"On the left here we have the stack of records of experiences the mind records as necessary for survival. On the right the stack of records the mind records as not necessary for survival.

"Now for the sake of certainty we will take an imaginary human being from birth. No sooner. We know the possibility exists that the being may inherit several trillion years of tapes, many of which may record number one experiences. We ignore this possibility. We know also that during the time the being lives in the mother's womb it's quite likely that the mother may fall or be kicked or have severe vomiting and thus cause a number one experience in the as yet unborn baby. We're quite sure of this but for the sake of this analysis we'll pretend that no number ones occur before birth.

"So we'll start with birth. In his stack 'necessary for survival' he has a bunch of records of his birth. Fine. Then presumably he has a few clear days or weeks. So in this other stack here, he has a bunch of records of experience *not* necessary to survival. Good. Then one day he gets dropped. Only a couple of feet but the poor kid feels for a few seconds that the ball game is over. Since psychologists tell us that babies under a year old spend most of their time in a state of semiconsciousness we can be quite sure that his slight fall and bump create a number one experience. Let's say that for the whole rest of the first year no more number ones. Were there any number twos or threes during that first year? Jack?"

"Sure. Probably quite a few. The kid's getting handled like in birth might even trigger off a number three."

"All right. Certainly there will be some number threes in that first year. Yes, Donna?"

"Would Joanie's being carried out into the cold air be a number three experience?"

"That's good. Yes, it might well be.... Now, the question I'd like each one of you to consider is this: about what percentage of Joanie's records would be number ones, twos, or threes in her first year as compared to her records unnecessary for survival? Just consider this question for yourself and give an estimate that you think would be true. All right, Jennifer?"

"You mean what percent of her experience would be associated with number one experiences?"

"Yes. Or with number two experiences. I want all of you to consider this question and to suggest a percentage. Okay. Let's see. Who's got an answer? Bob?"

"Twenty-five percent."

"Fine. Twenty-five percent. Leslie?"

"I'd say maybe only about five percent."

"Good. Elaine?"

"Twenty percent."

"Fine. Richard?"

"One goddamn hundred percent."

(Nervous laughter)

"Good. Donna?"

"Fifty percent."

"Okay. Silvia?"

"Ten percent."

"All right, good," concludes Michael, turning briefly away from the audience and then back again. "Let's assume for the sake of this example that the *lowest* percentage suggested—five percent—is the reasonable figure. Not that it's true. It's just the lowest reasonable estimate anyone gave. So in the first year five percent of all the baby's experiences are recorded in the stack necessary for survival. Now let's see what happens between the ages of one and, say, four. Let's assume Joanie has a pretty good life and only experiences one new number one experience—say an accident on her tricycle or falling down the concrete steps. Most kids will have more, but let's give our child just one. Of course, she will have a few new number two experiences—losses with strong emotion, losses associated with number ones—and she'll have a few more number three experiences. After all, she now has at least three number one experiences which have a whole raft of stimuli that might trigger number threes, and she now has several number twos with additional stimuli that might trigger number threes. The loss of her tricycle or dog or sailboat or brother or mother—any one of these might be a number two experience, and then any incident containing elements that existed in the incident of her losing her dog or sailboat or mother—like the crushed beer can in the gutter next to her dead dog in the example we went over—might well become a number three incident. Got it? WAKE UP OUT THERE! YOUR MINDS ARE TRYING TO PUT YOU TO SLEEP! . . . Do you get it? . . . Okay then. What percentage of her experiences between ages one and four would be ones, twos, or threes? Ask yourself that question."

There is a period of silence and lack of movement until a few tentative hands are raised.

"Yes, Judy?" says Michael, calling on a woman in the first row.

"I'd say it was now up to fifty percent."

"Fifty percent. Good. Jessie?"

"It seems to me that the older she gets the more and more of her experiences become number three, two, or ones."

"Good. That's true. What percentage of them during ages one to four would you suggest?"

"I don't know. A lot."

"What percentage?"

"Eighty?"

"Fine. Eighty. Ted?"

"Twenty-five percent."

"Thank you. Dick?"

"I get that it must be close to a hundred percent but that means—"

"Fine. One hundred percent. Anyone else?"

There is a silence in the room and no more hands are raised.

"Okay. The lowest figure we have now is twenty-five percent. Let's see what that means for Joanie's next year or two or three. First of all, can she possibly have any *fewer* than twenty-five percent during the fifth year of her life?"

Several no's are spoken in subdued voices. Some trainees seem to have lost totally the line of argument, though most are fully alert but subdued, a bit depressed, sensing the direction of the argument and not liking it.

"No," agrees Michael. "The percentage of her number ones, twos, and threes, those records the mind finds necessary for survival, those records that operate totally on the mechanical principle of identity, must continually increase. If after birth there are, for example, one hundred different stimuli that can trigger ones, twos, or threes, and at the end of one year there are, say, a thousand, and after four years, forty thousand, the number of experiences that can escape being number ones, twos, or threes keeps getting smaller and smaller, and the percentage of experiences which are number ones, twos, or threes gets larger and larger. In fact, taking the lowest percentage, five percent after the first year—which ignored the possibility of number ones, twos, and threes before conception and the probability of ones occurring during pregnancy—we see that in three years the percentage has multiplied five times to twenty-five percent. In the next three years it will grow at least at that rate, which means that—since five times twenty-five percent is one hundred twenty-five percent—by the age of seven at the latest, *all* of Joanie's experiences will be in the stack necessary for survival."

Michael pauses, looking from the trainees to the blackboard and back to the trainees with a strangely bland, indifferent expression. The room is silent.

"There's only one thing wrong with this analysis," he goes on with a frown. "We seem to have overlooked the idiotic logic of the mind. In actual fact, after the royal number one experience of birth, the child has at least a hundred stimuli which would trigger a one, two, or three experience. But with the mind's logic of identity each of these stimuli is immediately associated in the baby's mind with everything else it is related to. The doctor's hands get associated with men's hands, get associated with men's arms, get associated with men, get associated with human beings, and so on and on. The green of the hospital wall gets associated with green leaves, with trees, then with bushes, and so on. The hospital walls get associated with all walls, with all surfaces, and so on. If we honestly look at what happens from the moment of birth onwards we'll see that *everything* the baby experiences from then on is associated with pain, threat to survival, and relative unconsciousness, that everything the baby experiences from birth on is at least a number three experience and thus *all* of the baby's records are in the stack 'necessary for survival' and thus all of his behavior is of the mechanical stimulus-response variety."

Michael is sitting in his chair now leaning slightly forward, his expression absolutely neutral. He speaks from now on much more slowly, with long pauses between some sentences. Most trainees seem to be listening with bewilderment, disbelief, or depression.

"From the moment of birth onwards we come under the influence of the mechanical mind. From the moment of birth onwards everything is stimulus-response, stimulus-response, stimulus-response, stimulus-response. The mechanical mind using the logic of identities in its moronic effort to survive. From the moment of birth we are totally under the influence of the machine mind ... stimulus-response, stimulus-response, stimulus-response ...

"Earlier you all saw that when Robert tried to decide whether to raise or lower his hand, the hand just popped up or down or the decision just popped up into his head.... All mechanical ... No control ... All mechanical ... Stimulus-response, stimulus-response, stimulus-response, stimulus-response ..."

Michael pauses a long time, staring neutrally from right to left over the trainees. A deep silence seems to have come over the trainees, most of whom look gloomy.

"You're machines," he says nonchalantly after a while. "You've never been anything else except machines ..."

He pauses again, looking us over with complete indifference.

"Your lives are totally mechanical ... totally stimulus-response ... stimulus ... response ...

"Your lives are meaningless.... Machines aren't meaningful.... Machines don't have goals ... ideals ... morals ... meaning.... Machines just chug away ... mechanically ... trying to survive ... throwing off a few sparks now and then ... maybe gas fumes ... smelly exhaust ... but are totally meaningless ..."

Someone is now crying softly. Most of the trainees are sitting utterly still, faces masks of resistance or depression.

"You're machines.... You've never been anything else ...

"There's no control ... You've never had any control ...

"Your tragedies are just you playing your tapes ..."

He reaches back to take his thermos from the lectern and casually takes a drink.

"All your dramatic upsets," he goes on, smacking his lips, "are just your machine mind triggering off some past threat to survival. . . . The whole works is just stimulus-response, stimulus-response, stimulus-response ...

"You've spent your whole life trying to find an escape from

admitting you're a machine, your whole life trying to escape from admitting what is, is . . .

"You were a machine before the training. . . . You're a machine after the training. . . . No change . . . Two hundred and fifty big ones for no change. [Someone laughs softly.]

"You're a machine . . .

"Notice your minds sitting there fighting it. Your mind feeds you thoughts like 'It's too abstract' or 'It doesn't make sense.' . . . You yourselves *know* you're free because a thought just mechanically zipped through your mind *saying* you were free. And then another thought mechanically followed saying, 'Yeah, that's right, I'm free' . . ."

Someone else laughs, a staccato ratatat-tat, and Michael seems oblivious of it.

"And you're all sitting there saying to yourselves, 'Oh, it's just another one of the trainer's tricks . . . in a few minutes he'll switch everything around and he'll tell us we're not machines and by trying a few simple *est* processes we can all be better.' "

Three people laugh briefly, one loudly.

"It's not a trick . . . ," says Michael, drinking again from his thermos. "There's not going to *be* a switch. . . . This is all there is. . . ." A few other trainees begin laughing softly. Someone else is still crying.

"There ain't no more. . . . You're machines . . ."

A brief ripple of laughter flows through a group of trainees on one side of the room.

"Every thought that's popping into your head at this moment just pops. . . . You don't control it. . . . It just pops. . . . Effect effect effect effect effect . . . And the old machine mind keeps grinding away and that's all you are . . . machines. . . . You've never been anything else," he says, shrugging his shoulders in a comic 'so what?' manner while several trainees laugh.

"That's all there is . . . [Someone laughs again.]

"There's nothing to get. . . . I hope you get it . . .

Several people laugh, two very loudly.

"You've had it ... [Laughter]

"You've lost. There ain't nothing to get ... [Laughter]

"You've spent your whole fuckin' lives trying to hide from the fact that you're a machine ... to pretend you somehow had control over your mind. . . . Oh well," he says, again shrugging his shoulders, "Nothing to worry about ... [Laughter] ... Nothing's important. Everything is as worthless as everything else ... [Laughter]

"Now we can tell you what enlightenment is," Michael goes on with a slight upbeat to his blandness as if what he was about to say is one percent more important than what he has been saying. "Enlightenment . . . is knowing you are a machine . . ."

Laughter starts slowly and spreads across the room, growing into a giant wave and then receding.

"Accepting your machineness . . ."

He pauses a long time looking out at the audience with his bland bored expression.

"That's it . . ."

Loud laughter from a small percentage of the trainees dominates the room. Someone applauds too. Most are sitting stunned and bewildered.

"It's all a cosmic joke," one of the trainees says aloud.

"Yeah," says the trainer. "That's about it ... [Laughter]

"You've all paid two hundred and fifty dollars to get you're a machine. [Laughter] ... and that you've always been a machine . . ."

(Laughter)

As Michael now continues, from a third to perhaps half of the trainees are glowing and many laughing at everything he says. Another third to half are sitting glumly or in bewilderment.

"Enlightenment is simply knowing and accepting that you're a machine.... Big deal. [Laughter] ... You got it and it's nothing, right? [Laughter] ... Don told you last weekend that you'd get nothing out of the training. [Laughter] ... Well, you got it!" Michael concludes brightly, and an explosion of laughter follows. "There's nothing to get . . ."

He returns the thermos he has been holding to the lectern and wipes his mouth.

"Mankind struggling for three hundred and fifty trillion years to try to avoid simply being what he is. . . . No wonder he gets tired! [Laughter] It's tough being a machine when you're always trying not to be a machine. . . . Makes for a lot of squeaks, worn parts . . . smelly exhaust . . .

"Enlightenment is saying yes to what is . . .

"Enlightenment is taking what you get. . . . You might as well take what you get . . . because it's what you get! [Laughter]

"And you might as well not take what you don't get . . . because you didn't get it. [Laughter]

"Of course, some machines like to *not* take what they get . . . but naturally, they get it anyway. . . . Enlightenment [at the use of the word several people laugh] . . . is a big nothing. . . . Enlightenment is taking what you get . . . when you get it. [Laughter] . . . And not taking what you don't get . . . when you don't get it . . . [Laughter]

"What do *you* want?" Michael suddenly snarls at a trainee with his hand up. Michael is speaking in a totally new, farcically irritable voice, which brings a burst of laughter from the audience.

"I just want to say," says Tom, standing, "that this has been the greatest two hundred fifty dollars I ever spent . . ."

(Laughter, applause, and gloom)

"Big deal," says Michael, with a shrug of his shoulders. "A machine congratulating itself on being a machine. [Laughter] . . . Yes, Jane?"

"I have a question about the stacks," she says and is immediately interrupted by uproarious laughter from almost half the audience.

"It's too late, Jane, it's all over . . . [Laughter]

"It's all over. There ain't no more . . . ," concludes Michael.

(Laughter)

"But I'd like to ask a question about the stacks," insists Jane, followed by more laughter.

"Relax," suggests Michael, "and enjoy the tapes.... Yes, Terry?"

"Now that we're enlightened are we still assholes?"

(Laughter)

"An asshole," begins Michael with exaggerated dignity and solemnity, "is a machine that thinks he's not a machine." He pauses and squints back at the blackboard like Mr. Magoo. When he turns back his face bursts into an exaggerated idiotic smile. "An *enlightened* man [Laughter] is an asshole that *knows* he is a machine. [Laughter and applause]

"Richard?"

"Yes," says Richard, standing with a frown. "I don't understand what everyone is laughing about."

"Everyone's not laughing," Michael replies, looking surprised by the question. "You're not laughing. I'm not laughing."

"Yes, but most people are."

"Well, Richard, it's like this. The people who are laughing are laughing because ... they are laughing. And the people who aren't, aren't laughing because ... they aren't."

(Laughter)

"But what's *funny?*" insists Richard.

"It's quite simple," Michael replies. "A guy named Henri Bergson, a great French philosopher I'm told, once wrote a book proving that the essence of laughter is seeing human beings acting like machines. [Laughter] ... And some people in here are apparently seeing human beings acting like machines."

"But philosophically," begins Richard, but the word *philosophically* brings such a flood of laughter from some trainees that his next words are drowned out and he simply sits.

"Jerry?" says Michael, calling on the big man with the brush cut.

"Utterly, utterly, utterly amazing," Jerry says with a big

smile. "Why do I feel so good? I don't even agree with what you've been saying, but I feel like I'm floating two feet off the ground. But why? It's incredible . . ."

(Applause)

"Take what you get, Jerry. Some machines find that when they stop trying *not* to be a machine, life gets a little easier. . . . People who drive their cars full speed through life with their brake pedal pushed to the floor have a kinda . . . jerky ride. [Laughter]

"Where are *you* going?" Michael asks a tall man who has leapt up from his seat in the third row and is striding toward the back of the room.

"I *got* it! I *got* it!" he says with a grin. "It's great and I figured I'd go home."

(Laughter and applause)

"Sit down," says Michael with a mock-firm expression. "Your agreement is to stay till the training's over. Just because you know you're a machine is no reason to think the training's over."

"But I got it!"

"Big deal. Remember, you always *did* have it. There's nothing to get. Sit down."

Smiling broadly, the tall man returns to his seat.

"Okay. It's all over . . . ," says Michael, stretching and yawning an obviously fake yawn. "Enlightenment is knowing you're a machine. Enlightenment is taking what you get when you get it and not taking what you don't get when you don't get it. Werner says that what is, is." He pauses and looks quizzically at the audience. "Seems pretty likely, doesn't it? [Laughter]

"Buddha said it differently but it's the same. He said, 'You cannot escape the wheel of birth and death until you realize you are not the Doer.' . . . 'You cannot escape the wheel of birth and death until you realize . . . you are not the Doer.' The wheel, of course, was the first machine. [Laughter] . . . Yes, Jennifer?"

"I want to thank you. This last half hour has just freed me from five years of guilt over the death of my daughter."

(Applause)

"Phil?"

"Well, I'm depressed," says Phil firmly and looks it.

"Great," says Michael. "Take what you get."

"But I mean it's horrible to see all these people laughing at what I find totally depressing."

"Sure, it is," agrees Michael. "What you got is that there's nothing to get and it's depressing, right?"

"Yes!"

"Great! Take what you get. . . . Yes, Donna?"

(Applause as Phil sits)

"How can machines feel as good as I feel? It's impossible."

"Take what *you* get, Donna . . . when you get it. . . . If you don't get it . . . don't take . . . what you don't get."

Michael now stands up and strides away from his chair.

"Okay," he says. "At this point all of you are in one of three categories. Either you got it, and you *know* you got it; *or* you *know*, you're absolutely sure that you *didn't* get it; *or*, thirdly, you're not sure whether you got it or not. Okay? Three categories. Now I don't want you to bullshit me about this. Don't lie. You been lying all your lives. Time to stop. Don't do me any favors. I don't give a shit which category you think you're in. Just be honest.

"Either you got it and you *know* you got it—that's number one. Or you know, you're absolutely sure you didn't get it—that's number two. Or you may have gotten it or maybe not, you're not sure. That's number three. I now want everyone who got it and who knows they got it to stand up. That's right, stand up."

About half of the trainees and seemingly all those who were laughing now stand, most of their faces glowing, smiling. A few also stand with gloomy or bland expressions.

"Now everyone who got it and knows he got it but who doesn't *like* what he got, let them stand now too."

Several more people stand.

"And everyone who knows they got it but knows they had it before they ever came here stand up too."

A few more stand.

"And everyone who knows he got it but is too stubborn to stand up and admit that *it* is *it*, stand up."

Several others, smiling self-consciously or laughing, now join those standing.

"Now if you're sitting there and something I've said triggers something and you *know* you've got it, stand up."

Two more trainees stand.

"And lastly, everyone who knows he got it but wishes he hadn't, stand up."

(Laughter)

Ten more people stand. At this point fully three-quarters of the trainees are standing.

"Fine. Anyone else secretly knows he or she has got it?"

Two more stand.

"Okay. Everybody sit." And while the first group sits Michael strolls back and takes a drink from his thermos. "Now I want everyone who *knows*, who is sure he didn't get it to stand up."

Six trainees stand. Michael asks each of them, one by one, whether or not he's *sure* he didn't get it. Each assures him he's sure he didn't get it.

"All right, we'll deal with you six a little later. I'm going to ask you to sit but be sure not to forget who you are."

(Laughter)

"Okay, last category. Everyone who isn't sure whether he got it or not, stand up."

About twenty-five to thirty trainees now stand up.

"Fine. Now if when I'm talking to one of you standing, another one of you who thinks you're not sure suddenly is sure just go ahead and sit down. Marie, did you get it?" The trainer asks Marie, who is standing in the second row at the far left of the room.

"I don't know," Marie replies. "I'm not sure."

"Fine. What did you get?"

"I don't know."

"You must have got something."

"Well . . . I got that there's nothing to get . . ."

"YOU GOT IT!"

(Laughter and applause)

Marie sits, looking a little baffled, but smiling.

"All right, Larry. Did you get it?"

"I'm not sure. It seems too . . . simple, too . . . abstract."

"Fine. You got it and it seems too simple?"

"I'm not sure . . ."

"What did you get?"

"I got that, well . . . we're all machines . . . and well, we might as well relax and enjoy it."

(Laughter and applause, and Larry, suddenly smiling, sits)

"Okay. Barbara. Did you get it?"

"I'm not sure."

"Fine. What did you get?"

"Confusion. Total confusion."

"Great! Wonderful! You got total confusion. That's marvelous! What else did you get?"

"That's all. Total confusion. Murkiness. Blackness."

"That's fine, Barbara. Now let me ask you this: do you get that you got confusion?"

"Yes."

"And do you get that you didn't get clarity or laughter?"

"That's right, I didn't."

"And do you get that when you get confusion that's what you get?"

(Laughter)

"Yes."

"And that when you don't get confusion, that's what you don't get?"

"Yes."

"And that when you get what you get you get it?"

"Yes."

"Great! You got it!"

(Applause and laughter)

By this time about half of the original thirty have sat down.

"Barry? Did you get it?"

"I'm not sure. I thought I got it but everyone else seems to find it funny or marvelous and I find it depressing."

"Oh! You got it and you find it depressing!"

"I'm not sure."

"What did you get?"

"I got that we've been wasting our time hoping for something to bring us out of our mechanicalness ... there's no way out."

"You got it!"

(Laughter and applause)

"Donald? Did you get it?"

"I'm just standing to say that you've made us pay two hundred fifty dollars and four days of our lives to hear that we're all mechanical machines, that there's nothing to get, that we get what we get when we get it and not before then, and what is, is whether we like it or not, and that we've had all this all our lives and that there's nothing to get. It's the biggest ripoff I've ever heard of and ... it's also the best two hundred and fifty bucks' worth I've ever had."

(Laughter and applause)

Several of those who don't think they got it remain firm in their conviction, and Michael has to work with them for up to ten minutes (and with one for twenty minutes) before they sit down. Two or three sit with expressions implying they still haven't got it. In any case it is evident, as Michael says, that some people who get it find it's a release, while others find it's depressing—not only are they left out of the joy so many are showing, but to them it's utterly inexplicable that trainees should find it a liberating experience to be told they are machines.

But the removal of brakes is always a release, and many seem to find the experience they've just been through permits them to let go in ways they never have before; their vitality and animation during the next forty minutes gradually increases until the room is alive as never before during the training. Then Michael announces a dinner break, to be followed by his telling us all about the difference between an enlightened man and an unenlightened man, and all about sex and love and choice and decision.

Although the hotel buffet is unbelievably bad—unpalatable food that must have been carefully selected from all of the most undesirable places in the universe—the nine trainees at our big round table don't notice. Four are still floating a couple of feet off the ground, glowing and laughing and cheerfully making asses of themselves. The five others are watching with dignified restraint and suspicion: the joyful four *must* have cracked up or be faking it, pretending they got enlightened. They watch carefully, hoping to discover which.

"You know," says Tom, the bearded fellow with the beads who spent so much time arguing and now looks blissed out, "I remember now that I read in some article that *est* ends up telling us we're machines and I remember saying to myself: that can't be it, there must be a secret something beyond that. And yet, here we are and that's all there is, and suddenly it's all right."

"We're *not* machines," David says firmly from across from Tom. "I got that *whatever* is, is, and there's no sense in fighting it, but *est*'s theory that we're all machines is just nonsense, pure nonsense. There are so many holes in today's argument it looked like a sieve."

This statement is greeted with a moment of polite silence; then an older man named Hank, the one who periodically wanted to leave, says glumly, "Yes, I thought it was all . . . too abstract. I mean, he went too fast. We didn't have time to raise logical objections."

Two people, a man and a woman, begin laughing and then check themselves.

"I'm sorry," says the woman, Jennifer. "It's just that . . . well, you're right, you're absolutely *right*. I imagine the argument doesn't hold up very well to logic, but you see, those of us who laugh aren't laughing because we *believe* an argument. I don't *believe* I'm a machine. That's nonsense, right?"

"Well, that's what I think," answers Hank.

"Nonsense to *believe* I'm a machine," says Jennifer, beginning to laugh again, "but . . . but you see . . . it's just that I *experience* my mind as a machine," and she smiles and looks embarrassed.

"But why in hell is that *funny?*" David interjects sharply. "Human beings have been evolving for over one billion years —not three hundred fifty trillion years incidentally—to get beyond stimulus-response. And besides, the sort of behavioristic determinism lying behind this silly notion of our being machines went out of fashion twenty years ago."

"I wouldn't know about that, David," Jennifer replies. "All I know is that I operated for the last thirty years of my life under the belief that I had control, that I could change myself, and life has usually been . . . shit. Now I *experience*, I *experience* that I have no control, that all I can do is choose to accept what is—and I find the feeling marvelous. I understand that it makes no sense. But sense was one of the things I realize was screwing up my life."

"You know," David says, looking intently around at the faces at the table, half of them filled with joy, "it's as if you people had been *brainwashed.*" Four of them laugh. "*est* has done its job. I suppose you'll now become good little *est*ies and lead guest seminars and spend the rest of your lives *sharing* and *creating spaces* and sending Christmas cards to Werner."

Again David's outburst is met with a brief silence. Finally, Alan speaks. "What we do, we do," he says, smiling. "And if we don't do it, we don't do it."

"Gobbledygook!" David comments fiercely.

"If I do all that you say," Alan goes on mildly, "the universe will survive, won't it, David?"

"Yes. It's *you* I feel sorry for," David replies.

"But if I've been brainwashed into bliss, where is my problem?"

"You could be living freely in misery," says Tom, and he and Alan laugh.

"What happened to you when the trainer began telling us we're nothing but machines?" Tom asks David with obvious interest.

"At first I got sucked in," says David, and as soon as he begins talking about his experience, his face begins to lose some of its tension. "I mean I know that a lot of what we do and feel, especially upsets, comes out of past experiences which are more basic ... more basic to survival, one might even say. And then, long before he concluded that we must be entirely machines, I began to feel depressed. I began to feel trapped. And when he told us we were machines and that's all there is I was just numb. And people started laughing. . . . Jesus ..." David is staring at the artificial flowers in the center of the table but obviously looking deeply within at his own experience. "When people began laughing I felt ... incredible panic ... incredible panic ..."

He looks up across at Tom. He looks frightened and almost about to cry.

"There must be more to it. There *must* be more to it."

Tom looks back seriously.

"I can't help you, David. I got that that's all there is and I got a release. But you didn't get that and what you *did* get is exactly what *you* should have gotten."

David stares back.

"What do you mean, what I got is what I should have gotten?"

"Well," says Tom, frowning, "what you got ... is *there*, I mean it's what you got and nothing is ever going to change it. For you to try to get what I got or Barbara got or Hank, would be madness."

David is staring intently across at Tom. His eyes are blank, his fork is poking at some stale baloney, as his mind seems to be racing along.

"But ... what I got is that the theory is nonsense."

"Perfect," says Tom quietly. "It couldn't be any other way, could it?"

"... No ... but ... what is, is, I get that," says David, concentrating very hard, "but this business about a machine..."

"I don't think the machine business is all that important," Barbara says. "What counts is your suddenly letting go your resistance to things, letting things be as they are anyway."

David laughs sharply, then stops. His eyes briefly glow, then fade.

"Wait a minute," he says, beginning to smile, "wait a minute ... let me see ... I think I'm a machine ... right?"

"Apparently," says Alan.

"That's what's happening with me, right?"

"Yes," says Tom.

"And that's okay, right?" says David, smiling broadly.

"That's perfect," says Tom.

"I think I'm a nonmachine and that's perfect, right, and you assholes think you're machines and that's perfect for you, right?"

Everyone is smiling now and leaning toward David.

"Yes. Go on."

"So where's the problem?" David asks, smiling fully.

"You had the problem, remember?" Tom asks, puzzled.

"Oh yeah, that's right," says David. "I think you assholes are all brainwashed, right?" He laughs abruptly again. "And that too is perfect, right?"

"Right!"

"Right!"

"I GOT IT!" announces David, laughing. "We're all nonmachines, some of whom think they're machines, but we're all who we are and what we are no matter how hard we try so we might as well all relax and enjoy it."

"That's good!" says Barbara.

Then David suddenly frowns.

"But ..." he begins. "But ... [Still frowning] Ah ... [Smiling] What I'm getting now is a 'but,' right? And a 'but' is perfect, right?" He begins to laugh.

"Shit. It's simple. I've wasted all this time—four tedious, ball-breaking days—to learn that when I say 'but' I'm saying 'but.' " And he laughs.

Hank and Estelle, however, continue to sit at the table listening to the others with expressions of obvious gloom and dissatisfaction. Hank shifts his weight on his chair restlessly . . .

"The difference between the enlightened and the unenlightened man is nothing," says Michael amiably to the reassembled trainees, and they laugh, as they will with increasing frequency for the rest of the long evening. "The unenlightened man acts as the result of stimulus-response, stimulus-response, stimulus-response. The enlightened man acts as a result of stimulus-response, stimulus-response, stimulus-response. Big deal. The difference is nothing. The unenlightened man tries to do something about it. He's always doing something: when he's making love, he's thinking; when he's meditating, he's seeking enlightenment; when he's reading, he's seeking enlightenment. The enlightened man does nothing. The fully enlightened man *always* does nothing. Doing nothing is simply doing what you're doing when you're doing it. Doing nothing is simply accepting what is. What it is, whether we accept it or not, so you don't have to be too bright to be enlightened, you just come to accept what you are, accept what comes, accept what is, or, as we've been saying for ten days, take what you get .. when you get it.

"Now during the dinner break one of you asked me what all the fuss was for four days about experiencing things completely and they would disappear. Does this mean we can slowly but surely disappear our ones, twos, and threes, until eventually we've eliminated our machine mind?

"Absolutely. In theory all we have to do is re-create all our experience, fully experience our experience, and the records disappear from the stack. When we've disappeared all the records, we're mindless! [Laughter]

"Only one problem. According to the best estimates, we have about three hundred trillion tapes. [Laughter] Give or take a trillion or two. If we can eliminate, say, a *thousand* a day, we can then totally wipe the slate clean and be utterly mindless and totally liberated in just a little over eighty million years!

"But there's another advantage to fully experiencing experience as opposed to nonexperiencing experience. When you fully experience something, the record disappears and what are you left with? Space. And that's why when you fully experience something or re-create an experience you're left with a feeling of lightness. When you nonexperience something, you add to the stack and the burden you're carrying around gets heavier.

"Being enlightened is choosing what happens when it happens. Being enlightened is knowing you are what you are and aren't what you aren't and that's perfect. Being enlightened is saying yes to what happens, saying yes to your yes's and yes to your no's.

"It doesn't mean that because everything is perfect as it is we don't protest against war, or work to end poverty, or assist others who need assistance, or that we don't work to create a better society. No. Enlightenment means saying yes to what is for us, and if for us society is sick and needs changing then we choose to work to change the sick society. If what's so for us is that we fear death, then we say yes to our fear of death, we choose our fear of death and in *choosing* our fear we fully experience it. It may disappear and it may not. If it disappears we say yes to its disappearing. If we still have our fear, we say yes to our still having the fear.

"What has been transformed in you is not your fears or upsets. At least, not yet. What has been transformed is your ability to experience living so that the situations you have been trying to change or have been putting up with clear up just in the process of life itself, just in the process of choosing to let happen what happens.

"Sometimes your pains and fears and barriers will disappear and sometimes they won't. But your *experience* of them will now be totally different.

"In an experiment in California, terminal cancer patients, patients who knew they were dying and were usually in great pain unless heavily sedated, were given prescribed regular dosages of LSD over the last weeks of their lives. They all reported that the *pain* still existed, the knowledge that they were *dying* still existed, but their *experience* of the pain and of their dying had been transformed. The pain no longer bothered them. It didn't seem important. Their dying no longer bothered them. It didn't seem important. They were in complete contact with reality. They weren't hallucinating at all. Nothing had changed. They were experiencing the release of saying yes to what is.

"So too now with you. You've learned the secret those guys who spend twenty years isolated in a cave on a mountain eventually come back with: you've learned you aren't the Doer. You're the *source* and creator of all you experience, you're a God, but what you, the individual entity bouncing around inside the big universe you've created, what you do is totally out of your control.

"It's total nonsense. Total paradox. You are the source of all your experience and you don't have the least control. All you can do is choose what happens. When you learn to *want* what you get, you know what? You get what you want. From now on you'll *always* get what you want, always ... as long as you want what you get. [Laughter]

"It's all a cosmic joke, as one of you said. You don't *understand* a joke, you *get* it. So when someone outside *est* asks you about what *est* is all about, don't try to *explain* it to them. Explaining a joke is a sure way to bore people and make them think you're nuts. People either get a joke or they don't. If they don't, it's no big deal. Mankind has survived for three hundred trillion years without most people getting the joke. It'll survive till next week if you or some friend don't get it.

"If they don't get it, you know what that will mean? That they don't get it . . ."

"All right, then," says Michael a bit later to Elaine, who is seated on a chair beside him on the platform before the other trainees. "What I want you to do, Elaine, is to pretend I have here in my two hands two ice-cream cones, one chocolate, one vanilla. I want you to choose one or the other, chocolate or vanilla. Which do you choose?"

Elaine, smiling with her hands folded on her lap in front of her, replies, "Vanilla."

"Fine," says Michael. "Why did you choose vanilla?"

"I'm in the mood for vanilla."

"No," says Michael. "Here are two cones, one vanilla, one chocolate. Choose one."

"Okay," says Elaine, her smile a little nervous. "I choose vanilla."

"Fine. Why did you choose vanilla?"

"I chose vanilla because I like vanilla better than chocolate."

"No," says Michael. "Here are two ice-cream cones. Which do you choose?"

Elaine frowns. "I choose chocolate," she says.

"Good. Why do you choose chocolate?"

"I figured I'm not getting anyplace with vanilla, I'll try chocolate."

"No," says Michael firmly. "Look, here are two ice-cream cones, one vanilla and one chocolate. Choose one."

Elaine stares at Michael, at his two fists holding the imaginary cones, and then out at the audience.

"Well . . . but I *like* vanilla best!" she blurts out.

"Choose one, Elaine."

"VANILLA!"

"Great. Why did you choose vanilla?"

"Because I *like* vanilla."

"No," says Michael firmly. "That's reasonableness. Here's a chocolate cone. Here's vanilla. Choose one."

Elaine looks flushed and irritated, and she sits frozen for several seconds.

"I ... choose ... chocolate ... ," she says carefully.

"Good. *Why* did you choose chocolate?"

"I choose chocolate ... because ... I feel like eating chocolate."

"No, that's reasonableness. Here are two cones, vanilla and chocolate. Choose one."

Elaine is now clearly vexed. Many in the audience feel they know the response Michael is seeking and are squirming with impatience at Elaine's failure to come up with it. Elaine is now staring at the back of the room.

"Vanilla ... ," she says without much enthusiasm.

"Fine. *Why* did you choose vanilla?"

"I ... chose ... vanilla ... because ... I like vanilla ice cream better than any oth—"

"No! That's reasona—"

"BUT I LIKE VANILLA BETTER!"

"That's great, Elaine," says Michael. "I get that. You like vanilla ice cream better than chocolate ice cream. Right?"

"YES!"

"Fine. Here are two cones, one chocolate, one vanilla. Choose one."

"VANILLA!"

"That's great, Elaine. Now listen carefully, why did you choose vanilla?"

"I chose vanilla because I chose it!"

(Laughter and applause)

"Good. Why did you choose to come up on the stage for this demonstration?"

Elaine, looking pleased that she's escaped her torment, says, "Damned if I know."

"Why did you choose to volunteer for the demonstration?"

"Because I wanted to get as much as possible out of the training ..."

"No!" says Michael. "That's reasonableness, consideration, that's making yourself the *effect* of something. *Why* did you choose to volunteer for—"

"Because I DID!"

"Because you did what?" asks Michael.

"I chose to volunteer because I chose to volunteer!"

(Applause and laughter)

"That's very good," says Michael. "Now, Elaine, you can either stay on the platform or return to your seat with the other trainees. Choose one."

Elaine smiles.

"I choose to sit," she says, standing and moving off the platform.

"HOLD IT!" shouts Michael. "That's fine. *Why* do you choose to sit?"

Elaine stares back at him for five, ten seconds.

"It's quite simple," she says after a while and now smiling fully. "I choose to sit because ... *I choose to sit.*"

As Elaine proceeds to sit, the trainees applaud. Michael stands up and paces off to his right.

"Okay, more *est* nonsense. Anyone want to question or comment? Yes. Jack?"

"Now I know what Don was trying to tell me last weekend. I told him I was taking *est* because some friends had recommended it and he kept insisting that *I choose* to be here. At the time I pretended I understood. Now I *get* it."

"Thank you, Hank. Betsy?"

(Applause)

"Well, I *don't* get it. Elaine prefers vanilla to chocolate. Isn't that *why* she chooses vanilla?"

"It's why she chooses vanilla in the world of effect, effect, effect, in the world of unreality—code word reality—but it's *not* why people choose things in *reality*, in the realm of self-responsibility, in the realm of cause, cause, cause. In *that* realm, we *choose* things because we *choose* them."

"It seems to me a kind of trivial distinction to make," says Betsy.

"I'm afraid if the distinction between reality and unreality still seems trivial to you, Betsy, you may encounter some problems. Look. Most people say, 'I got mad because my friend lost my twenty dollars,' or, 'I ate vanilla ice cream because my palate always prefers vanilla.' They experience their friend or their body as cause and themselves as effect. It's a sure way to keep your life not working. In *est* we are cause in the matter. Our palate prefers vanilla, loves vanilla, but *we choose* ... either vanilla or chocolate; we choose what we choose, but we don't experience ourselves as simply the effect of our bodies."

"But I thought you said we were nothing but machines."

"I said *that*?" says Michael, making an expression of mock surprise. "Oh yes, I said that. And I said you were all machines because you *are* machines, and now that you get it you're *choosing* your machineness and acting as cause rather than at effect."

"Then we *do* have free will after all?" asks Betsy.

"We haven't mentioned 'will' or 'free' or 'free will' once in the training and we're not going to start now. 'Free will' is a concept and can only lead to trouble. Just *choose*, Betsy, *choose* what you get, choose what you choose, and take responsibility for what happens."

"Well, for myself, I think I'd always eat what I like. I'd probably have a thousand vanilla cones."

"That's great. If you got a vanilla cone would you choose a vanilla cone?"

"Of course."

"And if they only had chocolate cones and you got a chocolate cone, would you choose chocolate?"

Betsy stares up at Michael.

"Oh!" she says abruptly. "Now I get it," and she begins laughing.

"Why are you laughing?" Michael asks.

"I'm laughing," Betsy answers, smiling happily, "because I choose to laugh . . ."

Michael goes on to present to the trainees some of Werner's notions: about love and how people mess it up; about human beings as God who, being bored, must create games; and about the natural flow of the universe from "being" to "doing" to "having." (Most individuals, according to the latter notion, try to define themselves by what they *have*—money, cars, spouses—or by what they *do*—win races, act, manufacture plastic toys—rather than by what they in fact *are*. Being a successful ballerina, for example, begins not with having special shoes and dresses, or with doing special exercises, but with *being* a ballerina; the doing and the having will then follow from the being.) Finally, Michael leads us through a process in which we use our centers to create new experiences, and then we are given our last break before the graduation.

During the twenty-minute break a cluster of seven or ten trainees gather around Michael, who remains seated on one of the chairs. He has himself changed his "form": he now smiles and jokes with the trainees in a way he has not done prior to now. When someone tries to see what's inside the thermos he's been drinking from for two days, he pretends to hide the thermos and says sternly that only after graduation is anyone permitted to view the sacred liquid.

After several of the trainees have thanked Michael for being who he has been, Robert speaks.

"You know," he begins, "during the getting-it process about two hours ago I was really high. It was incredible. I'm beginning to come down now just a bit, though the energy in this room has been really fantastic tonight. But I was wondering whether I can expect highs like this often or whether I ought to begin preparing myself for my usual dull days."

"You don't have to prepare yourself for anything, Robert,"

says Michael, sipping from his thermos. "Your dull days will come whether you prepare for them or not, and your really high days will come only when you *don't* prepare for them."

"Yeah, but that business about being God has me a bit confused. What does our high this evening have to do with playing games?"

"Actually it really has to do with letting go of games that weren't working. Your getting it was a kind of temporary release from taking your mind's unworking games seriously. In actuality, each of us, as the sole creator of our universe, is a God, and because we have created all, everything is as important as everything else. When we're fully in touch with what already is and accept what is as more important than what isn't, then all games are over. There's nothing to do, nowhere to go, everything is perfect. Some guy said in an enlightenment poem that after he got *satori*, 'how superb a cup of tea!'" Michael smiles, sips his liquid and makes an exaggerated look of intoxicated pleasure. Then he frowns.

"But we Gods get bored with this perfection," he goes on, "and so we always end up pretending that something which *isn't* is more important than what is, and that's a game. As soon as you and I decide that being over there by the blackboard is more important that being where we are now, then we can have a race. As long as we're sitting here feeling perfect, being fully aware of our being Creator, then all is equally important. There's nothing to do, no game to play, we can sit for a while in bliss examining our navels. But we get bored. We decide to begin playing again. 'I'll beat you to the men's room,' I say and the game is on. When we begin playing we're back on the roller coaster."

Robert is frowning. Someone starts to ask another question and stops. Robert then says:

"You mean we could get off the roller coaster by staying in touch with . . . well, that everything is perfect the way it is."

"That's right. I know it sounds groovy, but being God gets boring. You notice that all the gods in Greek and Norse mythology are always taking human form to play games. So do Krishna and Shiva. Even Jesus is seen as God taking a temporary human form."

"So how are we supposed to play?" asks Hank. "It seems to me you're implying we should create an imaginary world."

"You keep forgetting: the world *is* imaginary," says Michael, looking briefly at a note delivered to him by the training supervisor. "The only question is who is going to do the imagining. Most people passively absorb the imaginary structures and game rules of others. The wise man creates his own. All games, all goals, all events are the creation of imagination. You can accept the world as others have created it, accept their goals and rules and play their games, or you can consciously create your own. In both cases, however, you and you alone are responsible for everything that happens."

"It bothers me," says Hank, "that you give such great power to the imagination."

"We don't give it. The power's there, being used every second whether we will it or not."

"But what about man's search for enlightenment or Ultimate Truth or God?" asks Tom. "Are you saying those are all worthless?"

"No," says Michael. "The search for Enlightenment or Reality with a capital R, for God with a big G, for Ultimate Truth is an interesting game ... until it's won. It's interesting until one has grasped Enlightenment, Reality, God, or Ultimate Truth. Then, as soon as you have, you find *that* game is over. If you then marry your insight you find that you're living with illusion. Maybe you don't notice it, but your neighbors do: 'Whatever does he *see* in her (or him)?' they say. What you decide is Ultimate Truth probably seems to your neighbor to be a trivial illusion."

"That's depressing," says Tom.

"Not at all," says Michael. "What we humans want is interesting problems and games, no more, no less. Not pleasures, not truths, not moral codes, not a state of happiness, but inter-

esting games. Mind, body, spirit: all love games. The trouble
with most humans is that they live in an imaginary world
where the desire for games doesn't exist as a conscious desire;
it must always come disguised as 'pursuit of truth,' 'a groovy
experience,' 'a meaningful relationship,' or 'an adventure.'
But there are no truths, or groovy experiences or relationships
or adventures without rules, goals, opponents, allies, and
cheering spectators: without games."

"I suppose the monk and the mystic then are playing
games?" asks Robert.

"The best, the best. Advancing along the Path, being beaten
back, making a sudden leap forward, even 'winning,' although
most mystics discover that 'winning' or 'having won' loses its
interest and they slip back into mountain-climbing up the Path
to score again."

"But what about those who are really enlightened?" asks
Tom. "Those who've really gotten it, people like don Juan or
Ramakrishna or Baba Ram Das, those who have entered what
I call the pathless path?"

"Well," says Michael. "They differ from the average human
primarily in that they don't play the same games over and
over, are never bored, and are continually creating entirely
new universes."

"Then they still compete?"

"Oh yes. Human life in any meaningful sense is impossible
without playing games, without contest. But they don't live
with the illusion that they are competing for anything worth
winning or *against* anyone other than an imaginary creation of
themselves."

"So to you," asks Hank, "I'm just part of your creation?"

"For sure. A most pleasant and intelligent creation."

"My intelligence you attribute to yourself?"

"Of course. I alone experience your intelligence. Without me
your intelligence doesn't exist."

"That's modest of you."

"I also create your stupidity."

"Thanks."

"Your stupidity for me. You create your own stupidity for yourself and the two stupidities rarely overlap."

"Then I *do* exist separate from you?"

"Sometimes," says Michael, standing, as the break is about over, "when I'm in the mood . . ."

Soon the trainees are joined by a hundred other *est* graduates who come especially for the occasion to be there and later to do a personality profile with one of the new graduates. This last part of the training is a high time for almost all the trainees, even for most of those who were glum or bewildered during the "getting it" at the end of the anatomy of the mind.

The graduation itself takes place in another room where each trainee does a personality profile, meets personally with the trainer, and receives a little book of aphorisms and a thank-you note from Werner. But in some sense the training ends before the trainees shift rooms, when Michael tells the trainees he'd like to say a personal word.

"For two days now," he says, looking as bright-eyed, alive, and high as the trainees, "I've been playing the role of trainer and you've been playing the role of trainee. And now I'm going to step down from the platform and return to playing the game of Michael, God pretending He's a human, interacting with you other Gods, also pretending you're humans. All of us will occasionally also play the role of God pretending to be an asshole. [Laughter]

"What I'd like to do now that I end the game of trainer," he says, stepping off the platform down onto the ballroom floor, "is to acknowledge both for me this weekend and on behalf of Don during last weekend, that all during these four days *you* have been training *us*. I wouldn't be where I am now if it weren't for each one of you and the spaces you've created for me during this training. I want you to know that for *me* you've been the trainer for this training and I want to thank you. I also want to say . . . I got it . . ."

A NOTE TO THE READER

The est *training, per se, doesn't exist. It is an absolutely unique* individual *experience. To work, it depends entirely on a person's being there with two hundred and fifty other people, listening, sharing, and suffering,* doing *the processes instead of reading about them, creating one's* own *experience instead of reading another's creation. The* est *training certainly cannot exist in any book. Through 1976 over 100,000* est *trainings have existed, one for each trainee or graduate who goes through an actual training. Your training cannot occur until you put your sole in the room, follow instructions, and take what you get.*

Part 2

"SO WHAT?"

"*Failure is always in the eyes of the beholder and each Master can only help us one step at a time along the Path to Enlightenment. For example, I once knew a man who, when he first began seeking liberation, thought that when he lost a game of chess he had failed.*"

"*That's typical of all of us.*"

"*After studying for two years with a famous Zen master he thought that when he won the game he had failed.*"

"*I see.*"

"*Still not satisfied, he studied for a year and a half with the great Sufi sage Narsufin and learned that when he lost but felt good about losing he had failed.*"

"*That's very good.*"

"*But then he went on to the Himalayas for three years and learned from the great Yogi Mayarishi that when he won but felt guilty about it he had failed.*"

"*That's tremendous.*"

"*Finally, he studied with Werner.*"

"*What happened?*"

"*He learned at last how to develop his pawns.*"

5

The Postgraduate Roller Coaster, or What Do You Do With It Once You've Gotten It?

"I met a holy man in the Himalayas who could see into the future, and he was training his disciples so they could do the same."

"Oh well," said Werner, "anybody can do that. Our way is much harder."

"What's that?"

"We get people to see the present."

"Before you took est life was a roller coaster; sometimes you were way up there and then whoosh!, you would dive down into a valley and be pretty low. Up and down. After the training, though, you know what life is really like. Now for you life is really a roller coaster: way up one day, way down the next. Up and down.

"There's a small difference though. Life is still a roller coaster, but now you get to be inside the car instead of always lying on the track."

—FROM AN *est* GRADUATE SEMINAR

Three days after the last Sunday of the training, the vast majority of the new *est* graduates gather in another hotel meeting room for their "post-training seminar."[1] It's like reunion time at a fraternity: everyone is smiling, shaking hands, embracing. Faces are aglow. Most present feel a great closeness to the others, who have shared the ordeal of the training and its exchanged intimacies. When Michael enters he is greeted with an enthusiastic standing ovation. Guests of the graduates are also in the room, but they soon leave to attend their own special guest seminar. For the first forty minutes of this session (half with the guests present) the graduates share their experiences since graduation. Michael simply calls on someone, who stands, shares, and sits. The acknowledging applause on this night is often lengthy and loud, and the many "in" jokes bring explosions of laughter, which must be baffling to the guests.

Diane is one of the first to speak. She stands flushed and happy and laughs once before she begins.

"I want you to know that after the training early Monday morning—you know, about three A.M.—a man approached me as I was walking toward my apartment and he said something stupid to me and I hit him! I hit him! [Laughter] You never saw such an expression on a man's face in your life! [Laughter] He seemed to be saying to himself what's New York City coming to if a man can't insult a woman at three in the morning without getting belted! [Laughter]

"I want you also to know that ... let's see ... Tuesday night a man I'd just met a few hours before kissed me and WOW! I mean I got it! [Laughter] And he got it too! He said later that if he'd known *est* was all about kissing he would have signed up long ago!"

(Laughter and applause)

Richard, tall, intense, a man who raised many objections on the fourth day:

"I'm a dentist and I felt the stupidest part of the training was that definition of the mind you kept repeating over and over last Sunday. This morning I was working on this patient

I've had for years—the only guy I know who no pain-killer seems to work on. I mean I usually shoot a year's supply of Novocain into his gums and still every time I pry open his jaw he screams.

"So this morning I was telling him about the *est* training and I told him about the definition of the mind, you know, 'the mind is a linear arrangement of multisensory total records of successive moments of now.' And I bet him a dollar he couldn't memorize those fifteen simple words before I'd finished drilling out his cavity. 'Say it to me again,' he asked, and I told him the definition of the mind again. And just before I started drilling I repeated it again slowly ... and after ten seconds I repeated it again. After I was half done and he had to spit, he asked me to recite it again and just before I drilled I did. Twice more I said it, drilling away at the biggest cavity the poor guy had had in years. Not a peep of pain out of him for fifteen minutes. When I'm done he looks up bright-eyed and although his mouth is swollen with the normal Novocain I'd given him and he talks as if his mouth were filled with a hundred marshmallows he says: 'I gah ih! The mine ith a multilinear record of total then-thory arrangements of moments of thucthethive nows!' [Laughter]

"He looked so pleased I was wondering if when he takes the training you could maybe change the definition so he won't be disillusioned ..."

Jennifer, well-dressed, and looking quite happy despite what she says:

"I'm confused. I guess I was confused during most of the training and I'm confused now. I was feeling great Monday, really great, and yesterday I was more depressed than I've been in years. This morning was great and this afternoon is horrible. I knew life was supposed to be a roller coaster but I mean really, since *est* it's a bit too much. I don't really see how I can have gotten it and got as depressed as I did yesterday."

"I've got a secret for you, Jennifer," Michael responds. "If you want to feel very, very depressed, all you have to do is try to recapture a very high high. If you'd like to get high just *try* to feel the worst depression you've ever felt. Life is going to be a roller coaster no matter what, and if you want to spend a lot of time diving to the depths, just try to hang on to the highs. If you think you'd prefer to avoid the extreme downs then you know what? You'd better start choosing them and stop resisting them. If you're confused, stay with it, choose to be confused, accept it, observe. Same with depression. My guess is you're running away from what's so for you and resistance is the road to ruin, or more accurately, resistance is a sure way to speed the roller coaster, especially downhill."

Raymond, short, thickset, graying, wearing a suit with a maroon turtleneck sweater:

"This is only the second time I've said anything since the training began. I'm afraid I spent most of the four days wondering why I was there and what the hell was going on. I slept a lot and when I did stay awake not much of it made any sense to me.

"And yet last Sunday something happened. I don't know what, but *something* happened. I got it all right. The first three days of this week—I'm a vice-president in this plastic firm I work at—and these last three days I've spent letting everybody in the entire plant know exactly what was what. Guys I should have straightened out years ago I straightened out. One secretary that seems to spend half the day breathing on her nails since I spoke to her Monday afternoon hasn't stopped typing. When one of the other vice-presidents and I and two other executives met, I found myself saying exactly what was so and everybody looked at me as if I were setting off firecrackers in church. This afternoon just before I left to come to this seminar the president of our firm called me into his office. He said to me, 'Ray, I want you to know I appreciate what you've been doing but I have one piece of advice: if you're planning to keep up this *est* business—and I hope you do—I want you, before it's too late, to begin taking karate and kung fu.' "

(Laughter and applause)

Andy, young, good-looking, wearing jeans and a tee shirt:

"All last week I was looking forward to turning on Sunday night after graduation. During the training I had almost an obsession about breaking my grass fast but I didn't. Then Sunday I was free but I was too high to want to turn on. Monday too. Tuesday night I didn't feel like it but some friends were over and passing joints so I took a few tokes. Well, you know what happened? The fuckin' joints brought me down. Pot was a downer. What do you make of that? Now I'm stuck with sixty dollars' worth of good dope I no longer want; I'm too cheap to give it away and too uptight to deal it. Since *est* ruined the dope I wondered if *est* would reimburse me the sixty dollars?"

Marcia, smiling:

"For years I've been saying someday I'm going to clean off my desk. I want to report that *est* works. This morning, after three days of being a graduate, I managed at last to see the face of the left rear corner of my desk. It's stained black! I never knew!"

Nancy, the woman who in the training complained about male chauvinism:

"I can't say I'm turning cartwheels about it but . . . I've left my husband. I entered the training feeling that if I got it I'll leave my husband and I took the training and I got it and I've left him. The big thing is that I couldn't leave him before the training because I had to be *right*—he had to be the villain and leave. Now I don't have to be right. It doesn't make any difference who seems right. Now all I want is a relationship that'll work and my marriage has been the most consistently nonworking relationship in history for five years.

"I want to say also that I take full responsibility for the shit I put up with for five years . . . ah . . . I mean the shit I *created* for five years. I had a period of bitterness this morning when I looked around the crummy one-room apartment I've moved into. I found myself blaming my husband for the crummy apartment! When I got in touch with the stupidity of that, I also realized that almost everything else I tend to blame him for is equally my responsibility. It was also my responsibility that I stayed with him. Well, two days ago I uncreated my marriage. I can't say I'm turning cartwheels about it, but ... it's what I got ...."

Tom, bearded, bright-eyed, shares for a minute and then concludes:

"... So I was really feeling enlightened ... way, way up there on the sixth or seventh plane moving through this world of Buddhas on West Fourth Street, smiling away, wondering vaguely why everyone wasn't showering flowers in my path or bowing or something, and vaguely hearing the voices of people walking on the sidewalks with me and really blissed out, and this voice suddenly shouts, 'Hey, ASSHOLE!' and you know what, I turned because I figured somebody was calling *me*."

(Laughter)

The training is complete, the trainee is now a graduate, and *est* lives on. He has been informed at the mid-training, on the fourth day of the training, and again at the post-training of a graduate seminar especially available for him. At the post-training he is urged to enroll, and most do; 75 percent of *est* graduates living within seventy miles of a city offering graduate seminars enroll in at least one such seminar.[2] The graduate is urged to bring guests to such seminars for their sakes as well as his own: they are told that bringing guests is a manifestation of a person's willingness to share and to commit himself, to participate in life.

At the beginning of 1976 *est* offered seven graduate seminar series—Be Here Now, What's So, The Body, About Sex, Self-Expression, *est* and Life, and Child-Parent—in various major cities in the United States. The three most frequently offered (and hence frequently taken) graduate seminar series are Be Here Now, What's So, and About Sex. Over the five-year history of *est*, Werner has expanded these graduate offerings steadily, revised the curriculum occasionally, and tended to increase slightly the number of special graduate seminars available, such as Making Relationships Work I and II and special Graduate Review Seminars.

According to *est*:

> Werner created the *est* Graduate Seminar Program to provide an experience and a supportive environment from which graduates can come into the world, take responsibility for its condition, and experience and contribute to the expansion of love, health, happiness and full self-expression through conscious participation, complete communication, acceptance of what is and the willingness to take responsibility for their lives, *est* and the universe.[3]

The essential features of most of these seminars are the same: extensive sharing of the graduates either with the whole roomful of other graduates or with each other on a one-to-one basis; some new data; and a large number of new processes, some similar to those of the training but most completely new and occasionally involving writing. The seminars are led by individuals who have moved through the training, have assisted at many trainings, have led guest seminars, and have been specially trained to lead both guest and graduate seminars. In some cases the seminar leader may be a trainer or someone in training to become one.

The mood of a typical graduate seminar session is closest to the last day of the training: people are relaxed with each other and with the leader, and the atmosphere is open and high. The sharing is unusually frank; the "space" is experienced by most as completely safe.

Most graduates indicate that the value of the seminar series depends not so much on its ostensible data content or on the processes introduced, but on the sharing on an intimate basis with others. One graduate summed it up in a seminar by saying, "I've just realized the reason everything Werner does works so well, why these seminars work so well for me, why just being on a bus with other *est* graduates is always so high: Werner has created safe spaces where we can all just be who we are. The whole thing is just safe space!"

Certainly that is an essential factor in the great success *est* has in assisting people to totally "transform their ability to experience living." But the contents of the individual seminars direct these "open spaces" into various specific areas.

Be Here Now, for example, is essentially about handling upsets. Its stated purpose is "to expand your ability to experience being where you are right now, with nothing added . . . and to enable you to move in the direction of experiencing life totally in present time."[4] The graduates learn to list *all* of their persisting recurring upsets, analyze when and where they occur and under what circumstances, and experience precisely what it is they experience at such times. Werner has designed each of the ten sessions to achieve a specific purpose, and a single seminar may not in fact mention the word *upset* more than once or twice.

The Be Here Now seminar, as its name implies, also introduces the graduates to further processes designed to assist them to be attuned to the present moment. In any case, the data, processes, and sharing are extensions and elaborations of elements of the standard training. Since the graduate is now in a new space, at the beginning of a new mode of experiencing life, what he experienced one way in the first four days of the training before he "got it" is now experienced differently.

The purpose of the What's So seminar series is "to support your ability to experience out the unconscious blocks and resistance to confronting the incomplete cycles in your life."[5] One of the assumptions of the training is that our lives are often run by unconscious decisions taken years ago and are thus burdened by hundreds of incompleted relationships, events, transactions. Werner Erhard himself is a rather remarkable example of someone who went back in his own life and "cleaned up" noncompleted relationships. He recontacted his first wife and their four children twelve years after he left them. Amazingly, he was able to reestablish a good working relationship with all five. All have taken the *est* training, and two of the children are currently living with Werner and his second wife and family.

The purpose of the About Sex seminar series is to "allow you to locate and dissolve any barriers between you and communicating about sex [and] to expand your ability to experience yourself as the cause of your sexual experience and not the effect."[6] In three of the first five sessions, films of various aspects of normal human and animal sexuality are shown, films that act to dislodge graduates from areas of resistance and stuckness in their individual abilities to communicate about sex and to take responsibility for their own sexual experience. The films stimulate vigorous discussion on the one hand and then intimate sharing on the other. By the fifth session, graduates are sharing personal sexual experiences with amazing frankness, and barriers to communication are clearly dissolved.

In *est*, what works is accepting what is, which in turn leads to "the expansion of love, health, happiness and full self-expression." In evaluating human sexual behavior the same standard is used: does the behavior "work"—does it manifest love, health, happiness, and full self-expression? Thus, having sexual relations with many others might work if those relations increase the love, health, happiness, and self-expression of those involved; or it might not work if the individual fails to relate to *anyone* intimately in a loving and joyful way. In most cases the seminar leader warns against the danger of people using their beliefs in "freedom" and "openness" as possible rationalizations of one's failure to relate oneself wholly to anyone. But in general all forms of human sexuality are shared and acknowledged without criticism: heterosexuality, homosexuality, masturbation, and all manifestations of each.

The other four graduate seminar series—The Body, Self-Expression, Parent-Child, and *est* in Life—are structured similarly to the three more frequently offered seminars already described. The Body aims at permitting the graduate to "locate, experience, and dissolve areas of blocked consciousness in the body" and to "enable you to move in the direction of experiencing your body as buoyant, radiant and alive."[7] The purpose of the Self-Expression series is to get the graduate "in touch with who he is *afraid* he is so that he will be free to be who he really is."[8] The Parent-Child series provides an opportunity for both parents and children to view and dissolve the patterns and belief systems that are unconsciously influencing their behavior and blocking the full experience of their love for each other. The *est* in Life series centers on getting graduates to take responsibility for dissolving the barriers they have to getting the job done.

In addition to these structured seminar series, *est* has offered over the years special graduate "events" and "workshops" aimed at specific problems or specific *est* graduates. There are Educator Workshops and special workshops for clergy and for psychotherapists. Werner has also videotaped two day-long events titled Making Relationships Work I and II, which are periodically presented in various parts of the country. Finally, each year Werner creates "special graduate events," which are usually designed to achieve certain specific effects: to aid the graduates in some way in their movement toward greater aliveness.

It is difficult to evaluate the results of the training and the postgraduate seminars except in a subjective way. We know, of course, that the sharing during the post-training and graduate seminars is *not* representative of all those who graduate from the training. Those who speak are generally filled with their experience of the success for them of the *est* training. Those who are less enthusiastic tend to share less often, and some graduates don't choose to attend the seminars at all, in a few cases because they think that the training was valueless.

Only two professional studies have yet been made of the results of the *est* training, one by Behaviordyne[9] and a second by Robert Ornstein and his associates.[10] Neither is in any sense inclusive, but both indicate that the vast majority of *est* graduates report quite favorably about the training.

The Behaviordyne study indicates that in general the majority of those graduates surveyed manifested "definite improvement in self-image," were "less anxious and dependent," and exhibited "fewer guilts and fears." This study, which involved ninety-three graduates in 1973, did not use a control group, nor was it able to get a truly representative or random sample of graduates.[11]

The study by Robert Ornstein and his associates was more extensive. The "*est* Outcome Study" sent out a major questionnaire, with 680 questions, to a random sample of 2,000 graduates. Graduates were asked to assess their general experience of the training on a scale of 1 (very unfavorable) to 7 (very favorable). Over *half* the respondents gave the training the highest possible score (7), the overall mean was about 6, and, if 4 can be assumed to be a rating of neutrality, almost 90 percent of the respondents indicated their experience was favorable (5, 6, or 7).[12]

Essentially, the respondents reported "strong, positive health changes since taking the *est* standard training, especially in the areas of psychological health and those illnesses with a large psychosomatic component."[13] The graduates reported most changes in their general physical and mental health; in headaches, hypertension, and sleep difficulties; in need for medication, drugs, and alcohol; in their energy level, work satisfaction, and significant relationships; and in numerous specific physical health problems often related to psychosomatic problems (for example, allergies, digestive problems, back pains, smoking, and sexual difficulties). The majority of respondents reported improvements in these areas. Only 7 percent reported "overall negative changes in physical or mental health," and

the study uncovered no evidence that *est* had harmed anyone.[14]

Ornstein's letter acknowledges that his study demonstrates
not that people's health changes as the result of *est*, but only
that they definitely say it does. Although his study is large
enough to be representative of the *est* graduates of that time
(1973), it wasn't designed to isolate the *training* as the vari-
able that has modified the health of the graduates, nor does it
eliminate the "placebo effect"—people reporting positively
about *anything* they are questioned about. However, a follow-
up analysis of the Ornstein data by Earl Babbie and Donald
Stone demonstrates that the beneficial effects of the training
reported seem to last or even *grow* over time, and that the
reports are as reliable as such reports can ever be. Yet they, too,
acknowledge that the highly favorable implications of the study
are not "proof."[15] In effect, we are left with what we can learn
from talking with any group of graduates: most report positive
changes from the training.

My own informal sampling of nearly a hundred *est* graduates is representative *only* of those who feel they have gained
positive value from *est*. My estimate is that at any given
moment, some 80 percent of *est* graduates would report that
they have benefited from taking *est*. Although I have given
emphasis in my dramatization to the "getting-it" process of the
fourth day, it should be understood that the benefits of the
training extend well beyond that. For one thing, many graduates later report they didn't get it at all during the training but
did get it one, two, or three months, or even a year, *after* the
training—while in a minor motorcycle accident, while mailing
a letter, while stuck in a traffic jam. Probably less than half the
trainees would say that their getting-it experience was exhilarating or that they had what we might choose to call an enlightenment experience.

Getting it means something unique for each individual, and
the permanent residual value of the training contains many

elements. In interviews with scores of those graduating over a two-year period I have found that graduates usually report one or more of the following five beneficial results:

First, the vast majority of graduates report in a general way that their lives are "better": they have more energy and enjoy things more. "Nothing overwhelms me as before," writes Marcia Seligson. "Nothing seems tragic or permanent; my energy —always high—seems limitless these days. I am more direct with people, and have a stronger sense of living in the moment."[16] Another graduate writes:

> I DISCOVERED TREMENDOUS ENERGY. . . . I see things differently—standing in the same mire, to be sure, but looking 180° outside my usual viewpoint. There is an energy releasing clarity to my vision, even when I am bogged down in the same old stuff.[17]

Second, some graduates report that persistent, recurring physical symptoms (such as stuttering, arthritis, asthma, sinus problems, back pain, other specific bodily pains, headaches, allergies) disappear. They attribute the disappearance either to the direct result of some specific *est* process or to the general influence of *est*. Says an executive at Columbia Pictures:

> "I'd been on five Valiums a day for a bad back. In the training I got to look at why I'd chosen to give myself that condition, in a concentrated way that I'd never done before, even in five years of analysis. Now I never take the pills and my back seldom pains me."[18]

The third beneficial result graduates report is an increased sense of responsibility. Taking responsibility for one's life necessitates the abandoning of a large number of destructive psychological games that were tied to the assumption that *other* people control our lives and are to blame for our failures. This new-found experiencing of self-responsibility, which some feel is the most important feature of *est*, results in clearing up debilitating relationships, especially those between husband and wife, by either improving them dramatically or ending them. The stuckness ceases as valuable relationships are renewed and valueless ones abandoned. *All* relationships benefit. Valerie Harper, of "Rhoda" television fame, has said:

After I took the *est* training, I continued with a graduate seminar and did a review training with Werner. Really, it has been the most valuable thing I've done in my life. All my relationships changed—I've experienced my parents as loving people, have experienced differently friends, family, coworkers, everything. It's like a peeling away, layers of junk being lifted. I feel like myself, and I've lightened up incredibly.[19]

Another graduate has said:

Since the training I've been more direct with everyone and I've been more approachable. By being more direct I've learned that the success of my communication depends as much on my willingness to *be* with people as on my ability to articulate my thoughts accurately and clearly.[20]

A successful woman executive discovered soon after completing the training that she hated the job she'd been working at for fourteen years and didn't like living with her husband of ten years. She says:

I kept quiet about my feelings for about a week and then I simply quit my job. Fourteen years and I quit. That evening I told my husband I'd quit, and he began complaining about my irresponsibility. After I'd let him run on for about ten minutes I told him I was leaving him too. He got even more upset. He said I could quit my job if I wanted after all, but that I couldn't leave him. I told him people were permitted to quit husbands just like jobs and I was done.

Up until that night he'd had nothing but contempt for *est*, never was interested in taking the training at all. Later that evening as I was quietly packing he came in and announced that he had phoned the *est* office and was taking the training. I asked him why. He said it was cheaper than hiring a lawyer for a divorce.

I still left.[21]

Fourth, many graduates report that they are less often run by the "yamayama" of their minds—they are more in touch with their own actual sensations, feelings, emotions, and other elements of their experience and better able to express them to others. Learning to be in touch with and to accept their actual experience—"what is"—allows them not to be run by upsets as frequently as before the training and helps them to express honestly what they feel. What *is* becomes more important than what was or what ought to be.

One graduate reports that "arguments with people changed from scary confrontations to opportunities to get to the root of grudges, bad feelings and misunderstandings I had been carrying around for years."[22] Another writes:

Another interesting thing happened a few months after the training, in June on the very first day of my massage class at the Joy of Movement Center in Cambridge. I wound up telling my students things about my former marriages, sex, abstinence, and about my grown children. And it all came out very natural and spontaneous. And these were things I wouldn't ordinarily tell even to my intimate friends. And right in the middle of my relating these thoughts and experiences, all of the class moved up a foot closer to me, smiling.[23]

Valerie Harper has said:

> The first thing I want to say about *est* is that almost all the effort has gone out of my life. I used to be in constant tension—I would struggle, strain and sweat to make things happen. Since I took the training, I've suddenly seen all the tension and the working-at-things, and I'm giving it up.[24]

These reported benefits of the *est* training are obviously not found in all graduates. Many single out only one or two as being particularly true for them. A small number indicate that the training was of no value. Since the only professional studies of *est* graduates yet made are not conclusive, an objective person is left with no *measurable* criterion to judge the results of the training other than that which the *est* corporation uses: namely, the number of graduates who take graduate seminars and the number of new individuals signing up for the training. Since both the percentage of graduates enrolling in seminars and the rate at which people sign up for the training have been increasing steadily since *est* was first presented in 1971, *est* can reasonably believe that the results of the training are quite positive. Whether in fact it is the *training* that is successful or *est*'s selling of the training cannot, however, be determined on the basis of the evidence. The only criterion the objective person is left with, then, is his own experience of the *est* graduates he meets or reads about.

I have left the fifth reported result of the training until the very end; because I consider it the most important, and because of its controversial nature, it will need a chapter of its own.

6

"Getting It," or Is Nothing Really Something?

Oboko, who didn't achieve enlightenment until he was in his fifties, wrote on that memorable day:

> *The moon's the same old moon,*
> *The flowers exactly as they were,*
> *My mind still goes on my mind,*
> *Yet see me glimmer on the pond*
> *And waver, yellow in the wind.*

When Nonoko finally achieved enlightenment, he wrote the following poem:

> *Why, it's only the movement of my eyes!*
> *And here I've been looking for it far and wide!*
> *Awakened at last, I find myself*
> *Not so bad after all!*

Werner Erhard has created in *est* a program that may be seen as in many ways the culmination to date of the "Easternization of America," a process that first became notable in the late fifties and early sixties. *est* has been described as "the logical extension of the whole human potential movement."[1] It is remarkable not only because of its phenomenal growth but also because *est* states that in only two weekends one can "get it"—by implication to some people at least, have an enlightenment experience. More important, for a surprising percentage of trainees *est* delivers on its promise.

Although the *est* organization always talks about "getting it" and prior to an individual's taking the training leaves the meaning of the phrase vague, Werner himself has said in one interview that "what [the graduates] get is an experience of enlightenment."[2]

Jerry Rubin writes that in *est* he "experienced a mini-satori. I got outside myself and looked at myself, seeing myself as another person might see me."[3] Liza Schwartzbaum, writing more emotionally, said:

> On the fourth day of the training, after a roller coaster week of manic elation and depression and after three training days of fear and pain and difficulty and bone-crunching boredom—on the fourth day I GOT IT!!!! In a brilliantly maneuvered flash my mind actually blitzed out. A rush of hollowness swept from my head down to my feet—like a cartoon of enlightenment—and in that instant I experienced it, NOTHINGNESS. . . .
>
> I knew, and I know and I carry a remnant sense of that instant of nothing-which-is-everything to all of my life now. For that, I appreciate profoundly the training which set up that experience for me.[4]

My own experience of getting it was different each time I took the training. The first time getting it was depressing, but the second time—four months later—I experienced a marvelously joyful, exhilarating, and long-lasting release—what might be called an enlightenment experience.

When we understand how Werner came to create the *est* training we will see even more clearly how central to the training is the getting it. Werner has explained that after a decade of immersing himself in many of the leading consciousness-expanding disciplines available—scientology, Mind Dynamics, Subud, gestalt therapy, Zen, Hinduism—he underwent an experience he has described as "catalytic," an "enlightenment experience."[5] Appropriately for an American guru, he had his enlightenment experience while zooming along in his car on a typical American freeway. About a month later, he says, "I got up and did the Training. I started *est*."[6]

Although it is tempting to argue that *est* was created so that Werner could make money, the argument founders on the fact that making money has never been a problem for Werner. There's little doubt in my mind that Werner must have had some sort of extraordinary experience to have created his training. No salesman would have dared to create anything like the *est* Standard Training. One can point forever at all the various processes, notions, techniques, and practices Werner has apparently borrowed from those disciplines in which he immersed himself, but the *est* training remains absolutely unique. It could have been created only by someone with complete confidence that he knew not what people think they want (what the salesman looks for) but what makes lives work, what permits people to escape from the prison they don't even know they inhabit. Werner experienced release from the tyranny of his mind, and the training creates for others a similar releasing experience. Although there are other ways in which the *est* training transcends the elements from which it is formed, the getting-it process of the fourth day—Werner's efforts to "blow people's minds"—is the most important.

Werner describes his own enlightenment experience as follows:

All my life I had been adding information to my store of information; I had been adding "experience" (what I really mean is records of experience to my store of records of experience), with the hope that something would happen in which I would either get to a critical mass and there would be an explosion or I'd find *the* secret, you know? And what happened that day was not any new information at all, but the system in which my information was contained was touched, so suddenly I went from knowing these four billion things to knowing a totally different four billion things. In other words, in one moment I knew nothing and came to know everything. A little unhumble to say that; you have to take that in the spirit in which it's meant. But literally, I knew nothing, I mean I went through this period where I absolutely didn't know anything, because I could see that every piece of information which I contained, even the information in my cells about how to function, were contained within a system that *precluded* aliveness. And my entire system of knowing—not what I knew, but the system with which I knew—dropped away and I came out of it on the other side having experienced literally nothing . . . so suddenly, like finding out *everything* in an instant.[7]

This description of his enlightenment experience indicates why Werner feels that 75 percent of what trainees get from the training happens on the fourth day, and why the anatomy of the mind is central to *est*.

But it is important to distinguish in this discussion between "getting it" and what is meant by an "enlightenment experience."[*] No one in *est* ever promises trainees enlightenment from the training, although Werner himself indicates that that's what graduates get. They do promise "getting it," and since the *est* trainer talks about enlightenment just after many of the trainees have had a joyful liberating experience of getting it, it is natural for these trainees to equate their getting it with enlightenment. But the trainer goes on to convince dozens of other trainees that they've gotten it even though they find what

[*] The distinction made here between "getting it" and "enlightenment" is my own, as is the description of each experience; Werner would probably say they are the same, and would not necessarily describe them as I have.

they got depressing or trivial or confusing. It is misleading to equate the experience of someone who feels gloom, anger, resentment, and disappointment during the getting-it period with that of someone who explodes into laughter at the cosmic joke and feels "high" for the next three days. Both persons may, as *est* maintains, have "gotten it"; but using language the way it is normally used, we cannot say that both have had an "enlightenment experience." Such an experience necessarily involves certainty, light, and lightness; the universe becomes clear and bright, and life becomes lighter. As a Zen master once put it, after enlightenment everything is exactly as it was before, except two feet off the ground.

Yet according to Werner, all trainees "get it," by which he means that at some time in the training (usually on the fourth day) they all break free from their identification with their minds and bodies and glimpse who they really are, which is actually who they have been all along. Says Werner, "The person de-identifies with his mind, de-identifies with his body; he de-identifies with his emotions, he de-identifies with his problems, he de-identifies with his maya, he begins to see that he is not the Play."[8] With this deidentification the person discovers the essence of the drama which is simply himself. "Self is all there is," says Werner. "I mean, that's it. We are trying to accomplish what is already so, that's why it is so easy. What is already so is ... you are."[9] The wall separating the trainees from who they actually are is partially disintegrated during the getting-it process. For some trainees only a few bricks are crumbled; for others, the wall may for the moment be totally demolished, resulting in what is here called an enlightenment experience. But in both cases, according to Werner, whether the trainee feels elated or depressed, there has been a fundamental change: the context in which the trainee experiences experience will be different. As the trainer says, the trainee's life has been turned around one hundred and eighty degrees.

What Werner calls "getting it" and says occurs for all trainees whether elated or not, and what I call an enlightenment experience and find occurs for only some of the trainees, is in any case the experience of the being letting go of his mind and body, ceasing to identify himself with the machine mind, and experiencing all as "self." Most of those who experience exhilaration on the fourth day of the training probably don't have the slightest idea why they feel so high, but Werner's explanation of the process seems sensible: even in the act of saying, "We're all machines" the trainee is in fact dissociating himself from his machine, his mind, and this dissociation is his enlightenment experience.

It is important to understand what Werner means by "getting it" and the way an enlightenment experience occurs, because the danger of reading about the *est* training is to see it as a series of intellectual positions that must be evaluated on the basis of their internal logic and external relation to other widely held intellectual positions. That approach has as little value as it would if applied to the Zen master's statement that the Buddha is two pounds of flax. *est*'s intellectual positions (such as "The mind is a linear arrangement . . ." and so on) are not basic to the production of enlightenment experiences, and to adopt them could be dangerous.

The easiest way to lose the feeling of lightness that is provided by fully experiencing experience is to form the *idea* that your mind is a machine or that you are perfect, and to begin living by the *idea*. Enlightenment is never an idea; it is always a mode of experience. Ideas may create opportunities for an enlightenment experience. An idea may seem to lead to many such experiences over a period of time, but sooner or later it becomes a deadening belief and creates a barrier to accepting what is.

The strange fact is that an enlightenment experience can come within a wide variety of events, disciplines, spiritual practices, and statements of ideas. No religion or philosophy seems to have a monopoly. To identify the enlightenment experience with any single spiritual practice, statement of an idea, or training is foolish.

The second time I took the *est* training, for instance, I enjoyed a marvelous "enlightenment experience," although the intellectual positions which, superficially, would seem to have allowed the release to occur (namely, Werner's anatomy of the mind) are very different from the techniques and intellectual positions that in my past have triggered similar experiences. That I could have experienced an enlightenment release in such seemingly diverse actions as reading and writing Zen parables, deciding to make decisions by casting dice, reading Castaneda's *A Separate Reality*, and experiencing the fourth day of the *est* training clearly raises the question as to what these actions have in common.

Werner's answer is that each acts to create a space which permits us to accept what is and fully experience experience. It is possible, however, to isolate what occurs a bit more precisely than that. To do this I'd like to offer a personal comparison of *est*'s getting-it process with three other enlightenment catalysts —the act of casting dice to determine one's course of action, a famous Zen parable, and a central passage of *A Separate Reality*.

In "die-ing" or "diceliving,"[10] a technique developed to assist people to "liberation," the dice-person—instead of always doing the thing he most feels like doing, or thinks is most *reasonable* to do, or *habitually* does mechanically—lists several possible alternative actions and, when the die arbitrarily designates one, he then accepts the designation and chooses it. The key to this exercise of "die-ing" is to say yes to whatever the die designates. The main notion behind the exercise of die-ing is that to escape from the mechanicalness of our reason and of our inherited habitual absurdities into fresh experience we must introduce chance into our lives. Another idea behind it is that we are all *multiple*, that anybody can be anybody, and that the diverse features of our multiple beings can best be uncovered and expressed by the introduction of chance. How could such nonsense have anything to do with enlightenment?

It is said that Gautama Buddha related the following parable:

> A man traveling across a field encountered a tiger. He fled, the tiger after him. Coming to a precipice, he caught hold of the root of a wild vine and swung himself down over the edge. The tiger sniffed at him from above. Trembling, the man looked down to where, far below, another tiger was waiting to eat him. Only the vine sustained him.
>
> Two mice, one white and one black, little by little started to gnaw away the vine. The man saw a luscious strawberry near him. Grasping the vine with one hand, he plucked the strawberry with the other. How sweet it tasted![11]

What does this nonsense have to do with enlightenment?

In Carlos Castaneda's *A Separate Reality* don Juan presents yet a fourth nonsensical "intellectual position" which in a way encompasses diceliving, enjoying strawberries, and saying yes to being a machine: the idea of "controlled folly." In one passage don Juan explains to his apprentice that all of his actions with everyone he meets are examples of his controlled folly. All actions are *folly* because, as don Juan "sees" it, each thing is as important as everything else; no one thing matters more than any other. His acts of *controlled* folly are at one and the same time totally sincere and yet always the acts of an actor. To the consternation of his disciple, he explains that he doesn't care whether his disciple becomes a "man of knowledge" or not; and his folly is *controlled* in that, while not caring, he nevertheless chooses to teach him. In fact all of don Juan's acts are controlled folly, he says, because he does everything even while "seeing" its unimportance.[12] How, we may ask for the fourth time, could this nonsense have anything to do with enlightenment?

The answer to this repetitive question is that enlightenment and nonsense are almost always linked. One can rarely have an enlightenment experience except under the impact of nonsense. *est*'s attack on man's belief systems during the first weekend of the training is essential to the later "getting it." Sense is our disease, the barrier to our full experience of life. Every time we laugh we are in a way experiencing a minienlightenment, a tiny letting go of some attachment to some bit of belief or sense. Full enlightenment, in these terms, is accepting what is, which leads to experiencing fully whatever one is experiencing.

The man dangling over the precipice with tigers above and below him and two mice gnawing on the vine that sustains him is man, and his enlightenment is to pluck the luscious strawberries before him.

Don Juan's statement that his acts are "sincere" but at the same time "only the acts of an actor" is nonsense, but what it clearly implies—as does the whole discussion of "controlled folly"—is that he has let go of his beliefs and does things as an actor does them.

The act of tossing a die onto a desk and permitting it to choose among six possible options is nonsense too. Yet, the "dice-person" will often experience a release in the very process of listing his options, since the act of turning over control of a "decision" to dice is an act of disidentification with the mind and of affirmation to whatever comes.

If we isolate what occurs in each of the four cases, we find that the individual lets go of his mind, his beliefs, his sense of who he has thought he was, and simply *is*. The diametrically opposed notions: "all is chance in the most accidental of worlds" and "all is stimulus-response in the most mechanical of worlds" create almost precisely the same psychological impact: namely, the disappearance of the illusion of the doer, of the illusion of there being someone who has control, of the illusion, created by beliefs, that there is something one *has* to do—in brief, the dissociation of the being from his mind and body.

When we are asked to examine our experience while making

a decision to raise or lower our right hand from in front of our face, we find that either the hand abruptly rises or falls without conscious thought, or a thought abruptly rises or pops into consciousness ("I think I'll raise it," or "I'll lower it," or "I wonder which I should do," or "This is a silly exercise"). Now we can take the intellectual position that those thoughts "pop up" completely by chance, like the random quanta of quantum physics, or that they pop up mechanically as the result of an unbroken mechanical causal chain. *Both positions are "nonsense."*

Both positions are useful for some tasks and useless for others. Both break down or become meaningless if applied too vigorously to all situations. Both "positions," however, undermine the idea that the being and his mind are the same and that there is a self that exists and has control but gets overwhelmed most of the time and *ought* to be doing things differently from the way they are being done. "You will never escape the wheel of birth and death," says the Buddha, "unless you cease to believe the illusion that you are the Doer."

An insight, as seen from the realm of fully experienced experience, is simply one illusion successfully breaking the stranglehold of another illusion. An "enlightenment experience" is the release experienced when the tension of fighting what is, is suddenly dissipated, and the being is released from taking his mind seriously. An enlightenment experience is saying yes to one's successive selves after a lifetime of saying no, saying yes to the luscious strawberry after a lifetime of worrying about illusory tigers. A guru is one who creates a package of nonsense, a package of illusions, which successfully smashes the life-inhibiting illusions held by the seeker. The guru's illusions must themselves be continually smashed if their "work" is to be continually achieved. Ideally the guru creates a package of *self-destructing* illusions that destroy the life-denying illusion of the seeker and "create a space" for him simply to be.

To compare the nonsense of "die-ing" to the more reasonable nonsense of the *est* training, it becomes clear that *ex-*

perientially the effect of making a choice by casting a die and acting on the die-chosen option can be identical to that of experiencing one's mind as a machine but *choosing* what you get. Late on the fourth day the *est* trainer tells the trainees that although both the enlightened and the unenlightened man are totally moving in the world of stimulus-response, stimulus-response, the enlightened man seizes a single space after the stimulus to *choose*, to say yes to the response. The response will occur in any case (what is, is), and the enlightened man differs from the unenlightened *solely* in choosing the response, in *choosing* what he gets . . . when he gets it.

That idea of a millisecond or tiny space in which to *choose* what is going to happen anyway is, of course, nonsense. As an intellectual position it is not worth defending. But it may be a *useful* idea; it may work to trigger the saying yes to life that is the core to all enlightenment experience.

Don Juan's controlled folly is his continuing to choose things even *after* he *sees* that nothing is important. The dice-person's controlled folly is his accepting the absurd random choice of chance rather than the "sensible," "caused" choice of his mind. The fleeing man's controlled folly is to enjoy a strawberry when he "should" be worrying about tigers. The *est* graduate's controlled folly is his continuing to choose things even after he *sees* that nothing is important and that things are going to occur whether he chooses them or not.

And so we come back to the warning that nonsense is usually integral to an enlightenment experience. Any rational analysis of the ostensible notions of the *est* training would not be relevant to whether or not it produces an enlightenment experience. One may find it interesting to examine the notions of *est*, but one should understand that whether the ideas hold up to internal or external consistency is not apparently important to the success of the training.

We are on equally uncertain ground if we attempt a rational analysis of how *est* produces its results. Rarely does substantial agreement among the trainees exist as to the lasting value of any one particular process or piece of data. Most trainees, for instance, complain of the boredom of having to listen to hour after hour of other people's repetitious problems; these same trainees, however, are excited when they themselves share their *own* experiences and realizations. Moreover, every now and then trainee John's listening to trainee Mary's probing into what's true for her will trigger in him an empathetic experience of great value to him.

We are faced with the paradoxical situation that trainees usually have to sit through immense gobs of processes, sharing, and data they experience as worthless nonsense (in some cases that which is experienced as nonsense exceeds half the training time) to get those moments that they experience as assisting them in transforming their lives. And the moment that liberates one trainee is often the same moment when sixty other trainees are sleeping or bored to the point of exhaustion.

In fact, the training seems to work in two general ways. First it works on the buckshot approach: by shooting enough processes and data and sharing, sooner or later every trainee gets hit. Second, the entire first three days of the training are a laying of groundwork for the fourth day to succeed. If you are feeling especially bored during the first three days you may be consoled by the thought that you are undergoing the type of indirect preparation that Zen masters often subject their disciples to: after cleaning the master's house and emptying the garbage for a year, the disciple receives a few enigmatic words and bingo!—*satori.* In the first three days of the training, Werner is letting you "clean the house" and "empty the garbage" so that on Sunday you can *get it.*

If I have made frequent comparisons between Werner's training and Zen the reason is that in my own experience the two are related. Werner himself has observed:

Although the *est* training is not Zen, some features of the *est* training coincide with Zen teaching and practice. Of all the disciplines that I studied, practiced, and learned, Zen was the *essential* one. It was not so much an influence on me; rather, it created space. It allowed those things which were there to be there. It gave some form to my experience. And it built up in me the critical mass from which was kindled the experience which produced *est*. It is entirely appropriate for persons interested in *est* to also be interested in Zen.[13]

In communications to *est* graduates he has frequently used Zen parables, or portraits of zany Zen monks, or Japanese watercolors to reflect the spirit of *est*. Werner's attacks on beliefs and reasonableness, his training's cheerful embracing of seeming contradictions, and its emphasis on getting it all reflect the spirit of Zen.

The major parallel with Zen, however, is not in meditation techniques nor in the use of an occasional koan or Zen parable but rather in the basic approach to human transformation: the master must use whatever beliefs, tricks, or techniques are necessary to create a space for the student to have the getting-it experience. Those who listen to the trainer and then repeat his words as "truth" have misunderstood the training and are misrepresenting the trainer. "You're an asshole" is not the statement of a belief; it's a clout on the head—a quite traditional Zen teaching device. As Werner once said:

> The Zen master technique was when the disciple was ready, you told it straight; when he wasn't ready, you hit him over the head, cut his arm off, or said jibberish. And the cutting arms off and hitting people over the head and talking what sounds like jibberish to them is an attempt to get them to give up their system of epistemology—the way that they have of knowing—so that they can know the same stuff in an entirely new way.[14]

The frequently expressed goal of the training, "to blow your mind," is only a colloquial expression for the traditional goal of Zen training: meditation eventually leads to a letting-go experience in which the false reasonableness of the mind explodes and the Zen student achieves satori. Both in satori and in getting it the individual has an *experience* in which hope and effort and trying and good and bad and getting it and enlightenment *all* wither into insignificance, and the student finds himself with what is, experiencing what is and high on what is. The intellectual content accompanying the enlightenment experience is not important, since the basic result is the disappearance of the intellect as the filter of experience.

Alan Watts has written of Zen: "The perfection of Zen is to be perfectly and simply human. The difference of the adept in Zen from the ordinary run of men is that the latter are, in one way or another, at odds with their own humanity."[15] Wrote the ninth century Zen master Lin-Chi:

> There is no place in Buddhism for using effort. Just be ordinary and nothing special. Relieve your bowels, pass water, put on your clothes, and eat your food. When you're tired, go and lie down. Ignorant people may laugh at me, but the wise will understand.[16]

Both Zen and *est* are quite firm about not confusing spirituality with thinking about God while one is mowing the lawn. For Zen and *est*, spirituality is mowing the lawn when you're mowing the lawn. Says Werner:

> You see, I think there is not anything *but* spirituality. So when you try to identify something that is more spiritual than something else, it is a lie. That's all there is, there isn't anything but spirituality. . . . Anytime we experience, it is a spiritual experience, because experience is spiritual.[17]

Some Zen masters express the same idea in a more *est*ian way even than Werner: "When it's time to get dressed, put on your clothes. When you must walk, then walk. When you must sit, then sit. Don't have a single thought in your mind about seeking for Buddhahood."[18]

Implied by both *est* and Zen is criticism of the chief Western religious traditions, which tend to emphasize belief, morality, and a spirituality separate from everyday reality. Everyday life is seen by these Western traditions as a *barrier* to the experience of God: retreat, prayer, meditation, self-discipline, asceticism are possible tools to increase one's experience of the Light, or God. What is, is mostly darkness. What is desired is union with Light. The religious man is he who is following certain religious practices that are seen as a path to the experience of God.

Both *est* and Zen are suspicious of dualities (good and evil, Darkness and Light, and so on) and place emphasis on experiencing a realm in which the dualities have ceased to exist.

In Zen and *est* one is not transcending everyday reality; one is, in fact, learning to *experience* it. The Zen initiate or *est* graduate is no longer run by the belief systems that incorporate the dualities and give a distorted, misery-making form to what is. God, or the light, were one willing to use such dualistic terms at all, would coincide with *what is.* But what is, is, whether we acknowledge it or not, and so "darkness" in this tradition simply doesn't exist: "darkness" is "what ain't."

Of course, a reasonable man might object that if *everything* is the Path, or if we're all perfect just the way we are, or if God is simply what is, then the world of illusion too must be the Path, and I'm perfect even when I'm totally immersed in misery-making illusion. And our minds rebel when the Zen master replies simply: "Very true: nirvana [the enlightened state] and samsara [the state of being ensnared in illusion] are one. Total and absolute enlightenment is nothing"; or when Werner agrees: "*est* isn't necessary; you're perfect just as you are."

The mind rebels and, if it insists on being right, lives unhappily ever after. If, on the other hand, the individual decides he'd rather have his life work than be right and reasonable, he will recognize the limitations of mind and learn to live with contradiction and paradox.

The sad fact is that the important experiences human beings cherish most—love and enlightenment, to name two—cannot be understood by the intellect. Possibly the most effective packaged enlightenment program is to be in a serious automobile accident and linger near death for a few days. By many accounts, the experience of being near death "transforms one's ability to experience living" so that problems clear up, and so on. It makes cherished beliefs seem trivial. Strawberries become important. Such a near-death experience may be successful in a higher percentage of cases than the *est* training. As Samuel Johnson once said, "Depend upon it, sir, when a man knows he is to be hanged in a fortnight it concentrates his mind wonderfully." The risk involved, however, makes auto accidents a relatively unpopular program for enlightenment.

We must sadly admit that no one seems to know *how* the types of transformation in human experience made possible by *est* or auto accidents or drugs or prolonged stays in a Zen monastery or dice-living occur. If we knew, we would be able to create a program to produce such experiences at less cost and with greater certainty than can be done by taking two weekends of *est*, by living in a Zen monastery for two years, or by arranging an auto accident.

7

The Criticisms of *est*, or We're All Perfect Just the Way We Are, But ...

"I have a few criticisms to make of est, *Werner," said the reporter.*

"That's fine," Werner replied. "And I want you to know I take full responsibility for creating all the things you don't like."

"You do?"

"Just as I'm sure you take full responsibility for not liking them."

est has become a phenomenon. In the past year hundreds of newspaper and magazine articles have appeared about *est* and Werner Erhard, nine or ten books have been published or will be published soon, and scores of *est* graduates, entertainment personalities, and authors—and Werner himself—have appeared on radio and television talk shows.

More significantly, the influence of *est* graduates on education, psychotherapy, religion, and the media is also increasing rapidly. Werner has developed and presented special work-shops for each of these four groups to discuss the ways in which some of the values and techniques of *est* can be brought

into each of the fields. Several experimental educational projects have been established throughout the country by *est*
graduates in teaching and school administration.[1] Hundreds of
psychotherapists are encouraging their patients to enroll in *est*,
and many clergy have indicated that *est* has opened up new
vistas in their own religious experience and practice. *est* is
working increasingly with members of the media to assure that
articles and books, whether critical or admiring of *est*, are
accurate and well informed.[2]

"Only in America" could we have this strange phenomenon
of a longtime businessman-salesman developing the most unusual and successful educational and revitalizing program in
recent times. "Zen and the Art of Selling Nothing" might well
be the facetious title of Werner's story of the discovery, devel-
opment, and selling of his training and seminars. His cheerful
acknowledgment that *est* is offering people the chance to discover only what they already have (or, more accurately, who
they already are), and hence there's nothing to get, reinforces
the tendency in some people to be extremely critical of him
and of *est*.

Trained from childhood to be suspicious of salesmen, we
Americans naturally bring a good deal of skepticism to our
appraisal of a man who has changed his name and in the past
sold cars and trained salesmen to sell encyclopedias. Although
Werner has made clear that *est* is neither a religion nor a
therapy, enthusiastic graduates of *est* treat him with the love
and awe normally associated with that of disciples for spiritual
teachers. When we now add our instinctive American suspicion of new religions to our suspicion of salesmen, we can
understand what formidable barriers Werner must overcome
to get people to examine his product honestly.

But probably the subtlest and most powerful barrier to the
honest appreciation of *est* is the disconcerting fact that *est* is
incomprehensible and valueless nonsense until one has taken
the training. To compound the problem, even after the training, which for most graduates is valuable, it is still incompre-

hensible. It is infuriating to deal with people who are happy and bubbly about something they seem unable to explain, something they blandly assert can only be "gotten" by taking the training. As a result Werner has been accused of being the greatest con man since the inventor of snake oil, and it is thus natural that he, his training, and the *est* organization have been submitted to both honest scrutiny and inaccurate attacks.

Because it seems to me that *est* is extremely important and valuable, I'd like to examine briefly the criticisms of *est* in order to separate those based on an accurate picture of *est* from those based on misinformation or misrepresentation, and to evaluate how serious are those criticisms based on accurate information.

The attacks on the training itself have been so superficial and based on such a misrepresentation of the training that it is difficult to grant them much weight. The most influential yet to appear is the argument that the training is a form of brainwashing.[3] As this criticism goes, the harsh physical conditions, the trainer's constant harangue, the total dependence of the trainees on the trainer, and the "fascist atmosphere" all set up a condition whereby ideas can be programmed into people's heads that wouldn't otherwise get in. The result is that the graduates all turn out to be Werner-worshipping robot *esties*.[4]

Although many graduates feel physical discomfort and experience the harangues of the trainer as intimidation, much of the training, indeed most of it, is the opposite of brainwashing. People are permitted to say whatever they want to the trainer about him and are always acknowledged by applause. They are never physically restrained from leaving the room if they choose. The various processes are usually designed to assist the trainee in getting in touch with buried material and experiencing himself as the *creator* of his experience. The third day of the training is entirely aimed at getting the trainees to experience responsibility for their own lives, hardly an ideal state of affairs from a fascist point of view. The fourth day of the training gets trainees to experience the mechanical quality of the mind, but, as Werner stresses, to disidentify with the machine mind, to be free of it.

Actually, the simplest refutation of the brainwashing charge is to get to know the *est* graduates themselves: on the whole, they seem more open to new experience, less attached to their beliefs, and more flexible than most other human beings. A brainwashed individual is, by definition, one who behaves compulsively and rigidly adheres to the belief system that has been forced into him. The frequently noted similarity in clothes and hairstyle between most of the trainers and Werner is hardly proof that the trainers are robots. In fact, such similarity of dress and mannerism is no more noteworthy in trainers than it is in actors playing Hamlet: in both cases a *prescribed role* is being played on stage, and dress and mannerism are part of the role. There are no prescribed modes of dress or hairstyle for *est graduates*, as a simple look around at any *est* graduate event makes abundantly clear.

The recurring reading during many of the processes of the long prose affirmation while the trainees are in a relaxed, meditative state is the only part of the training that could be seen as vaguely sinister or as brainwashing. *If* this long reading included such statements as "Werner is my Master and I shall not want," or "*est* is making me better and better every day," a case might be made. But the content of the affirmation is simply an extended catalogue of the positive notions that the training has been dramatizing throughout. It is not brainwashing to tell someone in a relaxed state that he is free, is good, and has important powers he will use only for ethical purposes.

A second criticism of the training is that *est* is dangerous because under unsupervised conditions, deep and "disturbing" material is contacted during some of the processes, and such material may lead some trainees to psychotic breakdowns.

Although I know of no such psychotic breakdown occurring, sooner or later one certainly will, just as sooner or later one will occur in the local A&P. *est* takes extensive safeguards against unstable people enrolling; for example, anyone who has ever been hospitalized for psychiatric reasons must obtain a letter from his therapist, and it is recommended he not take the training. In addition, anyone who has been in psychotherapy during the previous six months must inform his therapist and get his permission; if he is not "winning" in therapy, he is discouraged by *est* from taking the training. Such requirements obviously reduce the likelihood of unstable people being in the training. In any case, the trainer and the training supervisor are on hand at all times in the room to deal with upsets or a breakdown should one occur.

There is no doubt that on some occasions a trainee will find he is more anxious, tense, or depressed after the training than he was before. If one enters the training with the problem of general boredom, one may very well get in touch next with fear, and *after* the training have anxiety where before one had boredom. Or if one's barrier is anxiety and fear, one may peel the layer of onion and uncover an intense, disturbing anger and hatred. Or one may peel away anger and discover depression. If a graduate decides boredom was "better" than anxiety, he may feel he is "worse" after the training than he was before. If someone else feels fear is better than anger he too may experience that things have gotten worse. As we saw, *est* is careful to avoid claiming to be a therapy or promising that you will "get better." The vast majority of the graduates *do* feel that they're "better," though this is their own evaluation, as is that of those who feel they become "worse."

There is no doubt that *est* is potent medicine. If transcendental meditation is the marijuana of the human potential movement—abundant and tranquilizing—*est* is the LSD—explosive and potentially life-transforming. Because *est* is potent, some trainees are going to have deeper downs than they've had, just as they have higher highs, and just as patients in psychoanalysis may get "worse" before they get better.

What counts is the percentage of graduates who do have

breakdowns compared to the percentage of A&P customers or patients in psychoanalysis. How many graduates report highly favorable results from the training and how many report negative results? As long as the evidence is that the overwhelming number of graduates have found great value in the training, and as long as there is no evidence (and there is no evidence to date) that taking *est* is any more dangerous than shopping in the A&P, then any future psychotic breakdown in an *est* training, while it may be newsworthy, cannot be the basis for important criticism.

Another criticism of the training itself has more weight, especially since it has been voiced by Stewart Emery, who, from early 1973 to April 1975, was a successful *est* trainer—in fact, the first other than Werner to conduct a training. While Emery has acknowledged that the est training has value for almost all of the trainees, he has two criticisms: the notion that we are totally responsible for our experience is dangerous, and much of the *est* training is irrelevant to its success.

> I personally felt that a lot of the training was nonsense. . . . I thought the talk about reality, about the idea that you create it all, was just a heap of nonsense, and I still think that to tell people that they create everything is not the thing to do.[5]

It is not difficult to criticize the idea that we are all totally responsible for "reality," for everything that happens in our universe, for napalmed babies in Vietnam or the cancer of our child, *if* this idea is interpreted in a superficial way—which usually means that the idea becomes a belief rather than an experience. The notion that a Vietnamese child is responsible for his experience of being napalmed, while it is a philosophically consistent and defensible position, is, as are most philosophical ideas carried to their logical extreme, not very useful. Realizing that one creates one's own experience and coming to take responsibility for one's own life seem to be two of the most valuable results of the training. Applied to extreme situations, these *experiences* are still valuable, but as *ideas* they come to seem horrible or ridiculous. It is valuable to a hypochondriac to experience that he *creates* his own misery. It seems horrible to say that every child caught in a burning house or every person who died at the hands of Nazis was responsible for *his* experience. Furthermore, responsibility should not be confused with blame. It is a liberating notion to realize that when one's apartment is "robbed" (as society views the event), one does not have to experience the event as a loss—and if one does, one can take responsibility for so experiencing it. It is a false and debilitating notion to blame oneself for being robbed.

Emery's general reference to a lot of the training as "nonsense" raises a slightly different question. Earlier I pointed out that nonsense can have great value—in fact, may be inextricably linked with an enlightenment experience. Indeed, how can one use "sense" to blow the mind? On the other hand, the question legitimately arises whether there doesn't exist in the training a lot of valueless nonsense as well as valuable nonsense. Are there a few basic things in the training that do the good work and a lot that is just mumbo-jumbo and empty theatrics?

Paradoxically, only Werner knows. According to Ted Long, one of the most experienced *est* trainers, the evaluation of the training is being carried out in the actual training situation. The trainers and Werner generally meet together at least once a month to examine the usefulness of individual elements of the training. While the essence has remained constant, the training has continually evolved in form. Werner himself is the sole source of any changes, which he makes on the basis of his experiences in both the training and the special seminars he develops from time to time. Of course, in another sense the training is *always* changing because the trainees who come to it over the years have been changing.

The question of whether some of the training is mere window dressing can't be answered unless *est* begins experimentally varying the training and measuring the results with some sort of standardized questionnaire and later follow-up. At this point, *est* has no plans to undertake such a study.

Moreover, my own interviews with scores of graduates indicate that what is nonsense, mumbo-jumbo, or psycho-babble for one otherwise appreciative graduate may be one of the high points of the training for another. Sharing might seem to be the very essence of *est*, but many who never share still derive tremendous benefit from the training. While I found the personality profile valueless for me, a lawyer friend said that for him doing the profile graduation night was when he really "got it." Making an ass of oneself may be useless fun for some people and lead to a breakthrough for others. The anatomy of the mind puts many trainees to sleep and leads to an enlightenment experience for others. A trainee may get nothing from five consecutive processes and have an experience that will turn his life around during the sixth.

My guess is that if the *est* Standard Training has remained essentially the same for the last two years, it is because it works well the way it is now: no sense fiddling with the engine of a soaring aircraft.

The criticisms of the *est* organization are much more widespread than the criticisms of the training, but the basic rebuttal to them is the same in both cases: "perhaps you're right, but it works."

The *est* organization is not democratic (most American business organizations are not) but rather is authoritarian in a way that baffles many and antagonizes others. Werner Erhard expects staff members to be dedicated to serving *est*—which, because he and *est* are one and the same, means serving him. Late in the fourth day of the training, the trainer explains that Werner is in essence a power source serving masses of people, and individual staff members *supply* Werner with additional power. The power flows up from graduates and staff, through

Werner, out into the world. This is a perfectly reasonable way to explain the essentially Eastern phenomenon of a powerful being (usually a guru or spiritual teacher) attracting other powerful beings who nevertheless *choose* to channel their power *through* the leader.

Werner argues that learning to serve can be a valuable form of detachment from one's mind or ego or cravings, and the atmosphere in *est* offices bears this out. The *est* staff is hardly robotlike or subservient; it is open, joyful, alive. Werner's picture is not plastered prominently on the walls; as power sources go, Werner is certainly low-keyed. His continual acknowledgments to *est* graduates for creating the space for him to be him are undoubtedly genuine: he understands that they *are* supplying him with power, and that without them, *est* doesn't exist.

Another problem *est* faces is that it is a moneymaking organization in a field—that of self-help or enlightenment—that many people feel should not reap profit. Americans tend to feel that someone is "religious" or "helping others" on the one hand or "out for a buck" on the other, *but not both*. Were Billy Graham to own six Cadillacs and four houses, his position as spiritual teacher would, for some, be undermined. Spirituality, or helping others, we feel, ought to transcend material gain. From the moment *est* began to receive national exposure it has been perceived by some critics as a salesman's clever "sales pyramid."[6] It is certainly difficult for the organization to seem detatched from moneymaking on the one hand while making a lot of money on the other (the gross revenue—not profits—of *est* by the end of its first six years of existence will be close to $20 million).

There are some people who interpret Werner Erhard's having made a great deal of money from creating *est*, his living in a Victorian townhouse and driving a Mercedes, as an indication that his primary motivation for creating and expanding *est* must be to make more money. While Werner acknowledges that he has made and will continue to make good money from his work, nevertheless the heavy work schedule he demands of himself and his staff, the meticulous standards he maintains in the training and seminars, and his rejection of the opportunities for easy moneymaking projects that are inconsistent with *est*'s higher purposes all suggest he now has a stronger interest in serving people than in money.

The essential question in regard to money, however, is whether the product Werner is selling is shoddy or worth $250. When one considers other programs people seek to revitalize their lives—psychiatrists, growth centers, Arica, scientology, a Zen monastery, a Trappist monastery—one can only conclude that for most consumers, both before and after trying the *est* training, it is a "good buy": more aliveness is achieved at less cost than by other seemingly related offerings.

Another criticism about *est*'s moneymaking concerns the pressures some feel *est* puts on its graduates to bring guests to the graduate seminars and special events. The graduates are in fact the leading "salesmen" of *est*, and *est* has clearly created structures that encourage and guide them. Some graduates complain that seminar leaders communicate an authoritarian "Bring guests!" where their proper task is to remind graduates that sharing experience fully inevitably *creates* guests, since the graduate's experience of *est* is obviously positive or he wouldn't be attending the graduate seminar.

Werner has said in rebuttal that the graduate's active support of *est* is natural in that sharing experience is essential to a fully alive person. Moreover, it might be considered the duty of any "teacher" to create structures whereby his message or training is brought to as many people as possible.

We must also understand that any way *est* was sold would invite criticism. If *est*'s method of obtaining new trainees were to be altered from the voluntary proselytizing of its graduates to any of the usual commercial methods of promoting a new product—a big media event like the Houston Astrodome fiasco of Maharaj-Ji, a national advertising campaign such as that used by scientology or Arica, door-to-door or street-corner distribution of leaflets as is done by the Hare Krishna group and many Christian organizations—criticism would likely become sharper.

In the guru game and the enlightenment business it is *impossible* to do things in a way that doesn't strike many people as hypocritical or unethical. It's also impossible not to find followers who turn one off, who seem neurotic ninnies, pretentious assholes, or hoaxed simpletons. I personally found some of the training worthless; I have sometimes experienced the selling of *est* as obnoxious and some graduates as superficial or still helplessly out of touch with themselves. I find the *est* organization more authoritarian than my taste prefers. But all of my criticisms say as much about me as they do about *est*.

And it all doesn't make a bit of difference. We all manage to find warts on someone who is acclaimed as a spiritual teacher or great creator, and we will find ridiculous some of the movement's followers.

My own experience of *est* has been that in a misery-making society that offers thousands of self-help programs, religions, books, and gimmicks, *est* is the most effective, intelligent, and life-giving program I have encountered. While there are specifically religious groups whose followers manifest as much aliveness, love, and satisfaction as do *est* graduates, belonging to them necessitates the acceptance of certain religious beliefs or practices; as a result such programs are less likely than *est* to work for large numbers of people.

I cheerfully confess my agreement with those critics who have called Werner Erhard the greatest con man since the inventor of snake oil. Civilized human beings have been conned into making themselves miserable for a long time and it is clear that only the very greatest of con men could have invented a "nothing" that can con us out of continuing to make ourselves miserable.

est is a unique educational program. Unlike religions, therapies, and self-help programs, there is nothing to do, either in the training or after it—no practices, exercises, rituals, moral strictures, beliefs. It is complete in less than two weeks. And it leads a surprising number of the trainees to "getting it," which for some is clearly an enlightenment experience. *est* gives to most of its graduates what it values most: aliveness, joy, love, and self-expression. In a society not overly abundant in these qualities, that's not a bad contribution to make.

NOTES

Chapter 5

1. The material and sharing of the graduate seminars is not private and confidential and protected by copyright in the same way as are the data and sharing of the standard training.
2. According to Morty Lefkoe, manager of *est*'s Public Information Office.
3. From an *est* release to its graduates.
4. Ibid.
5. Ibid.
6. Ibid.
7. Ibid.
8. Ibid.
9. As reported in "A Physician's View of the *est* Training (Part II)" by John E. Emery in *The Bulletin* of the San Francisco Medical Society, Sept./Oct. 1973.
10. As reported in a letter dated March 15, 1976, sent to *est* graduates by Robert Ornstein, PhD, on the "*est* Outcome Study."
11. Emery, "A Physician's View of the *est* Training."
12. As reported in "What Have You Gotten After You 'Got It'?: An Evaluation of Awareness Training Participants," by Earl Babbie and Donald Stone, mimeo., p. 2. Babbie and Stone presented this analysis of the "*est* Outcome Study" to the American Psychiatric Association on May 13, 1976.
13. Ornstein, "*est* Outcome Study," pp. 1–2.
14. Ibid., p. 2.
15. Babbie and Stone, "What Have You Gotten After You 'Got It'?: An Evaluation of Awareness Training Participants," pp. 15–16.
16. Marcia Seligson, "*est*—The New Life-Changing Philosophy That Makes *You* the Boss," *Cosmopolitan*, June 1975, p. 205.
17. Lisa Schwarzbaum, "*est! est! est!* How I Got It, How I've Kept It and Why I Won't Go Back for More," *Mademoiselle*, November 1975, p. 205.
18. Seligson, "*est*—The New Life-Changing Philosophy That Makes *You* the Boss," p. 205.

19. Valerie Harper, "Rhoda Takes *est,*" *The New Age Journal,* no. 7 (1975), p. 46.
20. Eric Utne, "Rights and Responsibilities," *The New Age Journal,* no. 7 (1975), p. 35.
21. Personal interview with the author.
22. Peggy Utne, "Seeing Is Not Believing," *The New Age Journal,* no. 7 (1975), p. 38.
23. Al Valentine, "Before and After," *The New Age Journal,* no. 7 (1975), p. 47.
24. Valerie Harper, "Rhoda Takes *est,*" p. 46.

Chapter 6

1. Peter Marin, "The New Narcissism," *Harper's,* October 1975, p. 47.
2. Marcia Seligson, "*est*—The New Life-Changing Philosophy That Makes *You* the Boss," *Cosmopolitan,* June 1975, p. 204.
3. Jerry Rubin, "I'm Scared, You're Scared," *The New Age Journal,* no. 7 (1975), p. 42.
4. Lisa Schwarzbaum, "*est! est! est!* How I Got It, How I've Kept It and Why I Won't Go Back for More," *Mademoiselle,* November 1975, p. 205.
5. "Werner Erhard: All I Can Do Is Lie" (interview), *East West Journal,* September 1974, p. 5.
6. Ibid.
7. "Werner Erhard: An Interview with the Source of *est,*" *The New Age Journal,* no. 7 (1975), p. 29.
8. "Werner Erhard: All I Can Do Is Lie," p. 3.
9. Ibid.
10. The technique of die-ing was developed twenty years ago and first written about, for both comic and philosophic purposes, in my first book, *The Dice Man.* It has been translated into a dozen different languages and been read by close to a million people. Scores of readers have written me indicating the "liberating" impact of die-ing on their lives.
11. Paul Reps, comp., *Zen Flesh, Zen Bones: A Collection of Zen and Pre-Zen Writings* (Garden City, N.Y.: Doubleday & Co., Anchor Books, 1961), "A Parable," pp. 22–23.
12. Carlos Castaneda, *A Separate Reality* (New York: Simon and Schuster, 1971), pp. 99–100.
13. Werner Erhard, as quoted in Adelaide Bry, *est: 60 Hours That Transform Your Life* (New York: Harper & Row, 1976), p. 153.
14. "Werner Erhard: An Interview with the Source of *est,*" p. 28.
15. Alan Watts, *The Way of Zen* (New York: Penguin Books, 1962), p. 182.
16. As quoted in Alan Watts, *The Way of Zen,* p. 121.
17. "Werner Erhard: All I Can Do Is Lie," pp. 4–6.
18. As quoted in Watts, *The Way of Zen,* p. 171.

Chapter 7

1. There is an excellent mimeographed report available from *est* written by Robert W. Fuller and Zara Wallace and titled "A Look at *est* in Education," which describes in detail a half-dozen innovative educational programs created by *est* graduates in various parts of the United States.

2. For details about psychotherapists recommending *est* to their patients and the effect of *est* on clergy, see Adelaide Bry, *est: 60 Hours That Transform Your Life* (New York: Harper & Row, 1976), pp. 28–30, 78–81, 153–155.

3. See, for example, Mark Brewer, "'Erhard Seminars Training: We're Gonna Tear You Down and Put You Back Together," *Psychology Today*, August 1975, p. 88.

4. See, for example, Peter Marin, "The New Narcissism," *Harper's*, October 1975, pp. 46–47.

5. Stewart Emery, interviewed in *East West Journal*, December 1975, p. 12.

6. Mark Brewer, "Erhard Seminars Training: We're Gonna Tear You Down and Put You Back Together," p. 89.